DOMUS UNIVERSITATIS 1650

VERÖFFENTLICHUNGEN
DES INSTITUTS FÜR EUROPÄISCHE GESCHICHTE MAINZ
BAND 140

ABTEILUNG FÜR ABENDLÄNDISCHE RELIGIONSGESCHICHTE
HERAUSGEGEBEN VON PETER MANNS

FRANZ STEINER VERLAG WIESBADEN GMBH
STUTTGART 1989

LUTHER ON THOMAS AQUINAS

THE ANGELIC DOCTOR IN THE THOUGHT
OF THE REFORMER

VON
DENIS R. JANZ

FRANZ STEINER VERLAG WIESBADEN GMBH
STUTTGART 1989

CIP-Kurztitelaufnahme der Deutschen Bibliothek

Janz, Denis R.:
Luther on Thomas Aquinas : the angelic doctor in the thought
of the reformer / von Denis R. Janz. - Stuttgart : Steiner-Verl.
Wiesbaden, 1989
  (Veröffentlichungen des Instituts für Europäische Geschichte Mainz ;
  Bd. 140 : Abteilung für Abendländische Religionsgeschichte)
  ISBN 3-515-05434-0
NE: Institut für Europäische Geschichte ‹Mainz›: Veröffentlichungen
  des Instituts ...

Druck: Rheinhessische Druckwerkstätte, Alzey
Buchbinderische Verarbeitung: Adolf Hiort, Wiesbaden
Printed in the Fed. Rep. of Germany

For Chris and David

TABLE OF CONTENTS

TABLE OF CONTENTS

ABBREVIATIONS

CC   Corpus Catholicorum: Werke Katholischer Schriftsteller im Zeitalter der Glaubensspaltung. Münster: Aschendorff, 1919.

LW   Luther's Works: American Edition. 55 vols. St. Louis and Philadelphia: Concordia and Fortress, 1955-1988.

SCG   Summa Contra Gentiles

ST   Summa Theologiae

Viv   Thomae Aquinatis Opera Omnia. 34 vols. Paris: Viv, 1871-1882.

WA   D. Martin Luthers Werke. Kritische Gesamtausgabe. Weimar: Böhlau, 1883.

WABR   D. Martin Luthers Werke: Briefwechsel. Weimar: Böhlau, 1930.

WATR   D. Martin Luthers Werke: Tischreden. Weimar: Böhlau, 1912-1921.

Walch   Dr. Martin Luthers sämmtliche Schriften. Ed. Johann Georg Walch. 23 vols. St. Louis: J.J. Gebauer, 1880-1910.

PREFACE

This book has its remote origins in my earlier study on Luther's relationship to the late medieval Thomist school. Already there it became clear to me that a detailed study of Luther's view of Thomas Aquinas was a prime desideratum if we are to understand his relationship to the scholastic tradition. The proximate impetus was provided by the compilation of indices to the Weimar edition of Luther's writings, now continuing at the University of Tübingen. When the entries on Thomas and Thomism became available to me, my hesitation to undertake this study evaporated.

Over the past three years while this book was in process, a great number of colleagues and friends have encouraged me by their interest. Without them this book would be less than what it is in its present form. I owe a debt of gratitude to all of them, and most notably to the following: Walter Moore, for answering inquiries about Eck; Maria Grossman, for bibliographical help and for facilitating access to rare materials; Heiko Oberman, for suggestions and advice; Manfred Schultze, for supplying early access to the Weimar indices; Otto Pesch, for his encouragement and for sending me work of his own still in manuscript form; Harry McSorley, for lengthy discussion and helpful suggestions; John Payne and Kenneth Hagen, for their encouragement and advice; John Farthing, for giving me access to an early manuscript version of his book; Egil Grislis, for his interest and for making rare materials available to me; and Stephen Duffy and James Gaffney, for frequent consultations on matters linguistic and theological. I am also grateful to Loyola University for its generosity in granting a sabbatical leave and the research funds necessary for this kind of work.

Standard scholarly conventions are, for the most part, observed throughout this work. I depart from these occasionally for the following reasons. All references to Thomas Aquinas are to the Vivès edition. This edition was used there instead of the more modern Leonine edition because the latter edition is not yet complete. English translations of the *Summa Theologiae* are taken from the Benzinger edition. For Luther, references to the table talk are cited not by their designated numbers in the Weimar edition, but by volume, page and line. This was done for reasons of precision since some of the table talks are lengthy. All translations are my own unless otherwise specified.

It is an exhilarating and yet humbling experience to spend one's research hours in the company of intellectual giants such as Thomas Aquinas and Martin Luther. When these hours have become too long and the subject too all-engrossing, my two sons have constantly, and in their own unique ways, reminded me of the penultimate character of such pursuits. For this, and for their forbearance, I am deeply grateful; it is to them that this book is dedicated.

Denis R. Janz
New Orleans, LA
February, 1989

LUTHER ON THOMAS AQUINAS

Prospectus

It is often said that more books have been written about Luther than about any other figure in the history of Christianity. Among these, volumes bearing the title "Luther on ..." are only slightly less numerous than those entitled "Luther and ..." Authors of such works would do well, therefore, to say at the outset why they think another one is necessary.

The most obvious (and perhaps least convincing) reason for the present study is that, incredible as it may seem, it has never been done before. Books abound on Luther's view of a vast array of doctrines, persons, places and things; and yet Luther's view of Thomas Aquinas has never been seriously investigated. The reasons for this are many, but the most significant obstacle was the lack, until very recently, of adequate indices to Luther's massive literary corpus. The monumental task of reading through the 114 volumes of the Weimar edition with a view to finding every reference to Thomas daunted even the most assiduous Luther-scholars. Now, however, the burden has been significantly lightened by the compilation of modern indices, the most important of which is the index to the Weimar edition produced by the Tübingen Institut für Spätmittelalter und Reformation. Thus a comprehensive investigation of Luther's view of Thomas Aquinas has, for the first time, become feasible. Yet, the practicality of such a study, and the fact that it has never been done, are scarcely adequate grounds for doing it. The more cogent and compelling reasons for this study are of a theological and historical nature.

Thomas Aquinas and Martin Luther are arguably the greatest theologians in the history of Christianity. At the very least, all would concede that we are dealing here with two "classical" thinkers in the fullest sense of the term. If one can imagine them both being miraculously transported through time into the present, and a debate being staged between them, the event would be a theological sell-out. And understandably so: who would not want to witness this spectacular display of theological virtuosity? This book is a poor substitute. And yet it is as close as we can come to some indication of the shape such a debate would take, were it to occur.

Modern theologians have expended considerable effort in bringing the two into conversation. Most attempts to compare Roman Catholic and Protestant self-understandings sooner or later sharpen their focus by selecting major representatives of these traditions. And more often than not, the figures chosen turn out to be Thomas Aquinas and Martin Luther. Narrower theological studies have compared Thomas and Luther on a good number of doctrinal issues. Much as been written on what the "fundamental difference" between Luther and Thomas really is. And ecumenically-minded theologians are constantly searching for new avenues of rapprochement. For, rightly or wrongly, Thomas and Luther are inevitably regarded as the standard-bearers of Roman Catholicism and Protestantism. Thus the wider Protestant-Catholic dialogue is intimately related to the narrower conversation between Luther and Thomas. This study contributes to that wider dialogue by investigating the narrower one, and more specifically, by grounding the narrower one in history.

To bring Luther and Thomas into conversation means, of course, to compare two different constellations of ideas. But the single greatest problem with most theological comparisons to date is quite simply that they fail to take into account what Luther actually said about Thomas Aquinas. Thus, to cite only one example, a recent comparison of Thomas and Luther on baptism fails to ask what Luther had to say about Thomas' views on baptism. The comparison is therefore carried out in a wholly systematic and quite ahistorical way. The present work is, among other things, an attempt to fulfill this need, so that future systematic comparisons can at least take as their point of departure the historical foundation of Luther's actual view.

Besides such theological reasons for pursuing this study, there are also urgent historical reasons. For at least twenty-five years Luther-scholarship has been largely preoccupied with seeing Luther against his late medieval background. Thus research on late medieval nominalism, Augustinianism, Thomism and mysticism has thrown new and intense light on Luther and his break with the scholastic tradition he inherited. Yet Luther himself believed that among the scholastics, Thomas Aquinas was the greatest and most influential. Thus, if we are to fully understand Luther's abandonment of this theological heritage, we must understand his view of Thomas Aquinas. Though we now know a great deal about Luther's relationship to the various late medieval schools, we have not yet begun to understand his relationship to the person he acknowledged to be the "teacher of all teachers" in scholastic theology. It is the purpose of this study to lay the groundwork for such an understanding.

Since Luther never wrote a treatise "Contra Thomam", we do not have from him an organized and systematic critique of Thomas. Yet this scarcely means, as some have argued, that Luther was not interested in Thomas. Insofar as he was interested in scholastic theology, he was interested in the one he regarded as the most eminent scholastic; and insofar as he was interested in the Roman Catholic Church, he was interested in the one who, in his view, dominated not only its theology but its very life. Thus we find, scattered throughout Luther's writings, several hundred more or less substantive statements on Thomas Aquinas. This study attempts to be comprehensive in documenting all of them for the first time. But much more than this, it then attempts to analyze the accuracy of Luther's understanding and the cogency of his critique. In short, it uncovers and documents the evidence, and offers an interpretation. Readers may find the interpretation offered here bold and controversial, and yet, it is to be hoped, not entirely without value.

In what follows, the material is organized into four categories. First Luther has a moderate amount to say about the person of Thomas Aquinas. Chapter I examines these statements and attempts to draw some conclusions about Luther's view of Thomas' character. Second, Luther had much more to say about Thomas' theology. These largely critical statements are the subject matter of Chapter II. Here the data is so extensive as to warrant its division into some thirteen sub-topics, each dealing with a different doctrinal issue. Chapter III deals with Luther's view of the authority of Thomas in church and theology. This is the single issue which came up most frequently in relation to Thomas, and it was clearly of major significance to Luther. Finally, Chapter IV re-opens in a systematic and comprehensive way the much-debated question of Luther's knowledge of Thomas. Here the data from the preceding chapters bearing on this question is reviewed, new evidence is introduced, and an attempt is made to point the debate in a new direction.

Finally, it must be acknowledged that there are at the heart of a study such as this profound methodological problems which are specifically hermeneutical in nature. We would do well, therefore, at the outset to take cognizance of them and to make explicit the hermeneutical assumptions which are operative in what follows. The difficulty arises in the first instance because we are dealing with a corpus of theological texts written in the 13th century. This problem is complicated by the fact that we are also dealing with a 16th century interpretation of those texts, and that we are doing so from the vantage point of the 20th century. One way to largely avoid the difficulty would be to simply give a descriptive account of Luther's interpretation of Thomas. But this would be to abdicate the historian's responsibility, and to indulge our purely antiquarian interests at the expense of historical meaning. Surely more is required: description must be followed by analysis of Luther's interpretation of

Thomas. And such analysis must inevitably involve judgments about the veracity and accuracy of this interpretation. But then there immediately comes into play another factor, namely, our own 20th century interpretation of Thomas (and indeed a multiplicity of such modern interpretations). For whether we recognize it or not, our own interpretation of the text is the final criterion for assessing the accuracy of Luther's interpretation of the text. And this I would argue is perfectly legitimate insofar as our 20th century interpretation is based on the cumulative results of the modern historical-critical study of Thomas. The simple fact is that as a result of this modern historical project, we know far more about Thomas than anyone in the 16th century did. And thus we have a far better possibility than 16th century persons did of understanding the texts and discerning the intention of the author which lies behind them. This then must be the ultimate criterion for evaluating Luther's understanding of Thomas. All of this may well imply a notion of history as progress, perhaps even a confidence in the intellectual superiority of modernity over the past. And yet, while I must confess that these implications give me some discomfort, I know of no better way of proceeding.

CHAPTER I
LUTHER ON THE PERSON OF THOMAS

While most books on the history of theology never mention it at all, this history is riddled with loves and hatreds, sympathies and antipathies which are primarily personal in nature. Examples of this are not hard to find in eras which were less reluctant than our own in allowing free expression to such feelings. One thinks immediately of a figure like Jerome, who did not hesitate to speak of his great contemporary, Augustine, as "that little Numidian ant", or of the fateful clash of personalities between Peter Abelard and Bernard of Clairvaux. Nor was this kind of venom foreign to the intellectual world of the Reformation. Luther himself would have to be treated as a major figure in any history of theological insults.

Though such personal animosities are not uncommon in the history of theology, they have not counted for much in the writing of this history. Especially since the Enlightenment theologians and historians have been convinced that like or dislike of a historical figure's personality should not be allowed to influence one's judgment of his ideas. All would agree, for instance, that it would be foolish to dismiss Augustine's theology of the trinity on the grounds that certain aspects of his character are less than appealing. All would also agree that some of John Calvin's less attractive personal traits should not be allowed to obscure the greatness of his theological achievement. Person and idea must somehow be separated.

Whether or not this separation of a historical figure's character and thought is artificial and unjustifiable, there always remains a suspicion that on a deeper level the two are somehow related, and that therefore some attention should be paid to the personality of the thinker. Such attention to the personal loves and hatreds of an intellectual can add a human dimension to an otherwise disembodied mind, and perhaps even cast a new light on his ideas. It is for reasons such as these that Luther's comments on Thomas as a person are of great interest.

Before proceeding to an analysis of these statements, it will be useful to recall one stark contrast between the figures involved. Luther, as I have intimated, was amazingly forthright in expressing his loves and hatreds not only on the level of theology but also on the level of personalities. His writings are so full of this that one rarely suspects hidden and unexpressed personal disaffection looming in the background of some theological critique. In Luther's case, all such feelings seem to rise readily and unimpeded to the surface. This means that when Luther tells us what he thinks of Thomas as a person, we need not suspect that he is holding back for the sake of politeness.

We must also bear in mind that in contrast to Luther, Thomas shows an extreme reticence in expressing his personal likes and dislikes. In all of Thomas' vast writings, one finds "a little show of emotion" in four or five passages, and "some amount of temper" in two or three.[1] Aside from this, most of what we know about Thomas comes from the reports of others, especially from the hagiographical and legendary stories told about him after his death (1274) and before his canonization (1323). Thus, in contrast to other major theologians, there is an extreme paucity of information on Thomas' personal characteristics. And this means that while one may love or detest Thomas' theology, it is very difficult to love or detest Thomas as a person. This too must be taken into account.

Our description of Luther's view of Thomas as a person may begin with at least some mention being made of the several instances in which Luther refers to him in terms which can only be described as abusive. Without any explanation, Luther from time to time refers to Thomas as a "Sophist"[2], a "heretic"[3], a "blind cow"[4], "not worth a louse"[5], or a "beggarly

---

[1] M.D. Chenu, *Toward Understanding Saint Thomas*, (Chicago: Regnery, 1964), p. 122.

[2] WA 10 I 1, 115, 7ff (1522). Unless otherwise noted, translations are my own.

paunch"[6]. Other examples of this type of personal insult could be given, but to no real purpose here. They tell us little of substance about Luther's attitude toward Thomas. Anyone familiar with theological controversy in the 16th century is aware that such personal vituperation was standard fare on all sides. There are no insults which Luther hurled at Thomas that do not have a parallel elsewhere in the academic life of the early 16th century.[7] Yet those familiar with Luther's style know that he showed less restraint than most in employing such affronts. Indeed, Luther's name-calling rose to far more eloquent heights against some of his contemporaries than against Thomas. And consistent with his well-known general trend towards greater polemical excesses in his later years, most of these abusive references occur in his post-1530 writings. What all of this suggests is that the significance of such statements should not be overestimated.

Moreover, these kinds of abusive statements in Luther are counter-balanced by a very different kind of statement about Thomas. From time to time at different stages of his career, Luther spoke of Thomas in highly complimentary terms. Thus in 1518 Luther referred to Thomas as "this holy man".[8] Further, in 1520 Luther called Thomas "this great man".[9] Even the later Luther could speak of "the great Thomas Aquinas" (1533),[10] a man of "great genius" (1532/33),[11] and woefully misunderstood (1535-45).[12] Such positive statements about Thomas as a person, when placed alongside of the abusive ones, render the picture ambiguous. They should be regarded with no more and no less seriousness than the negative ones. And both the abusive and the complimentary ways of referring to Thomas should not be given the same weight as Luther's more substantive statements on the character of Thomas.

These more significant remarks occur on some fourteen different occasions in Luther's career. An analysis of such comments reveals that to some extent different aspects of Thomas' character were of concern to Luther at different stages of his career. This may be attributable to Luther's rapidly changing preoccupations on the front of controversy, or more simply to this penchant for repeating an interesting anecdote. All, however, give us a concrete indication of his views on the person of Thomas.

In the period between 1520 and 1525 Luther repeatedly calls into question the personal sanctity of Thomas. Is Thomas really a saint as the Church has said? The issue is first raised by Luther in his 1520 reply to Leo X's "Exsurge Domine". Here Luther uses this question in a purely hypothetical way to illustrate the point he is making, namely that disbelief in purgatory does not make one a heretic:

> I am not a heretic if I do not believe Thomas Aquinas to be a
> saint, even though he is canonized by the pope. So too those

---

[3]   WA 12, 625, 14ff (1523).

[4]   WA 40 I, 671, 14ff (1531). Is there an echo here of the "dumb ox" legend?

[5]   WATR 2, 193, 3 (1532).

[6]   "Bettelbauch." WA 46, 768, 12ff (1537/38).

[7]   The Thomists themselves were scarcely outdone by Luther in this regard. For examples, see James Overfield, *Humanism and Scholasticism in Late Medieval Germany*, (Princeton: Princeton Univ. Press, 1984), pp. 181 and 183.

[8]   WA 1, 658, 1ff.

[9]   WA6, 508, 23 (trans. from LW 36, 29).

[10]   WA 30 III, 562, 33.

[11]   WA 40 III, 112, 35ff.

[12]   WA 44, 136, 6ff. Cf. WA 1, 660, 5ff (1518).

who disagree with Thomas are not heretics even though his books
have been approved and confirmed by the pope.[13]

By the following year (1521) the question of Thomas' sanctity is no longer hypothetical. In controversy with the Thomists Ambrosius Catharinus and Silvester Prierias, Luther acknowledges "vehement doubt" on the question because "one smells nothing spiritual in him".[14] And in the same year, writing against Jacob Latomus, Luther expressed "most vehement doubts" on whether Thomas is among the blessed or the damned because he "wrote many heretical things and is the author of the reign of Aristotle, the ravager of pious teaching. What do I care that the bishop of bulls has canonized him?"[15] Luther's doubts on this score continued into 1522 when in a sermon on New Year's Day he allowed that if Thomas is a saint, he became one in a marvelous way since no one else has become one through his pernicious and poisonous teaching.[16] Two further sermons in 1523 and 1525 express this same doubt without further comment.[17] The issue then seems to pass from Luther's consciousness: no further explicit references are to be found in his writings.

While it would be too much to say that this question of Thomas' sanctity preoccupied Luther in the early 1520's, we cannot ignore the fact that Luther deemed the question worthy of comment no less than six times during this period. In evaluating the meaning and significance of this, it will be helpful to bear in mind several considerations. First, these particular comments on Thomas during this period must be seen within the context of Luther's heated controversy with the Thomist school which dominated his polemical agenda at the time.[18] Catharinus and Prierias were only two of the representatives of this school whom Luther treated with open contempt and conscious provocation. Calling into question the sanctity of Thomas was a surefire polemical tactic guaranteed to outrage his Thomist opponents. Another relevant consideration is that this issue arises for Luther in conjunction with an increasingly critical position in regard to papal authority.[19] This is already clear in 1520 when the issue is first raised in reply to Leo X's Bull. And the authority of the papal canonization is again called into question in 1521. We are not dealing here simply with the issue of Thomas' sanctity, but also with the issue of the papal authority to canonize. Thomas himself had written on the authority of papal canonizations, but how his views were to be understood was hotly disputed in the 15th and 16th centuries.[20] And this was perhaps in the back of Luther's mind

---

[13] WA 7, 149, 35ff (1520): "Sicut non credam Thomam Aquinatem esse sanctum, licet a Papa canonisatum, non sum Haereticus, quando et ii non sunt haeretici, qui Thomam negant, licet a Papa approbatum et confirmatum in suis libris."

[14] WA 7, 774, 14ff (1521): "De quo numero et S. Thomas Aquinas, si tamen sanctus est, nam vehementer dubito, cum adeo nihil olfiat spiritus in eo."

[15] WA 8, 127, 18ff (1521): "Nam de Thoma Aquino an damnatus vel beatus sit, vehementissime dubito, citius Bonaventuram crediturus beatum. Thomas multa haeretica scripsit et autor est regnantis Aristoteles, vastatoris piae doctrinae. Quid ad me, quod Bullarum Episcopus eum canonisavit?"

[16] WA 10 I 1, 497, 17ff (1522): "Ist Sanct Thomas heylig, als ich zweyffel, sso ist er freylich wunderlicher heylig worden, denn keyn ander heilig, umb seyner schedlichen vorgifftigen lere willen."

[17] WA 12, 414, 19ff (1523); and WA 17 II, 27, 25ff (1525).

[18] Cf. Leif Grane, "Die Anfänge von Luthers Auseinandersetzung mit dem Thomismus", in Theologische Literaturzeitung, 95 (1970), 241-250. Grane argues that from 1518 to 1522 the Thomist school was Luther's greatest enemy (p. 245).

[19] Scott H. Hendrix, Luther and the Papacy: Stages in a Reformation Conflict, (Philadelphia: Fortress, 1981), pp. 95ff.

[20] The relevant text in Thomas is Quodlibet 9, a. 16 (Vivès 15, 566-567). Cf. Max Schenk, Die Unfehlbarkeit des Papstes in der Heiligsprechung: Ein Beitrag zur Erhellung der theologiegeschichtlichen Seite der Frage. (Freiburg: Paulusverlag, 1965). After his extensive analysis Schenk concludes: "Thomas vertritt vorbehaltlos die These von der

when he made these comments. Finally, it is also worth consideration that Luther, until the end of his life, never ceased referring to Thomas as "Sanctus Thomas", "Beatus Thomas", or "Divus Thomas".[21] The titles are used interchangeably by Luther and they may merely represent the persistence of conventional ways of referring to Thomas in the later Luther. But on the other hand, one wonders whether, if he really believed that Thomas was not among the saints, Luther would not have eventually abandoned these titles.

Another kind of comment on the person of Thomas was made by Luther in 1532. While dining with friends and students on July 12 of that year, Luther is reported to have made the following remark on Thomas' girth:

> St. Thomas had such a large paunch that he could eat a whole goose at one sitting, and in order for him to have room to sit at the table, a hole had to be cut in the table to accommodate his paunch.[22]

Luther's recounting of this legendary material about Thomas at first sight may appear to be a critical remark in that it depicts the mendicant friar as a glutton. And indeed, Luther elsewhere intimates this when he refers to Thomas as that "beggarly paunch".[23] Such an interpretation, however, probably makes too much of a light-hearted moment: on occasions such as this, Luther's sense of humor often came to the fore. What we have here, then, is probably nothing more than an interesting anecdote told for the delectation of his students and friends.

In a much more serious context, Luther twice recalls another legend about Thomas, first in his *Operationes in Psalmos* (1519-21) and then again in his Galatians commentary of 1531. On both these occasions Luther holds the person of Thomas up for his students as a model of Christian humility: whenever Thomas heard himself being praised, he secretly made the sign of the cross under his cowl to remind himself of the sin of pride.[24] The context in which Luther tells this story, a discussion of humility, makes it clear that this is for Luther an unequivocally positive comment on the person of Thomas. Twice in the course of his teaching Luther holds Thomas up as exemplary in the virtue of humility.

Unfehlbarkeit des Papstes in der Kanonisation der Heiligen." (p. 177). Nevertheless, 15th and 16th century Thomists interpreted Thomas differently (p. 194).

[21] E.g. WA 1, 667, 11ff (1518); WA 1, 668, 12ff (1518); and WA 1, 665, 3ff (1518). The latest references to Thomas as a "Saint" occur in WA 45, 351, 20 (1537); WA 50, 251, 26 (1537); and WATR 4, 60, 12 (1538).

[22] WATR 2, 192, 14 - 193, 2 (12 July 1532): "Sanctus Thomas hatt so ein grossen bauch gehabt, das er auf ein mal eine gantze gans hatt konnen essen, und man hatt im mussen ein tisch auss schneiden, das er den bauch in das loch liget, raumb zu haben am tisch zu sitzen." Luther's knowledge of legends about Thomas comes perhaps from a volume entitled "Dulcis et brevis legenda de s. Thoma", which was available in the Erfurt libraries. Cf. Paul Lehmann, *Mittelalterliche Bibliothekskataloge Deutschlands und der Schweiz, Band 2: Erfurt*, (Munich: C.H. Beck'she Verlagsbuchhandlung, 1928), p. 557.

[23] WA 46, 768, 12ff (1537/38): "Bettelbauch."

[24] WA 5, 193, 23ff (1519-21): "Sic sanctum Thomam Aquinatem legimus, quoties sui laudem audiret, se sub veste sua cruce signasse, optima certe et pia reverentiae consuetudo." Cf. WA 40 II, 131, 1ff (1531): "Legitur de Sancto Thoma: quando audivit se laudare, semper crucem unterstrichen Christi, utrumque praestitit, quod Augustinus praecepit."

Another story about Thomas, recounted by Luther five times in the years 1532 and 1533, is more ambiguous.[25] The story appears in these years in sermons, table talk and in occasional writings. In its fullest version, Luther relates the legend as follows:

> The story is told of how a doctor [professor] met a coal peddler on a bridge in Prague. Out of compassion for the poor laity the doctor asked: 'Dear man, what do you believe?' The coal peddler answered: 'What the Church believes.' The doctor: 'But what does the Church believe?' The coal peddler: 'What I believe.' Later, when the doctor was about to die, his faith was so gravely tested by the devil that he could no where find peace until he said: 'I believe what the coal peddler believes.' Thus the story is also told of how the great Thomas Aquinas, at the time of his death, could not hold out against the devil until he said: 'I believe what is written in this book', and he held the Bible in his arm. But God does not reward us much for such a faith, since if these people believed nothing more than this, they both, doctor and coal peddler, believed themselves into the abyss of hell. Other spirits also believe themselves into hell by saying: 'Believe whatever it was that Christ taught; that is enough.' O yes, this is a fine and healthy faith, but such faith doesn't worry the devil at all.[26]

This version of the story appears within the context of a discussion of implicit faith. It is a critical comment on Thomas inasmuch as the story is used here to illustrate the inadequacy of an implicit faith which ignores the content of belief. The same kind of critique is implied in another version of the story which Luther used in a sermon in 1532: rather than Thomas merely saying 'I believe what is in this book', it would have been better if the book had been studied and its content absorbed.[27]

Yet Luther can also use the story in other ways. In a table talk probably stemming from this same period, Luther merely recounts the story without making any critical comment

---

[25] The editors of the version of the story in WA 48, 691, 18ff give the date as "unknown". However, since the other four versions of the story are from 1532/33, it seems likely that this one too comes from the same period. The version of the story given in WATR 2, 82, 11-15 (1532) gives the name "Thomas Müntzer" rather than "Thomas Aquinas" -- yet the editors acknowledge that most texts read "Thomas Aquinas." Again, since it is unmistakably Thomas Aquinas that the other four versions refer to, and since there is a discrepancy between different texts, I prefer here the reading "Thomas Aquinas".

[26] WA 30 III, 562, 27ff (1533): "Also sagt man, wie ein Doctor hab ein Köler zu Prage auff der brücken aus mit leiden, als uber einen armen leyen, gefragt: Lieber man, Was gleubstu? Der Köler antwortet: Das die Kirche gleubt. Der Doctor: Was gleubt denn die Kirche? Der Köler: Das ich gleube. Darnach, da der Doctor hat sollen sterben, ist er vom Teuffel so hart angefochten im glauben, das er nirgent hat können bleiben noch ruge [sic] haben, bis das er sprach: Ich gleube, das der Köler gleubt, Wie man auch von dem grossen Thoma Aquino sagt, das er an seinem ende fur dem Teuffel nicht hat bleiben konnen, bis das er sprach: Ich gleube, was inn diesem buch stehet, und hatte die Bibel inn armen. Aber Gott verleihe uns solchs glaubens nicht viel, Denn wo diese nicht anders haben denn also gegleubt, so hat sich beide, Doctor und Köler, inn abgrund der hellen hinein gegleubt, Dahinein gleuben auch solche geister, die da sagen: gleube den leib, den Christus meinet, das ist gnug, O ia, es ist fein und wol gegleubt, Solcher glaube schadet dem Teuffel nichts."

[27] WA 36, 318, 22ff (1532): "Si non scripturam in corde und ein wenig versucht hast, so wird dir das buch nichts helffen. Fiet tibi ut Thomae monacho u. da er nicht weiter kund, nam er das buch und dicebat: credo, quod in libro. Scripserat mundum plenum libris. Si in corde habuisset, wers viel besser gewesen."

whatsoever.[28]   Another version from 1533 appears within the context of a critique of the monastic life. Even such a life of devotion, Luther says, cannot bring certainty of salvation. Thomas Aquinas himself experienced grave doubt at the end of his life so that he finally had to say to the devil: 'I believe what is written in this book'.[29] Here it is important to notice that while it is set within the context of a critique of the monastic life, the story itself exemplifies victory over doubt and temptation. While Luther is critical of Thomas' teaching on the monastic life,[30] he casts no aspersions in this case on the person of Thomas.

The various ways, both critical and benign, in which Luther uses this particular story about Thomas illustrates a certain ambiguity in his view of Thomas' person, at least at this stage of his life. One can only speculate on why this particular story was of such great interest to Luther during these years. This speculation should be grounded on the fact that there are two themes in this story which were directly related to Luther's own experience.

The story deals first of all with the theme of "Anfechtung", an ambivalent term which Luther uses to refer to doubt, temptation to despair, anxiety, and dread in the face of death. Such Anfechtung was of course a life-long problem for Luther, beginning during his monastic period and recurring periodically until his death.[31] The increasing seriousness of his own illnesses after 1531, a greater foreboding about his own death, and a growing preoccupation with the devil may well have heightened these Anfechtungen and hence also his interest in this story in the early 1530's.[32] The "fact" that Thomas Aquinas had experienced something similar was perhaps of some comfort to Luther. Moreover, it should be noted that for Luther, such Anfechtung in the face of death is by no means a sign of weak faith. Christ himself, Luther liked to recall, was tempted to such despair. In fact, during precisely this same period of his life Luther asserted that without Anfechtung one cannot really know what the spiritual life is.[33] From Luther's point of view then, Thomas' experience of doubt was in no way a negative reflection on his faith.

The second theme in this story which no doubt attracted Luther's attention to it, is the theme of victory over these Anfechtungen through a faith grounded in the Bible. We have seen that in some versions, Luther depicts this victory as a hollow one. But on the other hand, it is still a victory won with the help of Scripture. This is interesting of course in the light of Luther's *sola scriptura* emphasis, but it is even more interesting in the light of Luther's critique of Thomas' use of Scripture. For Luther more than once accuses Thomas of preferring Aristotle over Scripture.[34] The story then may represent for Luther the triumph of Scripture over Aristotle in the person of Thomas Aquinas himself -- the one who, in Luther's view, introduced Aristotle into the schools.

---

[28] WA 48, 691, 18ff (date unknown): "Thomas Aquinas iam moriturus disputavit cum diabolo, et cum vinceretur ab eo, hatte er die bibel bey sich und sagte: En habes librum, bey dem bleib ich!"

[29] WA 38, 148, 13ff (1533): ". . .Sanct Thoma Prediger ordens, der doch selbs an seinem ende auch verzweivelt und sprechen must widder den Teuffel: Ich glaube, was inn diesem buch (meinet die Biblia) stehet. . . ." Note that Luther's own temptations to despair were most acute in his monastic period.

[30] See the analysis of this critique below, Ch. II.

[31] On Luther's Anfechtungen, see John von Rohr, "Medieval Consolation and the Young Luther's Despair", in Franklin H. Littel, ed., *Reformation Studies and Essays in Honor of Roland H. Bainton*, (Richmond, VA: John Knox, 1962), pp. 61-74; and C. Warren Hovland, "Anfechtung in Luther's Biblical Exegesis", in *ibid.*, pp. 46-60.

[32] On Luther's physical and mental condition after 1530, see Mark Edwards, *Luther's Last Battles*, (Ithaca, N.Y.: Cornell University Press, 1983), pp. 6-19.

[33] WATR 4, 490, 24-491, 1 (1530-40).

[34] WATR 1, 118, 1-3 (1532); WATR 5, 686, 15-17 (date unknown); etc. This issue is examined in detail below, Ch II.

10

Luther's interest in this story almost certainly stems from an affinity he felt with Thomas. Like himself, Thomas had experienced Anfechtungen. And like himself, Thomas had experienced victory over these assaults of the devil. In fact, Luther can describe his own victory in almost exactly the same terms as Thomas' victory. During precisely the period when Luther was telling and re-telling this story about Thomas, he described (in a table talk from the Spring of 1533) his own assaults of Anfechtung. He reports that he was often almost overwhelmed by these assaults, "But when I have taken hold of the Scriptures I have won."[35]

Thus Luther's repeated telling of this particular story represents an ambiguous comment on the person of Thomas. On the one hand it is a critique of a kind of implicit faith which is devoid of content. But on the other hand, it also depicts this eminent theologian at the end of his life overcoming the most violent onslaughts of Anfechtung with a simple appeal to Scripture, as Luther himself had done.

This same ambiguity in fact characterizes Luther's comments on the person of Thomas taken as a whole. On the one hand Luther can vilify Thomas in the most abusive terms, and on the other hand he finds in Thomas virtues which he holds forth as exemplary. His comments on Thomas' person range from vindictive criticism to good-natured humor, from the derogatory to the complimentary. What is clear from this survey is that Luther's view of the person of Thomas cannot simply be spoken of in negative terms. The open contempt with which Luther treated some of his Thomist opponents is absent in his treatment of Thomas himself. And the loathing which Luther had for some theologians is muted when it comes to Thomas. The view that Luther simply despised Thomas as a person is overruled by the evidence presented here.

Obviously there were vast personality differences between Luther and Thomas. Perhaps this is best illustrated by the story told of Thomas by his disciple, Bartholemew Capua. In the company of friends, Thomas was taken to survey the beauty of Paris from the elevated vantage point of the Cathedral St. Denys. Truthfully, he said, I would gladly give all the wonders of Paris for a copy of Chrysostom's commentary on Matthew.[36] Luther would not have paid such a high price for Chrysostom, that "blabbermouth",[37] but he would, he tells us, trade all of France or Venice for his Katie.[38] The personality differences speak for themselves, and, in the face of such differences, perhaps the most one could hope for is a grudging admiration. One indeed senses this in Luther. Thomas seems to have been for Luther an example of how great persons can at the same time be seriously mistaken. It is this image of Thomas as a person that lies behind Luther's theological critique, to which we now turn our attention.

[35] WATR 1, 238, 19. Tr. from LW 54, 93.
[36] Chenu, *Toward Understanding Saint Thomas*, p. 247, n. 23.
[37] WATR 1, 85, 3; 106, 4; etc.
[38] WATR 1, 17, 10ff.

CHAPTER II

LUTHER ON THE THEOLOGY OF THOMAS

1. Introduction

To anyone familiar with Luther, it comes as no surprise that he was critical of the theology of Thomas Aquinas. There are after all vast incongruities between the two great systems of thought propounded by these theologians, and it was natural that a person of Luther's temperament was not reluctant to point them out. However, the precise nature and extend of this critique has never been grasped by interpreters of Luther.

In the last hundred years, there have been of course a considerable number of attempts to spell out what the fundamental differences between Luther and Thomas are. While some of these attempts may well be correct in their identification of such basic intra-systemic disagreements, others are certainly mistaken. But what all have in common is that they in large measure bypass Luther's actual critique. Such comparative studies have most often taken as their point of departure Luther's well-known and programmatic-sounding statement about Thomas: that he is "the source and foundation of all heresy, error and obliteration of the Gospel".[1] And building on this statement, these analyses have been developed often with scarcely any further reference to the primary texts. Obviously such forays into comparative systematics remain largely speculative.

It is the aim of this Chapter to bring this whole discussion back to earth by examining Luther's actual statements on the theology of Thomas. Comparisons of Luther and Thomas, while they may well go beyond Luther's actual critique of Thomas, should at least begin there. The following thorough investigation of this critique, it is hoped, will provide this foundation. In doing so, it will inevitably alter some long-cherished notions about where the important dissonances lie between two of the most influential theological systems in the history of Christian theology.

The objection will immediately be raised that Luther's assessment of Thomas should not be seen in isolation from his more general critique of scholastic theology. According to this line of thinking, Luther attacked the whole of scholastic theology as being in some ways a fundamentally mistaken enterprise and Thomas' theology is only one instance of this. Luther's own theology was developed in conscious opposition to this whole theological tradition, and therefore his critique of an individual scholastic like Thomas was only of secondary importance to him. What Thomas actually taught on any particular doctrine was of minor concern to Luther, in comparison to the entire scholastic *modus loquendi theologicus*.[2]

Such an objection, it must be conceded, has an element of validity to it: the two critiques are obviously related in some way. But it must also be pointed out that the relation between Luther's critique of scholastic theology and his critique of Thomas is not a simple one. His general attack on scholastic theology is in itself, as Luther scholars know, highly problematic. While Luther from time to time lumps all the scholastics together, as in the title of his 1517 "Disputatio contra scholasticam theologiam," it cannot be said that Luther has an undifferentiated view of scholaticism. Even in this kind of general disputation Luther distinguishes between different kinds of "scholastics" and frequently names the ones he is attacking.[3] Moreover, until the end of his life Luther

---

[1] WA 15, 184, 32f (1524).

[2] This view is represented by Leif Grane, "Die Anfänge von Luthers Auseinandersetzung mit dem Thomismus", p. 247.

[3] So for instance, in the "Disputatio contra scholasticam theologiam", Luther names Scotus, Occam, Biel, *et al*. See WA 1, 224-228.

12

continued to distinguish not only between the *via antiqua* and the *via moderna* but also between the various schools within these scholastic *viae*: "via Thomae," "via Albertistae," "via Scotistae," etc.[4] Although Luther directs critical statements against scholastic theology in general, he is aware that all scholastics are not the same. This fact already calls into question the assumption that Luther's general critique of scholastic theology is in fact a critique of Thomas' theology.

This assumption that the two can simply be identified is further called into question by the realization that Luther consciously speaks in a very loose sense when he criticizes "the scholastics." When he accuses "the scholastics" of teaching something, he is often perfectly aware that there are exceptions. Thus, for instance, when he says that all the scholastics were inordinately influenced by Aristotle,[5] he is perfectly aware that some of them were not. He had after all read and commented on the *Sentences* of Peter Lombard and had found there nothing of Aristotle.[6] Likewise in attacking all the scholastics as "Pelagian", he was well aware that some were not: in his own view, Gregory of Rimini was a noteworthy exception.[7] Again, what this suggests is that when Luther attacks "scholastic theology", he speaks in consciously unnuanced generalities: we cannot assume that what he says about scholastic theology as such is intended to apply to Thomas Aquinas. The two critiques are not identical.

Clearly then, when Luther criticizes "scholastic theology" we must ask who Luther has in mind. Who is the primary target of such attacks? Often this question simply cannot be answered with precision. But it would be illegitimate to assume that in each case he has Thomas Aquinas in mind. A much more justifiable assumption would be that such attacks are directed against the kind of scholastic theology which Luther was trained in and which he knew best, namely that of Gabriel Biel.

For all these reasons, it is legitimate and even desireable in this context to disengage Luther's critique of Thomas' theology from his critique of scholasticism in general. That is after all what he himself does in singling out the theology of Thomas for specific criticisms.

From 1516 until the end of his life, Luther saw fit to comment on the theology of Thomas Aquinas on many occasions and in diverse contexts. These often caustic remarks themselves range from the most general to the highly specific. Occasionally Luther attacks Thomas' theology as a whole on methodological grounds: for example, Luther is critical of Thomas' use of Aristotle, his exegetical method, or the lack of an experiential dimension in Thomas' theology. Much more frequently the target of Luther's critique is a highly specific doctrine on which he disagrees with Thomas: e.g. Thomas' teaching on purgatory, Thomas' view of the angels, etc. In fact there are some thirteen different issues such as these on which Luther is critical of Thomas' point of view.

To thus divide Luther's critique of Thomas into a list of specific doctrines is of course somewhat arbitrary in the sense that many if not all of these doctrines are systematically related to one another. For instance, Luther's critique of Thomas on justification is systematically related to his critique of Thomas on law. Or, to cite another example, there is a systematic connection between his attack on Thomas' teaching on purgatory and his attack on Thomas' view of indulgences. In the final analysis perhaps every object of Luther's criticism is related in some way to all the rest. The systematic context of Luther's critiques, therefore, should not be ignored. Nevertheless, since Luther himself critiqued Thomas' theology in this kind of fragmentary way, it would be an artificial construct were we here to systematize Luther's critique of Thomas' theology

---

[4] E.g. WATR 4, 679, 3-5 (1540).
[5] E.g. WA 1, 226, 26f. (1517). Cf. WA 1, 227, 35f. (1517) against "the scholastics" and the exception Luther himself makes in WA 1, 228, 5f. (1517).
[6] Luther lectured on the *Sentences* in 1509/10.
[7] WA 2, 394, 31ff (1519).

for him -- to construct out of Luther's specific objections one general critique. In the description and analysis that follows, therefore, the specific issues on which Luther criticized Thomas are treated individually and distinctly.

These issues fall into two categories. On the one hand, there are those which can roughly be designated as methodological, and these are treated first. And on the other hand there are specific doctrines on which Luther criticizes Thomas, and these are treated next. Within each of these two categories, the order of subjects is arranged here according to the significance which they had for Luther, with the most important coming first. Obviously this arrangement reflects my own judgement and is open to dispute.

How can one gauge the relative significance which Luther attached to these various critiques? The criteria used here in making such judgments should be explicit from the outset. One supposition of this study is that the frequency and persistence of any critique *can* be an indication of the importance it had for Luther. Thus if Luther criticized Thomas' view on the veneration of images twice in his entire career, it is difficult to argue that this was very important to Luther. If, on the other hand, Luther over and over again attacked Thomas' view on another issue, and if this criticism was raised at various stages throughout the course of Luther's career, one would tend to assume that it was a relatively weighty issue in Luther's estimate.

Yet the frequency of a critique is only one of many factors to be considered. There can be no strict correlation between the number of times Luther addresses himself to an issue and its relative significance. One must remember, for instance, that at times Luther's critiques are determined by his opponents, as is the case in the indulgences controversy. The polemical agenda set by Thomist opponents in this case, has something to do with his oft-repeated critique of Thomas on indulgences. Here, in addition to the frequency of these critiques, one must also obviously pay attention to their historical and literary context. Thus, while frequency may give us an indication of significance, such matters cannot be determined simply by counting.

The other criteria used here for gauging the relative importance of issues for Luther are even more complex, and perhaps even more important. They have to do with matters of vehemence, cogency, thoroughness, veracity, etc. Estimations of relative significance are based on a combination of all these factors. And the rationale for such judgments is more or less explicit in my analysis of each of the issues that follow.

2. Experience

It is well known that in seeking to understand the precise role of experience in Luther's theology, one enters a veritable quagmire of paradoxical if not contradictory statements, the complexity of which has scarcely yet been fathomed. For Luther, experience teaches human beings of their sinfulness and yet the full dimensions of human sinfulness contradict our experience; faith is beyond experience and yet it is experienced; faith contradicts our experience and yet experience can be a theological proof; faith leads to experience and yet faith stands completely alone with experience; etc. What is clear amidst this "disturbing"[8] complexity is that experience plays a major if not decisive role in Luther's theological method. Theology is for Luther "an experimental wisdom, not a doctrinal one."[9] "Experience alone," he says, "makes one a theologian."[10]

On precisely this methodological issue Luther perceived a stark contrast between his theology and that of Thomas. While his own theology was at every stage intimately related to experience in a rich variety of complex ways, he perceived in Thomas' theology the total absence of any experiential dimension. And this perception was the basis for a variety of related criticisms levelled against Thomas especially in the 1530's.

Luther's first statement on this matter occurs in his *Rationis Latomianae Confutatio* of 1521.[11] Speaking in the context of penance, works righteousness, slavery to sin, etc., Luther says:

> . . .I have to some extent tested these spiritual matters in experience,
> but I clearly see that Thomas, and all those who write and teach
> similarly, have neglected this.[12]

Luther had indeed had intense experience in these things and here he calls on that experience as a validation of his way of speaking about them theologically. Thomas' "neglect" of this was evident to Luther from the fact that Thomas nowhere alludes to his own experience in his discussion of these matters. But more importantly, Luther means to suggest that if Thomas had deeply experienced these things, his way of speaking about them would be different.

It was not until 1532 that Luther returned to this theme in relation to Thomas. But in that year Luther raised the issue on four separate occasions. First, in a table talk early in 1532, Luther says that only Gerson wrote about "spiritual temptation"; others such as Thomas only wrote about bodily temptations.[13] By "spiritual temptation" Luther means the temptation to despair, to lose faith, to sin against the first commandment. This is the ultimate "Anfechtung" for Luther, beside which mere bodily temptations fade into insignificance. And it is experience of this which Luther thinks is lacking in Thomas (or at least Thomas does not write about it). Thus, as Luther

---

[8] Joseph Lortz, "Basic Elements of Luther's Intellectual Style," in J. Wicks, ed., *Catholic Scholars Dialogue with Luther*, (Chicago: Loyola U. Press, 1970), pp. 3-33, p. 10.

[9] WA 9, 98, 21 (1516).

[10] WATR 1, 16, 13 (1531).

[11] In a 1516 lecture of questionable authenticity we find an allusion which Luther will later make explicit: "Primum enim in contione verbum ex Thoma seu ex Aristotele est, et quia consequens non movet, nec ferire potest in homine interiore." WA 4, 537, 12ff (1516?).

[12] WA 8, 127, 18ff. Tr. from LW 32, 258.

[13] WATR 2, 64, 22-24 (early 1532): "Solus Gerson scripsit de tentatione spiritus, alii omnes tantum corporales senserunt, ...Thomas..." Cf. WATR 2, 468, 5-9 (early 1532), where the same thing is said. These are almost certainly reports of the same conversation.

adds further in the same passage, only Gerson is of value when it comes to the matter of soothing the troubled conscience.[14]

In a table conversation, in March 1532, Luther drew a further contrast between Gerson and Thomas. There are, according to Luther, two kinds of theologians, "men of conscience" such as Gerson, and speculative theologians such as Thomas.[15] Luther's earlier reference to Gerson suggests that by "men of conscience" Luther has in mind theologians who can speak effectively to the troubled conscience. Thomas, as a "speculative" theologian cannot do this; his theology in other words is insufficiently practical. In this sense too Thomas' theology lacks an experiential dimension.

Again in a table conversation, in July of that same year Luther expressed the same view, this time in the form of a maxim:

> Thomas is not worth a louse; and the same goes for his writings:
> Wash only my pelt and don't make me wet.[16]

Thomas' speculative theology is worthless in Luther's view because it merely dabbles in externals; it is powerless to reach the inner depths of the person. As Luther adds further in this same table talk, there is thus nothing in Thomas which would lead one to trust in Christ.[17]

On 5 September 1532 Luther returned to the same theme in a sermon preached at the castle church in Wittenberg. He recounts the legend of Thomas defeating temptation by professing belief in the Bible (discussed above, Ch. I). But it would have been much better, Luther adds, if Thomas "would have had it in his heart." Scripture must be "tried out" in the heart for it to be of any value.[18] Thus Luther seems to suggest that Thomas lacked inner experience of these truths; they remained for him merely objects of speculation.

Finally, in a sermon preached on 20 December 1533, we find a concrete example of how Thomas' "lack of experience" impoverishes his understanding of Scripture. Commenting on the words "Abraham begat" in Matt. 1:2, Luther asserts that he did this in no other way than by sleeping with his wife. This must have been unbelievable and unintelligible to a monk like Thomas who didn't have a wife. Experience enhances our ability to understand how God's work, word and holiness are carried forward by such earthly means.[19]

We recall though that Luther acknowledges at least one profound religious experience in Thomas, and he does this in his repeated telling of the legend alluded to above. For this legend tells of the grave "Anfechtung" which Thomas experienced at the end of his life (Cf. above, Ch. I). And we recall too that for Luther, without "Anfechtung" one cannot really know what the

---

[14] WATR 2, 64, 30 (early 1532): "Solus Gerson valet ad mitigandas conscientias."

[15] WA 2, 516, 9-11 (March 1532): "Duplices sunt theologi, scilicet viri conscientiae, Wilhelmus Parrhisiensis et Gerson; speculativi sunt Thomas, Scotus, Occam, Alexander, etc...."

[16] WATR 2, 193, 3f (12 July 1532): "Thomas ist nicht einer laus werdt; ist gleich mit seinem schreiben: Wasch nur den beltz und mach mir den nicht nass." Cf. WATR 1, 73, 28f (1531/32) where Luther applies the same maxim to Aristotle.

[17] WATR 2, 193, 5f: "Im gantzen Thoma ist nicht ein wort, das einem mocht ein zuversicht zu Christo machen."

[18] WA 36, 318, 22ff: "Si non scripturam in corde und ein wenig versucht hast, so wird dir das buch nichts helffen. Fiet tibi ut Thomae monacho u. da er nicht weiter kund, nam er das buch et dicebat: credo, quod in libro. Scripserat mundum plenum libris. Si in corde habuisset, wers viel besser gewessen."

[19] WA 37, 225, 11ff: "'Abraham zeuget' u. nihil quam quod cum uxore dormierit. Et mus ein garstiger Monch, S. Thoma, non habuit uxorem, fuit Monachus, eitel ungläubig, unverständig, qui nec dei opus, verbum nec Sanctitatem intellexit, quod nihil . . . etecontra. Hoc fit quotidie." In his commentary on the same passage (Catena super Matthaei Evangelium 1:2), Thomas mentions carnal generation but quickly moves on to the spiritual senses: e.g. Abraham begat Isaac just as faith begets hope, etc. (Vivès 16, 12-14).

spiritual life is.[20] Luther seems to think that Thomas' decisive religious experience came at the end of his life. Until that point Thomas himself lacked such experience and this is reflected in his writings. For one finds in his theology no experiential dimension and it is therefore powerless to speak to people's inner religious needs.

The accuracy of Luther's view of Thomas' personal religious experience need not concern us here. Though we know next to nothing about Thomas' own religious life, we might well surmise that Luther's view is somewhat exaggerated. What we do know is that in Thomas' theology experience does not play a central role. In seeing this, Luther's critique was an extraordinarily perceptive one. For what Luther perceives here is a fundamentally different way of doing theology.

The best framework from which to analyze this difference, it seems to me, is Otto Pesch's well-known distinction between existential and sapiential theology. As he formulates it,

> Existential theology is the way of doing theology from within the self-actuation of our existence in faith, as we submit to God in the obedience of faith. Its affirmations are so formulated that the actual faith and confession of the speaker are not merely necessary presuppositions but are reflexly thematized. Sapiential theology is the way of doing theology from outside one's self-actuation in the existence in faith, in the sense that in its doctrinal statements the faith and confession of the speaker is the enduring presupposition, but is not thematic within this theology. This theology strives to mirror and recapitulate God's own thoughts about the world, men, and history, insofar as God has disclosed them.[21]

In proposing this as "the ultimate level of opposition" between Luther and Thomas, Pesch finds few hints at such a distinction in either theologian.[22] But the critique that has been uncovered here directly substantiates Pesch's analysis. Experience is central to Luther's theology precisely because theology is done from within the experience of faith and has this experience as its theme. On the other hand, experience is to some extend programmatically excluded in Thomas because the central task of theology is not reflection on faith but the description of reality from God's point of view. In his critique of the absence of an experiential dimension in Thomas' theology, Luther was criticizing in fact a fundamentally different approach to theology. Luther's critique thus represents an awareness of their diverging theological methods. But Luther does not show an equally clear understanding of the consequence of this, namely, that such methodological differences, in Pesch's words, "necessarily produce diverse and even opposing dogmatic formulations about one and the same given reality."[23]

---

[20]WATR 4, 490, 24-491, 1 (1530-40).

[21] Otto H. Pesch, "Existential and Sapiential Theology -- the Theological Confrontation between Luther and Thomas Aquinas," in J. Wicks, ed., *Catholic Scholars Dialogue with Luther*, (Chicago: Loyola Univ Press, 1970), pp. 61-81 and 182-193, p. 76f. For further explanation see the entire essay.

[22] *Ibid.*, p. 65.

[23] *Ibid.*

3. Aristotle

The use of Aristotle in theology was one of the most important issues on which Luther attacked the very methodology of scholasticism. His views on this issue had already become clear in his 1517 "Disputatio contra scholasticam theologiam." Here approximately 20% of his complaints bore on the scholastic appropriation of Aristotle, and they were summed up succinctly in his famous thesis 50: "Briefly the whole Aristotle is to theology as darkness is to light. This in opposition to the scholastics."[24] From this point onward, Luther's opposition to the employment of Aristotelian thought in theology remained adamant.[25]

Important as this critique is for Luther, the tendency in the past to see it as a fundamental parting of the ways with Catholic theology has more recently been tempered by a new awareness of the immediate context. This includes, first, Luther's intellectual formation in the anti-Aristotelian environment of Erfurt,[26] and second, the already existing Augustinian and humanist critiques of Aristotle.[27] Indeed such critiques of the use of Aristotle in theology existed from the time of the "re-discovery" of Aristotle in the West -- that "sensational event"[28] of the late 12th and early 13th centuries. It should not be forgotten that this event was greeted with a massive resistance led by Bonaventure and culminating in official ecclesiastical censure.[29] Thirteenth century theologians no less than Luther could see the intrusion of Aristotle into theology as a betrayal of the gospel: in the words of one of them, "The spirit of Christ does not reign where the spirit of Aristotle dominates."[30] Resistance to the intrusion of Aristotle into theology, therefore, cannot be treated as something new and unique in Luther. Even the vehemence of Luther's critique should not be allowed to obscure the fact that Luther also had positive things to say about Aristotle.[31] While none of these considerations minimize the importance of Luther's critique, they are part of the context which is indispensable for understanding it.

Within this sweeping methodological critique of scholasticism, one aspect of it is of immediate concern here, namely, his critique of Thomas' use of Aristotle. What precisely did Luther have to say about Thomas on this matter, and what significance did this have in his evaluation of Thomas as a whole?

It was in 1518, and therefore at the very outset of his confrontation with Thomism, that Luther's critique of Thomas' use of Aristotle began. First, in his lectures on the 10 commandments published in July of that year, we find Luther deploring the confusion of opinions among the scholastic sects. The division of scholasticism into "Thomists, Scotists, Albertists and Moderni" means that scholasticism has become a "four-headed Aristotle."[32] All these scholastic schools seem

---

[24] WA 1, 226, 26f. Tr. from LW 31, 38.

[25] See for instance his 1536 "Disputatio de Homine," the definitive text of which can be found in G.Ebeling, *Lutherstudien II: Disputatio de Homine*, (Tübingen: Mohr, 1977).

[26] Karl-Heinz zur Mühlen, "Luther und Aristoteles," in *Lutherjahrbuch*, 52 (1985), 263-266, p. 265.

[27] Willigis Eckermann, "Die Aristoteleskritik Luthers: Ihre Bedeutung für seine Theologie," in *Catholica*, 32 (1978), 114-130, p. 114. Cf. Adolar Zumkeller, "Die Augustinertheologen Simon Fidati von Cascia und Hugolin von Orvieto und Martin Luthers Kritik an Aristoteles," in *Archiv für Reformationsgeschichte*, 54 (1963), 15-37; and Martin Grabmann, "Aristoteles im Werturteil des Mittelalters," in *Mittelalterliches Geistesleben: Abhandlungen zur Geschichte der Scholastik und Mystik*, 3 vols, (Munich: M. Hueber, 1926-56), II, pp. 63-102.

[28] M.D. Chenu, *Toward Understanding Saint Thomas*, pp. 31f.

[29] *Ibid.*, pp. 35ff.

[30] Absalom of St. Victor, Sermo 4, PL 211, 370; quoted in Chenu, *Toward Understanding Saint Thomas*, p. 35, n.25.

[31] WA 6, 458, 26ff (examined in detail below).

[32] WA 1, 509, 11ff: "...nam ibi sunt Thomistae, Scotistae, Albertistae, Moderni, et factus est quadriceps Aristoteles et regnum in seipsum divisum, et mirum quod non desoletur, sed prope est ut desoletur." Was Luther's reference to "quadriceps Aristoteles" the inspiration for Cochlaeus' later "septiceps Lutherus"? On Cochlaeus, see Gotthelf Wiedermann,

18

here to fall under Luther's judgment in this regard. Yet not unexpectedly, in his *Ad Prieratis*, published a month later, Thomism is singled out for special criticism. Here Luther accuses Thomas (and Prierias) of relying only on Aristotle for their opinion. The result of this mode of argumentation can only be a "probable" opinion, which is to say a doubtful one.[33] Thomism, in Luther's view, does this often enough to deserve the title of a "peripatetic theology" as opposed to his own Pauline theology.[34] Moreover, in his "Resolutiones" on the 95 theses, published almost simultaneously with *Ad Prieratis* Luther enunciated for the first time a complaint which was to come up again, namely, that the scholastics (including and especially Thomas) have misunderstood Aristotle, and have spread these misunderstandings throughout the Church.[35] Though Luther gives no specifics on this here, presumably he has in mind scholastic disagreement over the interpretation of Aristotle which has resulted in the "quadriceps Aristoteles"--obvious evidence of misunderstanding.

Meanwhile, in the Heidelberg Disputation held in April of 1518, Luther had launched his most aggressive attack yet on Aristotle's teaching and on its use in theology.[36] And this he had done without any reference to Thomas and the Thomists. His intention had been, as he explained shortly after the Disputation, to show that the scholastics had misunderstood Aristotle and that even when correctly understood, Aristotle is of no value for theology.[37] Early in 1519 this general attack on the scholastic tradition was sharpened by Luther to apply specifically to Thomas. In a letter to Spalatin of 14 January, Luther claims to have shown that neither Thomas nor any of the Thomists have understood Aristotle.[38] Setting aside Luther's to some degree characteristic exaggeration, it is of interest here that Luther now singles out Thomas and the Thomists from among all the "Aristotelian" scholastic schools. This is no doubt related to the fact that his major preoccupation at the time was the controversy with Thomism. And there are strong grounds for suspecting that the Thomists had given him good reason to single them out for such criticism. For example, Prierias' reply to Luther's *Ad Prieratis*, published in November of 1518, had spoken of Aristotle in the most extravagant terms: his truth shines brighter than the sun, and no falsehood has yet been found in him (except for his opinion on the eternity of the world).[39] Little wonder

"Cochlaeus as Polemicist," in Peter N. Brooks, ed., *Seven-Headed Luther: Essays in Commemoration of a Quincentenary, 1483-1983*, (Oxford: Clarendon, 1983), pp. 195-205. In his *Operationes in Psalmos* (1519-21), Luther again lumps Aristotle together with Scotists, Thomists and Occamists (WA 5, 371, 34ff.)

[33] WA 1, 664, 16ff.

[34] WA 1, 652, 31ff.: "...Sed sisto: nescio enim, an Thomistica Theologia hanc Theologiam unquam senserit: Paulina est enim, non Peripatetica."

[35] WA 1, 611, 25-30: "Nam in quantis, quaeso, B. Thomam etiam Scholastici errasse arguunt! Immo quod maius est, iam plus trecentis annis tot universitates, tot in illis acutissima ingenia, tot ingeniorum pertinacissima studia in uno Aristolele laborant, et tamen adhuc non solum Aristolelem non intelligunt, verum etiam errorem et fictam intelligentiam per universam pene ecclesiam spargunt..."

[36] See the philosophical theses (no. 29-40) of the Heidelberg Disputation, WA 1, 355, 1-25.

[37] WA 9, 170, 1ff. During this same period (1518-19), Luther was campaigning to have Thomistic studies dropped from the curriculum in Wittenberg. These included Thomas' Aristotle commentaries. See WABR 1, 262, 1ff; 325, 1ff; and 359, 1ff. Luther cannot have been wholly ignorant of these commentaries on Aristotle.

[38] WABR 1, 301, 19ff: "Caeterum Disputatio erat super Aristoteles et Thomae nugis. Ostendi ego nec Thomam nec omnes simul Thomistas vel unum Aristolele intellexisse capitulum."

[39] Walch 18, 418: "...den Aristoteles--den (so zu sagen) die ganze Naturbewundert und dessen wahrheit...heller als die Sonne ist, in dessen Lehre, sei sie in seinem die Gesetze des Denkens, oder der Natur, oder der Sittlichkeit betreffenden Schriften, bis jetzt noch keine Falschheit gefunden wurde, ausser dass er nicht für gewiss...die Meinung von der Evigkeit der Welt gehabt hat..."

then that Luther came to see Thomism as the champion of Aristotle. In comparison with such statements, Thomas' use of Aristotle seems extremely cautious.[40]

Two important works from 1520 carry forward Luther's critique of Thomas' use of Aristotle. First, in his *To the Christian Nobility* which was completed in June of that year, Luther asserts that his knowledge of Aristotle is superior to that of Thomas:

> I know my Aristotle as well as you or the likes of you. I have
> lectured on him and been lectured on him, and I understand him
> better than St. Thomas or Duns Scotus did.[41]

It should be mentioned here parenthetically that in this context Luther can also make a positive statement about Aristotle:

> I would gladly agree to keeping Aristotle's books, *Logic, Rhetoric* and
> *Poetics*, or at least keeping and using them in an abridged form, as
> useful in training young people to speak and to preach properly.[42]

A few months later, on October 6, Luther's *Babylonian Captivity of the Church* appeared. In this work Luther took issue with the attempt to make transubstantiation into an article of faith. He begins by recounting Pierre d'Ailly's opinion: more convincing reasons can be given for the view that real bread and wine are present on the altar, if only the church had not decreed otherwise. Luther adds that he has now learned what church decreed this--"the Thomistic--that is the Aristotelian Church."[43] This of course would be nonsense (as Denifle and Grisar gleefully pointed out), if the Church's "decree" on transubstantiation is taken to be the statement of Lateran IV in 1215. In response to this, Grane has argued that Luther was essentially correct in associating this dogma with Thomas since his influence on the fully developed theory was the determining one.[44] Moreover, we might add, it is very doubtful that Lateran IV intended to make transubstantiation into an article of faith, even though it used the term. Be this as it may, Luther goes on to say that this is a mere opinion of Thomas, and worse yet, one that is based on Aristotle.

> But this opinion of Thomas hangs so completely in the air without
> support of Scripture or reason that it seems to me he knows neither
> his philosophy nor his logic. For Aristotle speaks of subject and
> accidents so very differently from St. Thomas that it seems to me this
> great man is to be pitied not only for attempting to draw his
> opinions in matters of faith from Aristotle, but also for attempting
> to base them upon a man whom he did not understand, thus building
> an unfortunate superstructure upon an unfortunate foundation.[45]

---

[40] On Thomas' use of Aristotle, M.D. Chenu's treatment (*Toward Understanding St. Thomas*, pp. 31-39, 156-232) is one of the best.

[41] WA 6, 458, 18ff. Tr. from LW 44, 201.

[42] WA 6, 458, 26ff. Tr. from LW 44, 201.

[43] WA 6, 508, 11f.: "Postea videns, quae esset Ecclesia, quae hoc determinasset, nempe Thomistica, hoc est Aristotelica..."

[44] Leif Grane, "Luthers Kritik an Thomas von Aquin in De Captivitate Babylonica," in *Zeitschrift für Kirchengeschichte*, 80 (1969), 1-13, p. 7.

[45] WA 6, 508, 20ff. Tr. from LW 36, 29.

Thomas, according to Luther, based his opinion on Aristotle, and moreover failed to understand Aristotle correctly.[46]

In 1521 Luther's identification of Thomas and Thomism with the teaching of Aristotle receives even greater emphasis. In his response to the Thomist Ambrosius Catharinus, Luther speaks of Thomas and Aristotle as a single entity,[47] and Thomists such as Catharinus therefore are defending an "Aristotelean theology."[48] Moreover, in his *Against Latomus* of the same year, Luther clearly blames Thomas for the "reign of Aristotle" in theology.[49]

This reign of Aristotle in theology, so Luther explains in a sermon of 1522, has brought with it a corruption of the Pauline understanding of justification. Thomas errs when he follows Aristotle in saying that one becomes righteous by practicing virtue, i.e. by performing righteous acts. One does not become righteous by performing virtuous actions, but rather one is first made righteous by faith. Faith alone is the fulfillment of the law.[50] Here is a concrete example from Luther of how Aristotle, through Thomas, has distorted the Gospel. As Luther had put it a year previously (without mentioning Thomas), moral virtues have been put in the place of faith.[51] Thus, through Aristotle, the Christian understanding of grace and merit had been corrupted.[52]

Throughout the rest of the 1520's, Luther's critique of Thomas' use of Aristotle recedes into the background, except for two sermons in which he again reproaches Thomas for introducing this "paganism" into Christian theology. In these sermons Luther gives different versions of the same allegory. In the first, preached in 1523, Luther ascribes the allegory specifically to Thomas: Aristotle is like a beautiful bright slate and Christ's word is like the sun. Just as the sun shines on this slate enlightening it and making it more beautiful, so the divine light shines upon the light of nature and enlightens it. This "beautiful comparison" illustrates for Luther how pagan teaching has been introduced into Christianity.[53] In the second version, from a 1525 sermon, there are differences, but the point seems to be the same: in appropriating Aristotle Thomas imported paganism into Christian theology.[54]

Throughout the 1530's and 40's we find only a few references to Thomas' Aristotelianism. Thomas is again blamed for following Aristotle, but now for the first time, he is also accused of

---

[46] For more on transubstantiation, see the section on the Lord's Supper below.

[47] E.g., WA 7, 707, 30ff.

[48] WA 7, 738, 36ff.

[49] WA 8, 127, 19f.: "Thomas multa haeretica scripsit et autor est regnantis Aristolelis, vastatoris piae doctrine." Cf. the similar statement in WA 7, 739, 26-30.

[50] WA 10 III, 92, 17ff.: "Paulus sagt: Niemandt erfullet die gebott dann alleine der glaube. Die liebe ist nichts denn der glaube. Do irret Thomas mit den seinen, Das ist mit dem Aristoteli, die do sagen, durch ubung wirt einer virtuosus, wie ein Harpffen spyler durch lange ubung wirt ein gut Harpffen spyler, so meinen die narren, die tugende, lieb, keuscheit, demut durch ubung zu erlangen, est ist nit war, gleyssner und des teuffels merterer werden drauss....Derhalben haben sie geirret, als ich hab gesagt, Aristoteles und Thomas, das durch ubung tugentsam einer solt werden."

[51] WA 7, 737, 23ff.: "Invaluit enim et late potens facta est philosophia, ut Christo Aristolelem aequerit quantum ad autoritatem et fidem pertinet. Hinc 'obscuratis Sol' (iustitiae et veritatis, Christus, pro fide inductis moralibus virtutibus, pro veritate opinionibus infinitis)...." Cf. WA 7, 739, 26ff.

[52] Brian Gerrish puts it this way in his *Grace and Reason: A Study in the Theology of Luther*, (Oxford: Clarendon, 1962), p. 128. For Gerrish, this is the heart of Luther's critique of Aristotle and Thomas. For more on this critique see the relevant sections below.

[53] WA 12, 414, 19ff.: "...Zum ersten ist das die gröbste, das S. Thomas (ist er anders heilig) gelert hat, die kompt aus der heydnischen lere und kunst, die das grosse liecht der natur, Aristoteles geschrieben hat, davon sagen sie also, das er sey wie ein hübsche liechte tafel und Christus wort sey wie die Son, und gleich als die son auff ein solche tafel scheynet, das sie deste schöner leuchtet und gleysset, also scheynet auch das göttliche liecht auff das liecht der natur und erleuchtet es. Mit dieser hubschen gleychnis haben sie die heydnische lere auch in die Christenheit bracht..." I have not been able to locate Luther's source for this allegory.

[54] WA 17 II, 27, 25ff. Cf. the reference to Thomas' "paganism" in WA 12, 634, 9ff.

following Averroes, Aristotle's most prominent 12th century interpreter.[55] This new element in Luther's critique may indicate an advance in his understanding of medieval Aristotelianism in the late 1520's or early 1530's. However, Luther shows no awareness of the fact that Thomas at times sharply disagreed with Averroes' understanding of Aristotle.[56] This seems to speak against any deep familiarity with Thomas' commentaries on Aristotle.

A more significant development, perhaps, in this phase of Luther's life was Luther's new accusation that Thomas allows Aristotle to determine the way in which Scripture is interpreted. In a table talk from 1532 Luther outlines what he sees as Thomas' *modus operandi* in this regard:

> This is the procedure of Thomas: First he takes statements from
> Paul, Peter, John, Isaiah, etc. Afterwards he concludes that Aristotle
> says so and so and he interprets Scripture according to Aristotle.[57]

The same accusation is repeated in two other table talks, the precise dates of which are unknown but which also undoubtedly stem from the 1530's or 40's. Thomas indeed quotes Scripture, but in the end he sides with the opinion of Aristotle.[58] Again, Luther says that after citing Scripture, Thomas cites Aristotle's view and then agrees with Aristotle.[59] Even allowing for some conscious exaggeration in these statements from the table talk, Luther's concern in this matter is of high importance to him. Scripture must be allowed to speak for itself, and in its own language. The peril that all commentaries represent is that they will obscure Scripture and detain one from reading it. And this applies not only to the writings of Aristotle and Thomas but also to Luther's own. As he says in his *Lectures on Genesis* (1535-45):

> For this reason I myself hate my books and often wish that they
> would perish, because I fear that they may detain the readers and
> lead them away from reading Scripture itself, which alone is the
> fount of all wisdom. Besides, I am frightened by the example of the
> former age. After those who had devoted themselves to sacred
> studies had come upon commentaries of human beings, they not only
> spent most of their time reading the ancient theologians, but
> eventually they also busied themselves with Aristotle, Averroes, and
> others, who later on gave rise to the Thomases, the Scotuses, and
> similar monstrosities.[60]

---

[55] *In Esaiam Scholia* (1532-34), WA 25 219, 13ff. Cf. *Vorlesungen über 1. Mose* (1535-45), WA 43, 94, 3ff.

[56] E.g. the opusculum "De unitate intellectus contra Averroistas," c.2, where we have one of the few heated utterances of Thomas: "...to err with Averroes, who was not so much a Peripatetic as a depraver of the Peripatetic philosophy." Quoted in Chenu, *Toward Understanding Saint Thomas*, p. 192, n. 50.

[57] WATR 1, 118, 1-3 (8 June 1532). Tr. from LW 54, 39.

[58] WATR 5, 686, 15-17 (date unknown): "...Similiter facit Thomas, qui, optimos scripturae locos tractavit, tandem concludit cum sententia Aristoleles."

[59] WATR 5, 687, 31-33 (date unknown): "...Sic facit Thomas Aquinas, qui in suis libris disputat pro et contra; post scripturae locum addit: Aristoleles 6. Ethicorum aliter sentit. Ibi scriptura cogitur credere Aristoteli!"

[60] WA 43, 93, 40-94, 7. Tr. from LW 3, 305f.

For Luther, the correct *modus loquendi theologicus* is the language of Scripture. As Leif Grane has argued, by replacing this *modus loquendi Apostoli* with a *modus metaphysicus seu moralis*, Thomas unavoidably distorted the Gospel.[61]

This survey of Luther's critique of Thomas for his use of Aristotle raises a host of questions. Since it is a critique of Thomas' theological method, it has ramifications for other individual doctrines such as the authority of Scripture, transubstantiation, etc. While these will be considered in the relevant sections that follow, the primary concern here is Luther's rejection of this aspect of Thomas' method *per se*. What is the significance of this particular critique within Luther's general critique of Thomas? Without giving a definitive answer, the following observations point in the general direction that such an answer should take.

First, how is one to evaluate Luther's accusation that Thomas misunderstood Aristotle? The accusation itself presupposes that Luther himself understands Aristotle correctly. Some have argued that, indeed, Luther understood Aristotle very well.[62] This is not wholly implausible given the new critical attempt by 16th century humanists to retrieve the "Aristotle of history."[63] But the accusation also presupposes an accurate understanding of the way in which Thomas used Aristotle in the service of theology. And on this it seems clear that Luther's appreciation was incomplete. The scholastic procedure of *exponere reverenter*, which reached a pinnacle of subtlety and sophistication in the 13th century, was applied by Thomas not only to the Fathers but also to Aristotle. Far from being a facile attempt to harmonize contradictions, it was an admittedly ahistorical attempt to use a philosopher (in this case) for the sake of truth. Thus Cajetan could say that "Very often, [St. Thomas] glosses Aristotle as Philosopher, not Aristotle as such; and this, in favor of truth."[64] It was not as a historian that Thomas was interested in Greek philosophy but as a theologian. "Reverential exposition" of Aristotle in fact, meant, in the words of Roger Bacon, "correcting Aristotle through a pious and reverential interpretation."[65] Or as Alan of Lille put it, "An authority has a wax nose, which means that it can be bent into taking on different meanings."[66] Luther's shows no awareness that Thomas consciously refashioned Aristotle's "wax nose" for his own theological reasons. But was this misunderstanding, we may ask, unusual in the early 16th century? Even among the Thomists, Cajetan is the only one I know of who shows any degree of sophistication on this question. Other Thomists such as Prierias show a rather total lack of comprehension of the way in which Thomas employs Aristotelian thought. His statement that Aristotle's "truth shines brighter than the sun, and no falsehood has yet been found in him"[67] is absolutely alien to Thomas. Luther's lack of comprehension in this regard is thus equaled if not exceeded by that of Thomists themselves.

Second, what are we to make of Luther's accusation that Thomas allows Aristotle to control his interpretation of Scripture? This is no doubt an important critique and more will be said of this below in connection with Scripture. But is it as fundamental as Grane makes it out

---

[61] Grane sees this as the heart of Luther's critical reaction to Thomas' use of Aristotle. *Modus Loquendi Theologicus: Luthers Kampf um die Erneuerung der Theologie (1515-1518)*, (Leiden: Brill, 1975), p. 199.

[62] Zur Mühlen, "Luther und Aristoleles," p. 265. Grane ("Luthers Kritik an Thomas von Aquin, " pp. 12f.) argues that Luther follows Occam's interpretation of Aristotle.

[63] Zur Muhlen, "Luther und Aristoleles," p. 264.

[64] In his commentary on *S.T.* 2a2ae, q. 172, a.4 ad 4. Quoted in Chenu, *Toward Understanding Saint Thomas*, p. 207.

[65] Quoted in *ibid.*, p. 148.

[66] Quoted in *ibid.*, pp. 144f. Cf. E. Gilson's statement that the 13th century scholastics "are not to be blamed for having at once the name of Aristotle constantly on their lips, and for constantly making him say what he did not say. They would philosophize, not play the historian..." *The Spirit of Medieval Philosophy*, (N.Y.: Scribners, 1936), p. 425.

[67] Quoted above, n. 39.

to be? The first thing that must be recalled is that both Augustinians and humanists in the early 16th century criticized the scholastics (and Thomas) on the same grounds. They too argued that the Bible must obviously take precedence over Aristotle in theology.[68] Luther's critique on this issue, while it may have been more vociferous, was not unique.

A third and related consideration has to do with the question of whether, in Luther's view, it was precisely the use of Aristotle which led inevitably to the distortion of the gospel and to error on particular doctrinal issues. While Luther sometimes seems to say this, there are also indications to the contrary. The example of Bonaventure may be instructive here. Luther seems to be aware that Bonaventure opposed the use of Aristotle in theology. At least Bonaventure is never mentioned when Thomas and other scholastics are criticized for using Aristotle. And this omission is entirely appropriate given the fact that Bonaventure led the 13th century opposition to the use of Aristotle. Yet, as we shall see, Luther's critique of Thomas on many other specific doctrines explicitly includes Bonaventure. What this means is that for Luther, Bonaventure erred along with Thomas on many questions. Since, however, Bonaventure did not rely on Aristotle, it would be difficult to say that Bonaventure's and Thomas' common errors were a direct and inevitable result of reliance on Aristotle. The same could be said of Peter Lombard. As Luther knew, Thomas used Aristotle and the Lombard did not. Yet in many particular teachings, Thomas and the Lombard are said to hold the same erroneous opinion. Clearly these opinions are not a direct result of the use of Aristotle. All of this makes it highly problematic to say that, in Luther's view, it was precisely the use of Aristotle which led inevitably to error in theology and distortion of the gospel. For some who (as Luther well knew) did not use Aristotle were guilty of the same error and distortion. A more accurate statement of Luther's view would be that while some scholastic errors are attributable to the methodological mistake of using Aristotle, many others are not.

All of the above considerations imply that Luther scholarship has traditionally over-estimated the importance of this aspect of his critique of Thomas as a whole. And this is borne out by one final consideration. While the frequency of Luther's references to this issue need not necessarily be an indication of its significance, we cannot ignore the fact that Luther takes it up in a substantive way relatively infrequently. Thomas' teaching on penance, for instance, comes up at least twice as often, and Thomas' views on transubstantiation, baptism, purgatory, monastic vows, the papacy, etc. come up with approximately the same frequency. Needless to say, the way in which theology is done is important to Luther. But this aspect of his critique of Thomas should not be allowed to obscure the fact that in the final analysis, it is the teachings produced by the method which either distort or faithfully represent the gospel.

The entire matter of Thomas' reliance on Aristotle is perhaps best placed into perspective by Luther's discussion of transubstantiation in *The Babylonian Captivity of the Church*. Here Luther explains how Thomas arrived at his doctrine of transubstantiation with the help of Aristotle. This, it must be noted, is in itself an acceptable opinion, as long as other opinions are also tolerated. The fundamental problem here is not Thomas' teaching nor his use of Aristotle. Rather it is that this one opinion has now been transformed into a dogma of the Church by Thomas' disciples.[69] In other words, Thomas' appropriation of Aristotle, though unfortunate, was not disastrous for the gospel and the Church. What was disastrous was what later Thomists did

---

[68] See above, n. 27.
[69] WA 6, 508, 11ff.

with his opinions. Or, to put it another way, Thomas' utilization of Aristotle was disastrous for the Church only because his teachings based on Aristotle were made the measure of orthodoxy by his followers.[70]

[70] For more on this, see Ch. III below.

4. Scripture

It goes without saying that Luther's *sola Scriptura* principle was at the heart of his theological method. We have already seen this principle at work in his attack on Thomas' use of Aristotle. Yet one finds in Luther's critique of Thomas remarkably little on this matter of the authority of Scripture. Luther's focus here is rather on the related question of how Scripture is to be understood. Accordingly, while Luther does not ignore Thomas' understanding of the authority of Scripture, exegesis is the dominant perspective from which he criticizes Thomas' use of Scripture.

Luther's own proper academic discipline was what might today be called Old Testament theology. By far the greater part of his intellectual energies were spent, therefore, on biblical exegesis. Besides his strictly exegetical work, his polemical work too was an exercise in exegesis. For "after all, what he was defending against the theologians of Rome was a particular interpretation of the Scriptures, together with his right to maintain such an interpretation."[71] Similarly Thomas Aquinas' proper and primary academic work was in the field of biblical theology. His official title, "magister in sacra pagina" obligated him to lecture, hold disputations, and preach on Scripture.[72] "The extraordinary abundance of *Sentences* commentaries that have survived would seem to give the impression that the masters preferred the Lombard to the sacred text. But nothing could be further from the truth."[73]

One would expect, therefore, that Luther's critique of this fellow biblical theologian would involve exegetical issues at every stage. And indeed, this is the case. There is no particular theological issue in Luther's critique of Thomas which does not have in its proximate or remote background a difference in the understanding of the biblical text. But one is also led to expect from Luther a thorough-going methodological critique of Thomas' exegesis. And it is this critique which is of interest here. Accordingly the exegetical backdrop of particular theological issues in Luther's critique of Thomas will not detain us here.[74] Nor can the subtleties of Luther's exegesis,[75] or its relation to scholastic exegesis in general,[76] be treated here. The narrower task at hand is the documentation and analysis of Luther's view of Thomas' exegetical method. What is the substance of this critique, and do its dimensions fulfill our expectations?

While the seeds of Luther's disagreement with Thomas on this issue may already be found in his *Dictata super Psalterium* of 1513-15,[77] his actual critique began in 1518 in controversy with Prierias. Even here, however, the attack is for the most part implicit: though it is directed against the Thomists, it is intended at least to some degree to implicate Thomas. Luther begins his *Ad Prieratis* (1518) by clarifying his methodological foundation, one element of which is Augustine's statement that only Scripture is to be regarded as inerrant.[78] Here, however, Thomas is not

---

[71] Jaroslav Pelikan, *Luther the Expositor: Introduction to the Reformer's Exegetical Writings*, (Companion volume to *Luther's Works*), (St. Louis: Concordia, 1959), p. 41.

[72] Chenu, *Toward Understanding Saint Thomas*, p. 233. James A. Weisheipl, *Friar Thomas D'Aquino: His Life, Thought, and Work*, (N.Y.: Doubleday, 1974), p. 116.

[73] Weisheipl, *Friar Thomas*, p. 110.

[74] Insofar as these exegetical matters are explicit, they are treated in the relevant sections which follow.

[75] Although there have been many recent studies on this, Gerhard Ebeling's *Evangelische Evangelienauslegung: Eine Untersuchung zur Luthers Hermeneutik*, (München: Chr. Kaiser, 1942), is still fundamental.

[76] See, for example, James S. Preuss, *From Shadow to Promise: Old Testament Interpretation from Augustine to the Young Luther*, (Cambridge: Harvard University Press, 1969), and Hermann Schüssler, *Der Primat der Heiligen Schrift als theologisches und kanonistisches Problem im Spätmittelalter*, (Wiesbaden: Steiner, 1977).

[77] James Preuss, *From Shadow to Promise*, pp. 153-271.

[78] WA 1, 647, 22-25. Cf. the further analysis below in Ch. III, "Luther on the Authority of Thomas."

implicated: Prierias comes under attack for regarding *Thomas* as inerrant. The omission of Thomas from Luther's criticism here is entirely appropriate since Thomas quotes the same statement from Augustine and expressly says that only Scripture is to be regarded as inerrant.[79]

Further in this same work Thomas is more directly implicated in the critique of Prierias. Both, according to Luther, divide the most simple command of Christ to "Do penance" into three parts (penance as virtue, penance as sacrament, and penance as satisfaction). Is this, Luther asks, interpreting Scripture or tearing it apart? And what Scriptures, Fathers or reasons support this distinction?[80] Furthermore, these new distinctions then have to be defended by seven other new distinctions all of which are also supposedly contained in the words of Christ. But surely, according to Luther, Christ can be understood without the help of Thomas.[81] Also, in this treatise, Luther adds that Thomist theology (not Thomas) is too Peripatetic and not Pauline enough.[82] Prierias' highest authority is Thomas, while Luther claims Paul as his.[83] Finally, we find in this work one explicit and concrete example of Luther rejecting Thomas' exegesis. He rejects Thomas' understanding of the "keys" in Mt. 16:19 (quoted by Prierias) and opts instead for John Chrysostom's interpretation, without commenting on exegetical method.[84]

In the following years (1519-21) Luther lectured for a second time on the Psalms. Here we find Luther's first and only reference to Thomas' use of the fourfold sense of Scripture. By introducing these four senses (literal, tropological, allegorical and anagogical), Thomas and Lyra have in fact "divided the garments of Christ," recklessly tearing apart and mangling the Scriptures, so that everyone can find in it evidence for his own point of view. The result is that no stable or consistent understanding is left to us. And, Luther asserts, neither Thomas nor the Thomists have truly understood a single chapter of Paul or the Gospels.[85]

Luther's rejection of the fourfold sense of Scripture is well-known and need not detain us here. But how and why does Luther apply this criticism to Thomas? For Thomas too vehemently affirms the primacy of the literal sense: theological argumentation must rely on the literal sense alone and everything necessary to faith is contained in the literal sense.[86] Perhaps the answer lies

---

[79] *S.T.* 1a, q.1, a.8 ad 2.

[80] WA 1, 650, 18ff: "Primo, quis dedit tibi aut Divo Thomae hanc postestatem, ut verbum simplicissimum simplicissimi et unici doctoris Christi in tres divideres sectas? Hoccine est Scripturam interpretari, an potius dilacerare? Qua Scriptura, quibus patribus, quibus rationibus hanc distinctionem stabiles, quaeso?" For Thomas, if reason can show something to be false, it cannot be a correct understanding of Scripture. On this, see *S.T.* 1a, q.68, a.3.

[81] WA 1, 651, 6ff. Thomas would agree. According to him the Scriptures are addressed to uncultured people. *S.T.* 1a, q.91, a.1 ad 4. Cf. *S.T.* 1a, q.68, a.3, and 1a2ae, q.98, a.3 ad 2.

[82] WA 1, 652, 31ff.

[83] WA 1, 662, 17ff. Cf. WA 1, 674, 3ff. The question of how "Pauline" Luther's or Thomas' theology is depends of course on their and our interpretations of Paul. But it is not irrelevant to point out that in Thomas' works "Paul's epistles are quoted more frequently than the four Gospels together." Otto H. Pesch, "Paul as Professor of Theology: The Image of the Apostle in St. Thomas' Theology," in *The Thomist*, 38 (1974), 584-605, p. 589, n. 9.

[84] WA 1, 657, 14ff. For more on this see the section on Penance, below.

[85] WA 5, 644, 23-38: ". . .utpote Christo iam cum fide extincto, Apostolus eius, cum primis S. Thomas cum Lyra et suis in orbem vulgare coeperunt quadrigam illam sensuum scripturae, literalem, tropologicum, allegoricum et anagogicum, ac in has quatuor partes dividere hanc vestem Christi, ut unusquisque seorsum suos haberet autores, inquisitores et doctores, ceu milites strenuos et audaces scripturae corruptores. Quo studio id effecerunt, ut verba scripturae quidem haberent, sed sic dispartita et lacerata, ut prorsus nihil constantis intelligentiae, qua animas indueremus, reliquum nobis fecerint. Neque enim S.Thomas cum omnibus Thomistis universisque scholasticis doctoribus unius capituli vel in Paulo vel Evangelio vel quocunque libro scripturae intelligentiam germanam et legitimam unquam aut habuit aut docuit, ut evidens est experientia. Et tamen interim celebrant horum versiculorum decreta: Litera gesta docet, quid credas allegoria, Moralis quid agas, quo tendas anagogia."

[86] *S.T.* 1a, q.1, a.10 ad 1: ". . . Et ita etiam nulla confusio sequitur in sacra Scriptura: cum omnes sensus fundentur super unum, scilicet litteralem; ex quo solo potest trahi argumentum, non autem ex his quae secundum allegoriam dicuntur. . .Non tamen ex hoc aliquid deperit sacrae Scripturae: quia nihil sub spirituali sensu continetur fidei necessarium,

in Preuss' observation that in Thomas the *sensus litteralis* could mean at least three different things,[87] and thus Thomas and Luther understand the *sensus litteralis* differently. Another possibility is that Luther is not criticizing Thomas at all here, but rather the *Glossa Ordinaria*. This 12th century work Luther mistakenly attributed to Thomas Aquinas.[88] Perhaps then, in criticizing "Thomas'" use of the fourfold sense of Scripture, Luther in fact has in mind this medieval exegetical tool which he frequently used as a foil for his own exegesis. Indeed, this seems a likely possibility in light of the fact that Luther knew the *Glossa Ordinaria* well and had a dubious acquaintance with Thomas' Scripture commentaries.

Be this as it may, the thrust of Luther's critique in these lectures on the Psalms, is that in their free glossing and distinguishing, the Thomists (and Thomas?) snatch all power and authority away from the Scriptures. And even though the Thomists and the pope confess the authority of Scripture, they do not use it to refute Luther.[89]

During the same period (1519-21) Luther makes a further incidental comment in his *De captivitate Babylonica* (1520). Here he says that Thomas' opinion (on transubstantiation) hangs completely in the air without the support of Scripture or reason.[90] While most scholars today would agree that Thomas advocates a *sola Scriptura* principle,[91] this minor reference indicates that Luther did not think so. Yet the matter is more complicated than this. For as we have seen,[92] Luther is here arguing that since transubstantiation is not based on Scripture, it is an *opinio* and cannot be made into an article of faith (any more than consubstantiation can be). As for Thomas, though he thought it was important to believe in transubstantiation,[93] there are other indications that he would not have required belief in it as an article of faith. For elsewhere Thomas accepts in principle the sufficiency of Scripture.[94] Furthermore, he holds that it is necessary to believe only that which is in Scripture.[95] Extra-biblical traditions which are not biblically based, says Thomas,

---

quod Scriptura per litteralem sensum alicubi manifeste non tradat." For an example of Thomas' distaste for allegorical exegesis, see *S.T.* 1a2ae, q.102, a.2. Chenu has said that "De facto, it is probably never of his own that Saint Thomas proposes a mystical sense." (*Toward Understanding Saint Thomas*, p. 254.)

[87] Preuss, *From Shadow to Promise*, p. 55. By the late Middle Ages the terminology had become so chaotic that almost anything could be called the *sensus litteralis* (*ibid.*, p. 176).

[88] WA 48, 691, 18ff.

[89] WA 5, 645, 34ff: "Verum ubi ad subsumptionem et minorem venitur, mox merum ludibrium e scriptura faciunt milites isti ea licentia glossandi et distinguendi, ut totius scripturae eludant vim et autoritatem. Neque enim hodie vel Papam vel Thomistam per scripturas revincas, etiam si confiteatur scripturae autoritatem...."

[90] WA 6, 508, 20ff: "Haec autem opinio Thomae adeo sine scripturis et ratione fluctuat, ut nec philosophiam nec dialecticam suam novisse mihi videatur."

[91] Stephan Pfürtner has shown how the development in Thomas' understanding of the exclusive authority of Scripture culminated in the statement, ". . .sola canonica Scriptura est regula fidei." *Lectura super Johannem*, cap. 21, lect. 6, n.2 (Vivès 20, 375). Cf. Stephan Pfürtner, "Das reformatorische 'Sola Scriptura' -- theologischer Auslegungsgrund des Thomas von Aquin?", in Carl-Heinz Ratsschow, ed., *Sola Scriptura - Ringvorlesung der Theologischen Fakultät der Phillipps-Universität*, (Marburg: Elwert, 1977), pp. 48-80, p. 55. According to Pfürtner, "'Sola Scriptura' ist für Thomas Auslegungsgrundlage seiner gesamten theologischen Theorie" (p. 57). Hermann Schüssler comes to the same conclusion (*Der Primat der Heilgen Schrift*, p. 50).

[92] See the section on "Aristotle" above.

[93] In regard to the position known as consubstantiation Thomas says: "Unde haec positio vitanda est tanquam haeretica." *S.T.* 3a, q.75, a.2. Note, however, Thomas' broad definition of "heresy" which can even include "inordinata locutio circa ea quae sunt fidei" (*S.T.* 2a2ae, q.11, a.2 ad 2). Cited in Jared Wicks, "Roman Reactions to Luther: The First Year (1518)," in *Catholic Historical Review*, 69(1983), 521-562, p. 529, n. 32.

[94] *S.T.* 2a2ae, q.1, a.10 ad 1: ". . . in doctrina Christi et Apostolorum veritas fidei est sufficienter explicata." It is because of heresies that further explication in creeds, etc., is required.

[95] *Quaestiones de quodlibet* XII, q.16, a.26 ad 1 (Vivès 15, 607): "Hoc tamen tenendum est quod quidquid in sacra Scriptura continetur verum est: alias qui contra hoc sentiret esset haereticus. Expositores autem in aliis quae non sunt fidei, multa ex suo sensu dixerunt, et ideo in his poterant errare; tamen dicta expositorum necessitatem non inducunt quod

are not binding.[96] And Church teaching is to be believed only insofar as it represents what is in Scripture.[97] Church teaching authority thus stands under the authority of Scripture, at least in principle.[98] Thus Thomas might well have agreed with Luther that if no basis for transubstantiation could be found in Scripture, Christians are not required to hold to it.

In 1522 Luther again took the occasion to comment on Thomas' exegesis, this time in his "forward" to Philip Melanchthon's *Annotationes in epistolas Pauli ad Romanos et Corinthos*. Filled with enthusiasm for Melanchthon's commentary, Luther wants to apply to him what the Thomists say of Thomas, namely that no one wrote better on St. Paul.[99] Even Jerome's and Origen's commentaries are inept nonsense compared to Melanchthon's.[100] For Jerome and Origen and Thomas, Luther adds, wrote commentaries in which they gave their own rather than Paul's opinions.[101] This general statement on Thomas' exegesis tells us little, but it is the first positive indication that Luther was aware of Thomas' Pauline commentaries. And he was also aware of the Thomists' high regard for these commentaries, a regard which resulted in the reprinting of these commentaries at least three times between 1522 and 1532.[102]

In the following year (1523) we find Luther making only one comment related to Thomas' exegesis and again it is an incidental one. In relation to the imperial diet's mandate to preach the gospel "according to the exposition of the Scriptures as approved and accepted by the holy Christian Church,"[103] Luther's opponents had interpreted this to mean that such exposition must conform to that of the scholastics, namely Thomas and Scotus. This interpretation Luther was unwilling to accept, for the mandate said nothing about Thomas.[104] Obviously, Luther was unwilling to accord normative status to Thomas' exposition of the Scriptures.

In a sermon on Genesis 29 from about the same period, Luther seems to cite a concrete example of Thomas' exegesis. While Jacob had initially been endowed with the gift of chastity, he had been told that his seed would multiply. Setting himself to the task, he took wives and thus became a highly spiritual man, "no matter what Thomas says in his distinctions and parts." This story is instructive, Luther concludes, for the freeing of consciences from false doctrines.[105] This allusion suggests that in Luther's view, Thomas taught that Jacob became "less spiritual" when he abandoned chastity. But can such a view be found in Thomas? We do not have from Thomas a

---

necesse sit eis credere, sed solum Scriptura canonica, quae in veteri et in novo testamento est."

[96] *Catena Aurea Super Matthaeum*, cap. 23, n. 11. (Vivès 16, 398): Speaking of an extra-biblical tradition concerning Zacharias, Thomas says, "Hoc tamen quia de Scripturis non habit auctoritatem, eadem facilitate contemnitur qua probatur." Cf. Schüssler, *Der Primat der Heiligen Scrift*, p. 49, n. 25.

[97] *De Veritate*, q.14, a.10 ad 11 (Vivès 15, 37): ". . .omnia media per fides ad nos venit, suspicione carent. Prophetis etiam et Apostolis credimus ex hoc quod eis Dominus testimonium perhibuit miracula faciendo....Successoribus autem eorum non credimus nisi inquantum nobis annuntiant ea quae illi in scriptis reliquerunt."

[98] Pfürtner, "Das reformatorische 'Sola Scriptura'," p. 57. Pfürtner argues that potentially at least, Thomas' *sola scriptura* was an ecclesiastical-critical principle, as it was for Luther. (p. 73).

[99] WA 10 II, 309, 12ff: "Ego quid impii Thomistae suo Thomae mendaciter arrogant, Scilicet neminem scripsisse melius in S. Paulum, tibi vere tribuo."

[100] WA 10 II, 310, 4ff.

[101] WA 10 II, 310, 12ff: "Sola Scriptura, inquis, legenda est citra commentaria. Recte de Hieronymo et Origene et Thoma hisque similibus dicis. Commentaria enim scripserunt, in quibus sua potius quam Paulina aut Christiana tradiderunt."

[102] Hubert Jedin, *A History of the Council of Trent*, (St. Louis: Herder, 1957), vol. 1, p. 366.

[103] Quoted in Heinrich Bornkamm, *Luther in Mid-Career, 1521-1530*, (Philadelphia: Fortress, 1983), p. 303.

[104] WA 12, 63, 13ff.

[105] WA 14, 405, 1ff: "Si datur hec gratia alicui, quae data est Jacob, antequam duceret uxores, wol im, si modo scit, wo er hin gehort. Audivit Jacob locum de semine dilatando suo, ideo stellt er sich darzu, et antea dotatus castitate u. Ideo fuit vir magni spiritus, dicat Thomas quicquid velit in suis distinctionibus et partibus. Hoc fit et scriptum est, ut conscientiae liberae reddantur, quae captae fuerunt falsa doctrina...."

commentary on Genesis, nor can this view be found in the *Glossa Ordinaria*. Nor does Thomas say this in the *Sentences Commentary* or the *Summa Theologiae*. Rather it is in the *Summa Contra Gentiles* that Thomas comments directly on this matter: but here he speaks of Jacob's perfect virtue *despite* his unchastity. While Thomas argues against those who place the state of matrimony on the same level as the state of continence, he sees Jacob as an exception: his abandonment of chastity did not compromise his perfect virtue.[106] Thus, while Luther intimates that Thomas disagrees with him, they are in fact in agreement. Despite Luther's misunderstanding, this reference to Thomas' view of Jacob's virtue is the first positive indication that Luther knew and used Thomas' *Summa Contra Gentiles*. Luther's recollection (albeit faulty) of this detail from the book suggests that his knowledge of it was not merely superficial.

From the year 1527 we have another reference, though more obscure, to Thomas' exegesis. In a lecture on Titus 2, Luther focuses on the words "in everything act faithfully" (v. 10). These are simple words, Luther says, "and I do not have to read St. Thomas on them."[107] Whether Luther actually did or not is a difficult question.[108] However it is more likely here that Luther is merely using Thomas' name to refer to the complexities of scholastic exegesis which unnecessarily complicate a simple text. Again perhaps, Luther may be referring to that standard exegetical tool which he mistakenly attributed to Thomas, the *Glossa Ordinaria*.

Further, in his expositions of the book of Isaiah, Luther comments on Thomas' views four times. Two of these comments from his 1527-30 lectures on Isaiah attack Thomas' views on baptism (in Luther's explanations of Isaiah 28:13-15 and 42:7-8).[109] Thomas' expositions of these passages in his Isaiah commentary say nothing about this, nor does the *Glossa Ordinaria*. Luther's third comment from these same lectures attacks Thomas' view on the veneration of images (in connection with Isaiah 44:15).[110] Again, neither Thomas' Isaiah commentary nor the *Glossa Ordinaria* raise this issue. Finally, in his *Enarratio* on Isaiah 53 in 1544, Luther again cites Thomas. Here, however, it is specifically Thomas' exegesis of the text which is at issue. Luther says that Lyra, a certain Andrew (possibly Andrew of St. Victor), and Thomas Aquinas interpret the "suffering servant" as referring to the people. This is an impossible "Judaizing" interpretation: the text, according to Luther, speaks of the Messiah.[111] The source of Luther's opinion here is unclear. All of the many references to Isaiah 53 in Thomas' *Summa Theologiae* interpret the passage Christologically. And in his commentary on Isaiah 53, Thomas interprets the "servant" throughout as referring to the Messiah.[112] It is therefore almost inconceivable that Luther could have read Thomas' commentary on Isaiah.

Finally we must take note of the fact that Luther regarded Thomas as the author of the *Glossa Ordinaria*. This is mentioned in an undated Table Talk comment which probably comes

---

[106] *SCG* III, 137 (Vivès 12, 439): "Nec obstat quod alique perfectissimae virtutis viri matrimonio usi sunt, ut Abraham, Isaac et Jacob, quia quanto virtus mentis est fortior, tanto minus potest per quaecumquae a sua altitudine dejici." Thomas here argues against those who put the state of matrimony on the same level as the state of continence.

[107] WA 25, 50, 14ff: "'In omnibus' iterum occurrit particulari servituti....Non dicit: hoc fac, sed 'in omnibus' age fideliter, das sind simplicia verba, non opus, ut legam S. Thomam druber."

[108] Thomas' interpretation of these words is much the same as Luther's. See *In Epistola ad Titum*, cap. 2, lect. 2 (Vivès 21, 545f.)

[109] WA 31 II, 163, 12ff; and 315, 24ff. For more on this, see the section on Baptism, below.

[110] WA 31 II, 349, 23f. For more on this, see the relevant section below.

[111] WA 40 III, 713, 26ff: "Diabolus blasphemavit Dominum nostrum Jesum Christum per Iudaeos deprauantes sic scriptores etiam inter Christianos. Lyra quendam vocat Andream, qui Iudaisavit, et Thomas Aquinas: ii istum 'servum' populum exponunt. Sed textus non potest intelligi nisi de una persona Messiae...."

[112] See *In Isaiam*, cap. 53 (Vivès 19, 32-34). The same is true of the *Glossa Ordinaria* (PL 113, 1296). While Luther's accusation is mistaken, it is in itself significant. For here Luther is in fact accusing Thomas of abiding too closely to the *sensus litteralis*.

from the 1530's.[113]   While the authorship of the *Glossa Ordinaria* is still debated, it clearly comes from the 12th century.   It was frequently reprinted in the 15th and 16th centuries, usually together with the *Postillae* of Nicholas of Lyra and the *Additiones* of Paul of Burgos.[114]   Luther had a copy in Wittenberg[115] and used it extensively.   As we have already seen, Luther's attribution of this work to Thomas raises the possibility that he ascribes certain exegetical views to Thomas which Thomas did not in fact hold.   Further, it suggests that Luther did not read extensively in Thomas' biblical commentaries, for in those commentaries Thomas cites the *Glossa Ordinaria* along with other Patristic and medieval authorities.

This review of Luther's comments on Thomas' use of Scripture has made it clear that on the issue of the authority of Scripture Luther's critique is a limited one.   This may be surprising, since for centuries, confessional polemics have emphasized, as a fundamental divergence, Luther's *sola Scriptura* vs. "Catholic" Scripture and tradition.   That this is a fundamental divergence between Luther and Thomas is simply not born out by Luther's critique.   Of course, it would be an ahistorical oversimplification to say that Luther's *sola Scriptura* principle means exactly what Thomas' *sola Scriptura* principle means.   But it is also an oversimplification to assume, as many have, that the difference here is fundamental.   For both teach that the Church and theology stand under the authority of Scripture.[116]   Luther's apparent lack of concern about this issue would therefore seem to be justified.   Perhaps in this case Luther understood Thomas better than some of his subsequent interpreters.[117]

This is not to say that Luther was unconcerned about the way in which other scholastics treated the authority of Scripture.   This was perhaps especially true in relation to the Thomist school.   A brief survey shows that while some Thomists accurately reflected Thomas' view, others did not.   Paul of Burgos (d. 1435), for example, taught that whatever goes against a determination of the Church cannot be a correct understanding of Scripture.[118]   Here Thomas' *sola Scriptura* principle clearly loses its ecclesiastical-critical function.   Johannes Capreolus (d. 1444) also ties the authority of Scripture and the authority of the Church so closely together that they can never be at odds.[119]   Johannes Tinctoris (d. 1469), on the other hand, argues that greater assent is due to Scripture than to the Church.[120]   And Johannes Werd (d. 1510) seems to follow Tinctoris.   He

---

[113]   WA 48, 691, 18f: "Thomas Aquinas est autor glossae ordinariae..."

[114]   On the *Glossa Ordinaria* and its place in medieval exegesis, see Beryl Smalley, *The Study of the Bible in the Middle Ages,* (Notre Dame: Univ. of Notre Dame Press, 1964), pp. 46-66.   The work is printed in PL 113 and 114.

[115]   Ernest Schwiebert, *Luther and His Times,* (St. Louis: Concordia, 1950), p. 251.

[116]   "In der grundsätzlichen Forderung nach theologischer Sprache und Reflexion 'allein' aus der Schrift als ihrem eigenen Grund...bestehen zwischen dem Verständnis des Thomas und demjenigen Luthers unverkennbare Übereinstimmung."   S. Pfürtner, "Das reformatorische 'Sola Scriptura'," p. 72. Cf. H. Schüssler, *Der Primat der Heiligen Schrift,* pp.49f. It should also be noted that neither Luther's nor Thomas' *sola Scriptura* principles prevent "dogmas" (articles of faith grounded in Scripture) from themselves playing a normative role in exegesis. On this, see Harry McSorley, "Luther: Exemplar of Reform--Or Doctor of the Church?", in Egil Grislis, ed., *The Theology of Martin Luther,* (Winnfield B.C.: Woodlake Books, 1985), pp. 27-52, pp. 50f.

[117]   The consistency of Thomas' adherence to his *sola Scriptura* principle is a different question.   His theory of the treasury of merit and indulgences might be an example of a lapse in this regard.   Also cf. Luther's accusation that Thomas prefers the authority of Aristotle to the authority of Scripture (discussed above under "Aristotle").   But one can find notable lapses in Luther's application of the principle as well.   His apparent acceptance of the immaculate conception could be seen as an example of this. (WA 17 II, 288, 5-16).   Thomas expressly rejected the immaculate conception because Scripture asserts that all human beings are in need of salvation. (*S.T.* 3a, q.27, a.2). Cf. the discussion of Luther's interest in the legend of Thomas' final victory over doubt through trust in the Bible (above, Ch.I.).

[118]   J. Preuss, *From Shadow to Promise,* pp. 90f.

[119]   H. Schüssler, *Der Primat der Heiligen Schrift,* pp. 259f.

[120]   *Ibid.,* pp. 260f.

takes up the question of whether the Church is to be believed if it taught that the dog of Tobit had no tail (something which this book does not specify). His answer is in the negative: we believe the Church only insofar as it teaches what is in Scripture.[121] Prierias, Luther's Thomist opponent, moves in the opposite direction, subordinating the authority of Scripture to the authority of the Church.[122] Even so brief a survey as this shows that there was on this question diversity within the Thomist school.[123] But precisely those Thomists with whom Luther was to some extent familiar (Burgos, Capreolus and Prierias) do not adequately represent Thomas' *sola Scriptura* principle. Luther's attack on the Thomists (especially Prierias) in this regard was therefore justified.

Our review of Luther's comments on Thomas' use of Scripture has also made it abundantly clear that we find in him no thorough or sustained critique of Thomas' exegetical method. Although exegetical issues are always involved in Luther's critique of Thomas on every issue, the various complaints catalogued here do not amount to the kind of penetrating critique one might have expected. If Luther understood scholasticism at its most fundamental level as false exegesis, as some have argued,[124] there is no evidence for it here. At least when it came to Thomas Aquinas, it would be difficult to argue that exegetical method was Luther's main concern. Or, to put the matter differently, it was the results of exegesis more than the exegetical method itself which seems to have mattered most to Luther.

Luther's lack of interest in Thomas' exegetical method is also understandable from another perspective. For he saw himself in some basic way to have simply left the scholastics and their exegesis behind. In a sermon in 1531 Luther tells us that he could not find his teaching and preaching in Thomas, etc. He found it rather when he left this behind and listened to Scripture alone.[125] There was little reason then for Luther to concern himself about Thomas' exegetical method.

Yet Luther did not do his own exegesis in an historical vacuum. His exegetical work would scarcely have been possible had he not relied on the exegetical tools available to him. Thus he was willing to use Erasmus' exegetical work even though he had low regard for him as a theologian.[126] And similarly he was even willing to use exegetical tools developed by Thomists: Paul of Burgos (d. 1435) and Sante Pagnini (d. 1541) are two examples of this.[127] Evidently not even Thomist exegesis was totally devoid of value for Luther.

Thus in the final analysis, Luther's stance vis-à-vis Thomas' exegetical method is shrouded in ambiguity. Any comparison of their respective biblical commentaries immediately reveals major differences in how the text is approached and handled. Yet nowhere in Luther do we find a sustained methodological critique of Thomas' exegesis. Only in isolated and infrequent comments does Luther attack Thomas' exegetical method. Again, it is the concrete results of exegesis that seem to be of far greater interest to Luther than exegetical method itself.

---

[121] *Ibid.*, p. 261.

[122] *Ibid.*, pp. 261f. Cf. Preuss, *From Shadow to Promise*, pp. 133-137.

[123] This is Schüssler's conclusion (*Der Primat der Heiligen Schrift*, p. 262).

[124] E.g. Leif Grane, *Modus Loquendi Theologicus*, p. 174.

[125] WA 34 II, 148, 7ff.: "Meam doctrinam et praedicationem non potui assequi in omnibus libris, in Aristotele, apud Scholasticos, Thomam, Scotum, donec wurde abgesondert a turba et ipsum [Scripturam] solum audivi."

[126] Grane, *Modus Loquendi Theologicus*, p. 118.

[127] On Burgos, see A. Kleinhaus, "Paulus von Burgos," in *Lexikon für Theologie und Kirche*. 8, 230; and J. Preuss, *From Shadow to Promise*, pp. 86-101. Cf. Luther's favourable comment in WA 43, 234, 39f. On Pagnini, see Paul Oskar Kristeller, *Medieval Aspects of Renaissance Learning* (Durham, N.C.: Duke University Press, 1974), p. 148. Cf. Luther's favourable comments in WA 42, 219, 16f. and WA 53, 647, 27-29.

5. Penance and Indulgences

The centrality of penance for Luther's personal and theological development has long been recognized by his interpreters. As Reinhold Seeburg put it almost a century ago,

> Luther's decisive religious experiences were gained in connection with the sacrament of repentance....This is the point of view from which the work of Luther must be considered in the history of doctrines. All his ideas. . .constitute a complex of religious conceptions which were developed under the pressure of and in opposition to the sacrament of repentance.[128]

From his early scrupulosity in regard to the sacrament in the monastery, to his so-called "Reformation breakthrough" in 1518, to his 1530 treatise on "The Keys," to his final denunciation of Catholic penitential practice in the Smalcald Articles (1537) and in his late autobiographical reflections -- at all these stages and indeed throughout his career penance stands in close proximity to the center of Luther's personal and theological concerns. This alone might lead us to expect from Luther a thoroughgoing and persistent critique of Thomas' views on penance. But is this expectation fulfilled when we look at what Luther says?

The evidence in this case is rendered problematic by the historical context in which it is found. Luther's attack on Thomas' teaching stems primarily from the year 1518, though there are a few isolated references even in the later Luther. It will be helpful, therefore, to recount the pertinent events of this important year in Luther's career. After the 95 theses "On the Power of Indulgences" were posted in mid-November of 1517, the first public assault was mounted by a pair of Dominican Thomists, Konrad Wimpina and Johannes Tetzel.[129] Wimpina had written a series of counter-theses against Luther, and on 20 January 1518 Tetzel vigorously defended them at a Dominican convocation in Frankfurt (on the Oder).[130] By mid-March of that year the theses had reached Wittenberg and upon reading them Luther composed what some regard as his "first great literary achievement," his "Sermon von Ablass und Gnade."[131] Preached and printed in late March, this sermon as we shall see represents Luther's first confrontation with not only these Thomists' view of indulgences but also that of Thomas. By late April or early May Tetzel had written a refutation in which he denounced Luther's "Sermon" in its entirety.[132] And in early June Luther published a defense of his "Sermon" entitled "Eine Freiheit des Sermons päpstlichen Ablass und Gnade belangend." Now, however, a third Thomist entered the lists against Luther: the Italian Dominican and Master of the Sacred Palace, Silvester Prierias, published his *De potestate papae*

---

[128] Reinhold Seeburg, *Text-Book of the History of Doctrines,* tr. C. Hay, (Grand Rapids: Baker, 1977; first published 1895-1898), Book III, pp. 224f.

[129] I follow here the chronology established by Martin Brecht, *Martin Luther: His Road to Reformation, 1483-1521,* tr. J. L. Schaaf, (Philadelphia: Fortress, 1985), pp.175-237. Cf. the careful reconstruction of the events of 1518 by Jared Wicks, "Roman Reactions."

[130] Brecht, *Martin Luther,* p. 207. The theses are printed in *Lutheri opera Latina var. arg.* 1, 296-305, and in German translation in Walch 18, 82-93.

[131] The judgment is Brecht's (*Martin Luther,* p. 208). The editors of the Weimar edition followed Köstlin in giving October 1517 as the writing date and February 1518 as the publication date. Internal evidence, however, indicates that Luther was responding to the Wimpina-Tetzel theses and thus that Brecht's dating is correct.

[132] Printed in *Lutheri opera Latina var. arg.* 1, 306-312. German translation in Walch 18, 274-295.

dialogus in June, having written it he tells us in three days.[133] Luther's reply to Prierias, *Ad dialogum Silvestri Prieratis de potestatae papae responsio*, appeared in August.[134] In addition, his *Resolutiones* or explanations of the 95 theses, first drafted in February, was also published in August. And finally, in October Luther personally confronted the weightiest of his Thomist opponents, Cardinal Cajetan.[135] These are the names, events and documents which form the historical context for Luther's critique of Thomas' teaching on penance and indulgences.

When we consider this context, two things are immediately clear. The first is that Luther's critique on this issue emerged out of a controversy with Thomists. He confronted in 1518 a veritable Thomist phalanx: Wimpina-Tetzel-Prierias-Cajetan. This was Luther's first real theological opposition and it forced him to engage the thought of Thomas Aquinas as he perhaps had never done before. It is understandable therefore that in the course of this controversy Thomas' name comes up frequently. Whether Luther actually turned to the writings of Thomas himself, or relied only on these Thomists' representations of Thomas' position is a question which remains to be answered.

Then it should also be noted that Luther's critique is an unfinished one. Since it stems primarily from 1518, it clearly does not represent his final word on the subject of penance. The view of penance on which this critique of Thomas is based had yet to undergo a substantial development which cannot concern us here. It would serve no purpose to speculate on what the late Luther might have said about Thomas' views on penance. Luther's actual critique at this early stage will have to suffice. And it is in itself of great interest, first, because it represents the starting point of a lifelong "Auseinandersetzung" with the thought of Thomas, and second, because it sheds light on the question of Luther's understanding of Thomas.

The actual critique begins not with Thomas' views on the sacrament of penance itself but with a subsidiary issue, namely indulgences. The Wimpina-Tetzel theses attacking Luther's 95 theses "On the Power of Indulgences" forced him almost immediately to confront the teaching of Thomas Aquinas on this subject, for Wimpina and Tetzel, as Dominican Thomists, claimed to represent the teaching of their 13th century master.[136] This Luther did, most pointedly and extensively in his reply to the Wimpina-Tetzel theses, the "Sermon von Ablass und Gnade" of late March 1518. Here Luther for the first time explicitly situated his early views in relation to those of Thomas Aquinas.[137]

Though this sermon has been the subject of much scholarly attention, no one to my knowledge has pointed out that it is directed against Thomas and his followers. The opponent is named in the very first sentence: "First you should know that some new teachers such as the Master of the Sentences, St. Thomas and their followers divide penance into three parts. . ."[138] Here "new teachers" does not refer to representatives of the *via moderna* but to these doctors of

---

[133] Printed in *Lutheri opera Latina var. arg.* 1, 344-377 German translation Walch 18, 310-343. According to Walch (vol. 18, p.18), the Pope himself criticized Prierias' book saying he should have spent three *months* on it.
[134] The Latin original is in WA 1, 644-686. Printed in German translation in Walch 18, 344-411.
[135] On this, see Brecht, *Martin Luther*, pp. 246-265; and especially Wicks, "Roman Reactions". Cajetan had prepared several position papers prior to this encounter some of which can be found in Jared Wicks, *Cajetan Responds: A Reader in Reformation Controversy*, (Washington: Catholic Univ. Press, 1978). Cf. Luther's report of the proceedings, the "Acta Augustana", in WA 2, 6-26. For additional literature, see my *Luther and Late Medieval Thomism: A Study in Theological Anthropology*, (Waterloo: Wilfrid Laurier Univ. Press, 1983), p. 125.
[136] Whether they faithfully represented Thomas' teaching in their theses is, as we shall see, highly dubious.
[137] On another topic, he had already done so implicitly in his 1517 "Disputatio contra scholasticam theologiam". On this cf. Janz, *Luther and Late Medieval Thomism*, pp. 24-27.
[138] WA 1, 243, 4-6: "Zum ersten solt ihr wissen, dass etlich new lerer, als Magister Sententiarum, S. Thomas und ihre folger geben der puss drey teyll . . ."

the *via antiqua*. And their views are to be measured against what Luther calls "the old holy Christian teachers," namely the Church Fathers.[139] Throughout the rest of the sermon then, Luther uses words like "they," "their," etc. to refer back to these "new teachers." It is fair to say therefore that the entire sermon is directed against them. But what of the "Magister Sententiarum," Peter Lombard, mentioned along with Thomas and his followers, as the opponent? The sermon deals with indulgences and Lombard, as Luther no doubt knew, said nothing about indulgences. The reason, I would suggest, why Lombard's name is mentioned here is because the introduction to the sermon briefly outlines the theology of penance as it is found in Lombard and Thomas as a backdrop for the main issue at hand, indulgences. But when Luther addresses that main issue, Peter Lombard's name is obviously irrelevant. Thus we can say that the *only* explicit opponent in this sermon is Thomas and his followers.

The sermon takes the form of twenty theses, the first five of which situate indulgences within a theology of penance. To begin with, Luther tells his audiences that these teachers divide penance into three parts: contrition, confession and satisfaction. Luther is not sure that this distinction is grounded in Scripture or the Fathers, but this is here beside the point.[140] The important thing to understand is that indulgences have to do with the third part, namely satisfaction.[141] These "new teachers," furthermore, subdivide satisfaction into three parts: prayer, fasting and alms; and the various works of satisfaction are then subsumed under one or another of these categories.[142] None of these teachers doubt that such works of satisfaction are replaced by indulgences, and so after receiving such an indulgence, no other good work remains to be done.[143] "Many," according to Luther, go further to suggest that indulgences do more than simply replace the required works of satisfaction: they are of the opinion that indulgences also remove the punishment for sin demanded by the divine justice.[144] Here then is Luther's description of the foundation on which these "new teachers" -- Thomas and the Thomists -- build their teaching on indulgences.

Before going on to consider Luther's critique, we must first inquire into the accuracy of his description. Does his description in fact represent Thomas' view?[145] Thomas does indeed follow what was by his time a scholastic convention in dividing penance into contrition, confession and satisfaction.[146] He does, as Luther says, treat indulgences under the heading of satisfaction.[147] And Thomas argues that the works of satisfaction are suitably enumerated under the headings of prayer, fasting and alms.[148] But does Thomas teach, as Luther says, that after receiving an indulgence no good work of satisfaction remains to be done? On this question we find some

---

[139] WA 1, 243, 9-10.

[140] WA 1, 243, 4-11. Brecht is incorrect in saying that this first thesis sweeps away the traditional understanding of the parts of penance (*Martin Luther,* p. 208). Luther is not attacking this here: ". . . doch wollen wir das itst sso lassenn bleyben. . ." (WA 1, 243, 11).

[141] WA 1, 243, 12-14.

[142] WA 1, 244, 1-6.

[143] WA 1, 244, 7-10.

[144] WA 1, 244, 11-14.

[145] It should be understood from the outset that it is no simple matter to determine the precise nature of Thomas' teaching on indulgences. His mature and definitive word, the *Summa Theologiae,* does not treat this question. The young Thomas elaborated his views on indulgences in the *Scriptum* (IV *Sent.,* d. 20, in Vivès 10, 564-582), and this section was added after his death to the *Summa* as questions 25-27 of the *Supplementum.* The mature Thomas treated the issue briefly in 1269 in his *Quodlibet* II, q. 8, a. 16 (Vivès 15, 395-397), and again in 1273 he touched on it in his *Expositio Orationis Dominicae* (Vivès 27, 194). For the chronology of Thomas' writings, see J.A. Weisheipl, *Friar Thomas D'Aquino.*

[146] S.T. Suppl. qq. 1, 6 and 12.

[147] S.T. Suppl., q.25. Cf. *Quodlibet* II, q.8, a.16 (Vivès 15, 396): "indulgentia . . . cedit in locum satisfactionis."

[148] S.T. Suppl., q.15, a.3. This division is already found in the Lombard, IV *Sent.,* d.26, c.3.

obscurity in Thomas. For, on the one hand, Thomas states that the amount of remission through an indulgence depends only and entirely on the one granting it, and thus according to some of Thomas' interpreters, indulgences are understood here more as a replacement than as a completion of works of satisfaction.[149] But on the other hand, Thomas says that even after receiving an indulgence, penitents should not omit the works of satisfaction imposed on them since they are still of remedial and meritorious value.[150] And furthermore, though it may be implied in some things Thomas says, he nowhere states that after receiving an indulgence no good works remain to be done. Thus we find an ambiguity in Thomas himself on this point: Luther's interpretation is not the only one possible but it is a plausible one.[151] Finally, Luther is correct in saying that for Thomas, indulgences are effective for the remission of divine punishment.[152] Thus one finds in Luther's description of the foundation of Thomas' teaching on indulgences no glaring inaccuracies. We can say that it is substantially correct.

In the remainder of his sermon, Luther goes on to offer his critique of what these "new teachers" are saying about indulgences. He begins with an appeal to Scripture: the divine justice demands only true contrition and conversion for the forgiveness of sins, and this includes the works named above (prayer, fasting and alms). While "some doctors" have required some punishment or satisfaction in addition to this, no Scripture can be adduced to substantiate such an addition.[153] What Luther is alluding to here is the lack of a Scriptural warrant for indulgences.

He then goes on to examine further the question of divine punishment. God does indeed punish, says Luther, sometimes in order to bring about contrition in the sinner. But it is not in anyone's power to lift this punishment.[154] Luther's critique of Thomas on this point is an important one for he reiterates it first in his August 1518 reply to Prierias and then again in his August 1518 *Resolutiones* on the 95 theses. Against Prierias, Luther disputes Thomas' "new understanding" of Matthew 16:19 on the power of binding and loosing given to Peter. He prefers the interpretation of the Fathers, especially Chrysostom: the faithful should regard Peter's binding and loosing as though Christ himself were doing it, but this does not mean Peter can "loose" something in heaven.[155] Moreover, Luther confronts Thomas' argument (repeated by Prierias) to the effect that if loosing on earth would not at the same time loose in heaven, such loosing would hurt the sinner more than it would help him, since the satisfaction required after death would then be greater.[156] Thomas' argument is wrong, according to Luther, because the Church can remit only those penitential works which it imposes; remitting these cannot bring on worse punishments

---

[149] S.T. Suppl., q.25, a.2 ad 1; and Bernhard Poschmann, *Penance and the Anointing of the Sick,* (N.Y.: Herder, 1964), pp.224f.

[150] S.T. Suppl., q.25, a.1 ad 4: "Tamen consulendem est eis qui indulgentias consequuntur, ne propter hoc ab operibus poenitentiae iniunctis abstineant: ut etiam ex his remedium consequantur, quamvis a debito poenae essent immunes; et praecipue quia quandoque sunt plurium debitores quam credant." Cf. q.25, a.2 ad 2.

[151] The Tetzel-Wimpina theses emphasize the advantage of indulgences over works of love: they are a quick and complete way of making satisfaction. Works of love, on the other hand, increase merit (Theses 72 and 73 in Walch 18, 87).

[152] Thomas takes this position in S.T. Suppl., q.25, a.1: "Et ideo aliter dicendum est, quod valent, et quantum ad forum Ecclesiae et quantum ad iudicium Dei, ad remissionem poenae residuae post contritionem et absolutionem et confessionem, sive sit iniuncta sive non." But strictly speaking, indulgences do not involve "remission of punishment": "Ad secundum dicendum quod iste qui indulgentias suscipit, non absolvitur, simpliciter loquendo, a debito poenae: sed datur sibi unde debitum solvat." (S.T. Suppl., q.25, a.1 ad 2); and again, ". . . quia nihil de poena dimittitur, sed unius poena alteri computatur." (S.T. Suppl., q.25, a.2).

[153] WA 1, 244, 15-24.

[154] WA 1, 244, 25-30. What had first appeared as Thesis 5 in the disputation "On the Power of Indulgences" (WA 1, 236, 7-9) is here specifically directed against Thomas.

[155] WA 1, 657, 14ff.

[156] S.T. Suppl., q.25, a.1. Cf. Prierias' use of this argument in Walch 18, 363ff.

after death since over these the Church has no power.[157] Repeating this objection to Thomas in his *Resolutiones* on the 95 theses, Luther again forcefully states that punishments other than those imposed by the Church are not remitted through the power of the keys.[158]

On this particular point, there can be no doubt that Luther understood Thomas' position correctly. Thomas does in fact interpret Matt. 16:19 to mean that "whatever remission is granted in the court of the Church holds good in the court of God."[159] Indulgences therefore, in a manner of speaking, remit punishment whether it is enjoined by the Church or not. And yet we must recall that for Thomas, strictly speaking, in an indulgence "no punishment is remitted, but the punishment of one is imputed to another."[160] In the final analysis though, the sense of Luther's critique still stands: he disagrees with Thomas over whether the Church has jurisdiction over divine punishment.

Continuing then with Luther's comments on divine punishment (in his "Sermon von Ablass und Gnade"), Luther observes that it is not clear just what God's punishments are: perhaps they are precisely the good works mentioned (prayer, fasting and alms). Thus, Christians should willingly bear the punishment and do these good works rather than seek to be released from them through indulgences.[161] On this, Thomas agrees that indulgences should not be an easy way to escape works of satisfaction: for him, the imposed penitential works are still of great value and they should not be omitted even after receiving an indulgence.[162] These works of satisfaction are in fact "more meritorious [than indulgences] in respect of the essential reward, which infinitely transcends the remission of temporal punishment."[163] Thus the view which Luther criticizes here does not seem to be that of Thomas.[164]

Luther next takes up the distinction made by "some of the new preachers" between punishment which is healing (*medicativa*) and punishment which makes satisfaction (*satisfactoria*). Dismissing this as "chatter," Luther maintains that all divine punishment is for our betterment.[165] Thomas does indeed make a distinction like this.[166] But clearly he could agree with Luther that in some way, divine punishment is always for our benefit.[167]

---

[157] WA 1, 658, 1ff.
[158] WA 1, 568, 1ff.
[159] *S.T.* Suppl., q.25, a.1.
[160] *S.T.* Suppl., q.25, a.2. Cf. q.25, a.1 ad 2.
[161] WA 1, 244, 31-39.
[162] *S.T.* Suppl., q.25, a.1 ad 4, quoted above, n.23.
[163] *S.T.* Suppl., q.25, a.2 ad 2: ". . . quamvis huiusmodi indulgentiae multum valeant ad remissionem poenae, tamen alia opera satisfactionis sunt magis meritoria respectu praemii essentialis: quod in infinitum melius est quam dimissio poenae temporalia."
[164] In the Tetzel-Wimpina theses, indulgences are better than the works of love insofar as they make satisfaction more quickly (Thesis 75, in Walch 18, 87f). In his early June defense of this sermon ("Eine Freiheit des Sermons vom Ablass und Gnade"), Luther returns to the related question of whether the works of satisfaction remitted through indulgences are those which Christ has commanded. Though some claim the authority of Thomas for this view, Luther says that Thomas has not been rightly understood here: Thomas does not say this (WA 1, 384, 14-22). Luther's judgment in this case is correct. The Tetzel-Wimpina theses argue that Christ's command to do penance, since it refers to the sacrament, includes the works of satisfaction (Theses 3-5, in Walch 18, 82), and these works of satisfaction can be replaced by indulgences.
[165] WA 1, 244, 40-245, 4.
[166] The early Thomas alludes to this distinction in *S.T.* Suppl., q.12, a.3. A clearer analysis is given by the mature Thomas in *Quodlibet* II, q.8, a.16 ad 3 where he says that satisfaction is either *punitiva* or *medicativa*. Indulgences can stand in the place of satisfaction insofar as it is *punitiva*, but not insofar as it is *medicativa*. Note the difference between the distinction which Thomas makes and the distinction as Luther describes it. Luther's description seems to follow the terminology of the Tetzel-Wimpina theses, e.g. thesis 71 (Walch 18, 87).
[167] Cf. his general discussion of satisfaction in *S.T.* Suppl., q.12.

In the following theses Luther calls into question the argument that indulgences are necessary since adequate satisfaction for sins cannot be completed in this life. According to Luther this cannot be since God and the Church do not require the impossible.[168] Moreover, according to the view Luther is attacking here, the satisfaction which cannot be completed in this life can be made up for in purgatory or through indulgences. While Luther does not here reject this as false, he does see this as groundless and unproven speculation. For him no one can make satisfaction for his sins; God freely forgives and demands nothing but amendment of one's life.[169] If the object of Luther's critique on this point is Thomas, it is misdirected. Thomas does not argue that since satisfaction in this life is impossible indulgences are necessary.[170] Rather for him, humans can never make adequate satisfaction to God if satisfaction denotes quantitative equality. But God mercifully requires only a satisfaction of proportionate equality -- something which is possible. Man remains always in God's debt, "but it suffices that man repay as much as he can."[171] And clearly what Luther requires, righteousness of life, is close to what Thomas means by "satisfaction of proportionate equality." On this point, the real object of Luther's critique seems to be a Thomist misinterpretation of Thomas.[172]

Luther goes on in his sermon to say that indulgences are allowed for the sake of lazy Christians. Their use should not be discouraged but should also not be encouraged. One should rather contribute to the building of St. Peter's out of love for God, and besides, helping one's neighbor is more important than the building of St. Peter's. Again, indulgences are for "sleepy" Christians.[173] For Luther, good works are clearly of more value than indulgences. But is this a contradiction of Thomas' view of their value? It seems that Thomas would concur with Luther here. First, as we have seen, Thomas teaches that penitential works are still important even for those who have gained indulgences.[174] And second, he also teaches that works of satisfaction are more meritorious than indulgences.[175] Those in religious orders, for instance, merit more with regard to eternal life by observing their rule than by gaining indulgences.[176] In these senses, good works are of more value than indulgences for Thomas. Only a few months later, in August of 1518, Luther in fact acknowledged this to be the case in his *Resolutiones* on the 95 theses: "St. Thomas and St. Bonaventure say indulgences are not commanded and are less important than good works."[177] Here Luther correctly understands Thomas' teaching, and we must therefore say that the object of his critique on this point is not Thomas' teaching. Most probably this critique is directed against some of Thomas' followers such as Tetzel.[178]

---

[168] WA 1, 245, 5-17.

[169] WA 1, 245, 18-25.

[170] The Tetzel-Wimpina theses do not seem to explicitly take this position either.

[171] S.T. Suppl., q.13, a.1.

[172] The Tetzel-Wimpina theses speak of satisfaction without the qualifications one finds in Thomas.

[173] WA 1, 245, 26-246, 14. Luther echoes here the views of Albert the Great and Bonaventure who wished to allow indulgences "only to worldly-minded religious and not to the fervent." Poschman, *Penance*, p. 226.

[174] S.T. Suppl., q.25, a.1 ad 4.

[175] S.T. Suppl., q.25, a.2 ad 2.

[176] S.T. Suppl., q.27, a.2 ad 2.

[177] WA 1, 609, 9ff. Tr. from LW 31, 218. Here, however, Luther points out the apparent contradiction in what he says is the teaching of Thomas and Bonaventure. If indulgences are the application or dispensing of the merits of Christ, and if our good works are of more value than indulgences, then are we not forced to say that our works are of more value than the merits of Christ? In these few intervening months, Luther's thought on indulgences has developed in an increasingly critical direction.

[178] The Tetzel-Wimpina theses concede that works of love are more meritorious; but indulgences on the other hand can more quickly and entirely make satisfaction. And since "spiritual alms" are of more value than "bodily alms," the better way of helping the poor is with indulgences (Theses 72-77, in Walch 18, 87f.).

It should also be mentioned in this context that unlike some of his interpreters, Thomas lays down a stringent set of conditions on which the efficacy of an indulgence depends.[179] First, the recipient cannot be in mortal sin; true contrition and confession are prerequisites.[180] Second, the granting of the indulgences must promote "the good of the Church and the honor of God."[181] And third, there must be on the part of the recipient both charity and "piety which includes the honor of God and the profit of our neighbor."[182] Thus "sleepy Christians," to use Luther's term, would hardly qualify. Luther's statements leave little doubt that at this early stage he would have approved of the conditions laid down by Thomas, conditions which seem to have been forgotten by some of his followers.

Luther continues in his sermon to say that indulgences are not commanded but adiaphoristic. Moreover they are not meritorious.[183] As to the first point, while some of Thomas' followers may have taught that indulgences are commanded, Thomas himself did not. In fact, in a somewhat obscure passage, Thomas seems to teach that indulgences can add nothing to what is already gained by charity: speaking of indulgences Thomas says, "Now one person's good is applied to another in two ways: first, by charity; and in this way, even without indulgences, a person shares in all the good deeds done, provided he have charity."[184] What this suggests is that for the one who has charity (and this we recall is a prerequisite for indulgences), indulgences are not only adiaphoristic but in fact superfluous. This interpretation, however, stands in apparent contradiction to what Thomas says elsewhere, namely that "indulgences avail much for the remission of punishment" though "works of satisfaction are more meritorious."[185] While there is a lack of full consistency here, and while one can find countervailing emphases, Thomas generally does speak of indulgences as being in some sense meritorious.

Luther is also unsure whether indulgences rescue souls from purgatory. Although "some new doctors" hold this opinion, the Church has not officially decided this question.[186] While Thomas does not speak explicitly on this, there are some suggestions that indulgences can be applied to souls in purgatory, at least *per modum suffragii*.[187] What is clear is that most Thomists from at least the 15th century on held that indulgences were applicable to souls in purgatory, and the question of the Church's official teaching was to some extent settled by papal grants of indulgences for the dead in the 15th century.[188]

The sermon concludes with the observation that the scholastic opinions being discussed are just that -- opinions. There is no unanimity on them and they do not yield certainty. Therefore Luther's opponents (the Thomists) should not brand him a heretic.[189] They have "never smelled the Bible, never read the Christian teachers [Fathers of the Church], and never understood their

---

[179] In the Tetzel-Wimpina theses, contrition is unnecessary (Theses 30, 31, 64; in Walch 18, 84 & 86), and the other conditions are not mentioned.

[180] *S.T.* Suppl., q.27, a.1. Cf. *Quodlibet* II, q.8, a.16.

[181] *S.T.* Suppl., q.25, a.2.

[182] *Ibid.*

[183] WA 1, 246, 15-20.

[184] *S.T.* Suppl., q.25, a.2 ad 5.

[185] *S.T.* Suppl., q.25, a.2 ad 2.

[186] WA 1, 246, 21-26.

[187] On this, see the discussion in *S.T.* Suppl., q.71, a.6, and Poschmann, *Penance*, p.228.

[188] Poschman, *Penance*, p.228.

[189] Luther's statement echoes Thomas' opening comment in his discussion of the effect of indulgences: "Respondeo dicendum quod circa hoc est multiplex opinio." (*S.T.* Suppl., q.25, a.2). Though Thomas argues forcefully for his position, he tacitly admits that it is one among many. On the other hand, the Tetzel-Wimpina theses brand all but the most extravagant understanding of indulgences as "error."

own teachers [Thomas]."*190* This exaggerated polemic given in conclusion to his sermon contains an important element of truth. For it is clear, as we have seen, that on a number of points Thomas' views were not faithfully represented by his followers. There is indeed some truth to Luther's allegation that the Thomists have not understood Thomas.

The young Luther's critique of Thomas on indulgences is largely complete in the March 1518 sermon we have analyzed. However, five months after writing this sermon, Luther as it were added two more items to this list in his reply to Prierias' *De potestate papae dialogus*. In this work Luther attacks first Thomas' understanding of the power of the keys in relation to indulgences. Again the exegesis of Matt. 16:19 stands in the foreground, but this time the issue is whether this passage grounds the so-called "Petrine privilege," i.e., the exclusive right of Peter and his successors to grant indulgences. According to Luther, Christ's words about binding and loosing are a general law given not only to Peter but to all priests and the whole Church.*191* For Thomas, of course, the power of the keys with regard to indulgences is given to Peter alone and to bishops only by papal authorization.*192* But by this time, as we have seen, Luther was calling into question the more fundamental issue of the efficacy of indulgences in remitting divine punishment. In the present context he is simply disputing what he takes to be Thomas' questionable exegesis of Matt. 16:19.*193*

The second aspect of Thomas' teaching on indulgences that receives critical attention in Luther's reply to Prierias is the theory of the treasury of merit. At this stage the issue is merely raised as a question: Thomas teaches that the treasury of the Church is the merits of Christ insofar as these are satisfactions, but this is not proven, nor can it be proven by referring to the practice of St. Gregory who granted indulgences. Luther will wait for a determination on this matter by a council of the Church.*194* The question is raised again almost simultaneously in Luther's "Resolutions" on the 95 theses (August 1518), only here Luther acknowledges his doubts. And these doubts raise for him the question of whether Thomas erred in this respect, a possibility which Luther is already willing to entertain.*195* By 1520, in his reply to the articles condemned by Leo X, Luther can simply dismiss the treasury of merit as a figment based not on Scripture but on Thomas.*196* Luther is substantially correct in his description of Thomas' teaching on the treasury of merit. For Thomas the merits of Christ are in fact the superabundant treasury of the Church, and he did refer to "Blessed Gregory," though hardly in order to "prove" the theory.*197* Luther's understanding of Thomas in this case is correct.

With this, our survey of Luther's critique of Thomas on the subject of indulgences is complete. The later Luther of course modified his own views on the subject of indulgences. Whereas in 1518 he still expressed doubts about his views,*198* by 1530, for instance, he could issue

---

[190]   WA 1, 246, 27-38. Tetzel, in his reply to Luther's sermon, turns all these charges back against Luther (Walch 18, 295).

[191]   WA 1, 655, 3-15. Cf. Prierias' attack on Luther in regard to this issue in Walch 18, 317f.

[192]   S.T. Suppl., q.26, aa.1 & 3.

[193]   Luther's teaching on the keys of course underwent substantial further development, as is clear from his 1530 treatise "Von der Schlüsseln," WA 30 II, 435-507.

[194]   WA 1, 680, 39-681, 6.

[195]   WA 1, 610, 29-611, 26. This important passage is analyzed below in connection with Luther's view of the authority of Thomas.

[196]   WA 7, 124, 26-28.

[197]   S.T. Suppl., q.25, a.2. The fullest statement of this theory is to be found in his *Expositio Orationis Dominicae*, (Vivès 27, 194). Prierias had referred to Thomas' use of Gregory (Walch 18, 334).

[198]   In a letter of 13 February 1518, Luther said of his 95 theses: "Nulla vero pertinaciter assero. Tamen omnia Eccleaiae sanctae suoque iudicio submitto." (WABR 1, 139, 52-54). For further expressions of doubt at this stage, see Wicks, "Roman Reactions," p. 530, n.38.

a much more sweeping and vehement denunciation of indulgences.[199] But the later Luther did not return to a critique of Thomas on this issue. The critique of Thomas is an early one, developed specifically in the context of his controversy with the Thomists. In fact it is doubtful that the young Luther would have attacked Thomas on this issue were it not for the fact that his opponents were Thomists. By constantly appealing to Thomas, these Thomists in a sense forced the young Luther to confront the teaching of Thomas.

This, however, does not necessarily mean that when these Thomists attacked him in the name of St. Thomas, Luther immediately resorted to the writings of Thomas himself. There is no direct evidence in this controversy to support such a claim. But how accurate then was Luther's understanding of Thomas on this issue? Keeping in mind the ambiguities within the writings of Thomas himself, all that can be said is that at some points Luther's understanding is accurate and at some points it is not. But it is important to see that in those cases where Luther's understanding is inaccurate, he almost inevitably was adopting an interpretation of Thomas given by his Thomist opponents. Thus many of his "disagreements" with Thomas on this issue would have been undermined by a closer examination of Thomas himself. Interesting in this connection is the fact that Luther suspected his Thomist opponents had not understood Thomas correctly, as we have seen. Though he did not follow up on this suspicion, it was to some extent justified.

In other cases, as we have seen, Luther's understanding of Thomas, though not nuanced, was substantially accurate. In these cases Luther's disagreements with Thomas were real ones. But it is important to see these disagreements not in the context of Lutheran-Catholic polemic but in the context of the late medieval "Wegestreit." The critique of Thomas' view of indulgences, insofar as it met Thomas' position head-on, was undertaken in a context of widespread discussion and argument over how indulgences were to be understood.[200] While it is true that some opponents such as Tetzel and Prierias could characterize Luther's critique as heretical, other more judicious Thomists such as Cajetan refused to do so.[201] And Cajetan, like Luther, quickly recognized that the issue of indulgences was grounded in the larger issue of the sacrament of penance.

Though the theology of penance and the theology of indulgences are intimately related, it is fair to say that the former occupied Luther's thought throughout his life while the latter did not. Or rather, one might say that developments in his theology of penance rendered indulgences unimportant for the later Luther. But, while penance remained close to the heart of his theology at every stage of his development, his critique of Thomas on this issue stems primarily from the young Luther. And once again, this critique was developed in the context of controversy with the Thomists.

Just as Luther's "Sermon von Ablass und Gnade" was the central locus for his critique of Thomas on indulgences, so his *Ad dialogum Silvestri Prieratis de potestatae papae responsio* was the central locus for his critique of Thomas on penance. In this work (and in a few later works) Luther places his developing theology of penance in conscious opposition to that of Thomas Aquinas. Written in August 1518, a scant six months after his reply to the Wimpina-Tetzel theses, this work is a reply to Silvester Prierias, Master of the Sacred Palace and Inquisitor of Heretical

---

[199] In his "Vermahnung an die Geistlichen, versammelt auf dem Reichstag zu Augsburg" (1530); WA 30 II, 268-356, especially pp. 281-286. Meanwhile in 1525, it should not be forgotten, Luther had in *De Servo Arbitrio* dismissed indulgences as "trifles" (WA 18, 786, 26-31).

[200] The earlier discussion is documented in Nikolas Paulus, *Geschichte des Ablasses im Mittelalter: Vom Ursprunge bis zur Mitte des 14. Jahrhunderts*, 2 vols., (Paderborn: Schöningh, 1922-23). Also in 1518, the Sorbonne issued a critique of practices connected with indulgences. On this, see Wicks, "Roman Reactions," p. 522, n.3.

[201] Wicks, "Roman Reactions," p. 549: "In contrast with Silvester Prierias, Cajetan did not brand Luther's teaching heretical."

Pravity in Rome. In June of that year Prierias had written, in reply to the 95 theses, his "De potestatae papae dialogus."[202] Here Prierias had clearly drawn the lines of battle. On the one side stood Luther, "heretic," "arch-heretic," "devil," "blasphemer," etc.[203] And on the other side stood Thomas, cited as though he were, in Prierias' later words, the "light of the world."[204] It is not surprising then that Luther, in his reply, engages the teaching of Thomas. Once again, he was pushed to do so by the polemical context.

Luther's critique begins with what scholastic theology generally held to be the first part of the sacrament of penance, namely contrition. Prierias had argued that attrition (or insufficient sorrow for sin) was transformed into contrition (or sufficient sorrow) by the power of the keys. Though he had not explicitly ascribed this teaching to Thomas, he had left the impression that it was Thomas' view by inserting the phrase "according to the interpretation of the saints."[205] In his reply, Luther says that this is "perhaps" the teaching of Thomas, but it is incorrect.[206] Attrition does not become contrition but grace alone produces contrition in the penitent.[207]

Luther's tentative ascription of this position to Thomas is justified, not only in view of "certain obscurities and inconsistencies" in Thomas' theology of penance,[208] but also in view of the fact that the mature Thomas never dealt with the whole doctrine of penance.[209] Yet on this particular question Thomas is clear: "attrition can in no way become contrition."[210] And since contrition is to be understood as the act of an infused virtue, its source and principle is the grace of God.[211] Later Thomists, as Poschmann has shown, adopted the view Luther was criticizing, and Prierias was clearly one of them.[212] But the teaching he rejects is not that of Thomas.

Luther further engages the thought of Thomas with regard to the nature of contrition. In thesis 40 of the disputation "On the Power of Indulgences" Luther had asserted that true contrition is such that it seeks and loves penalties. Prierias had attacked this thesis saying that according to the teaching of Thomas this is true only if the penalties bring with them some reward or benefit, and that penalties and indulgences are better than penalties alone.[213] Luther responds first by pointing out a contradiction: one cannot love and seek penalties (satisfaction) and indulgences simultaneously, for indulgences take the place of satisfactions. Second, Luther agrees with Prierias and Thomas that in *this* life punishment is not willingly accepted if it brings no reward or benefit.[214] Third, Luther laments the miserable result of Thomas' inconsistencies, namely, that this thesis is approved in Italy and damned in Germany.[215]

---

[202] The text of this work can be found in *Lutheri opera Latina var. arg.* 1, 344-377. A German translation can be found in Walch 18, 312-345.

[203] Walch 18, 17.

[204] Walch 18, 19.

[205] Walch 18, 318.

[206] WA 1, 659, 1-2: "Dicis enim, quod attriti virtute clavium, iuxta sanctorum interpretationem (forte sancti Thome), fiunt contriti. . ."

[207] WA 1, 659, 17-23.

[208] Poschmann, *Penance*, p. 169.

[209] The *Scriptum* is the only work in which Thomas dealt with the whole doctrine of penance. His treatment in the *Summa Theologiae* breaks off after seven questions and the Supplementum then reproduces sections from the *Scriptum*.

[210] *S.T.* Suppl., q.1, a.3.

[211] *Ibid.*

[212] Poschmann, *Penance*, pp. 181ff. According to H. Oberman, Biel too held this view. *The Harvest of Medieval Theology* (Grand Rapids: Eerdman, 1967), pp. 159f.

[213] Walch 18, 329.

[214] WA 1, 674, 3-26.

[215] WA 1, 674, 26-28: ". . .Nisi quod iterum doleo Divi Thomae vicem et miseram suae discordiae sortem, quia hanc conclusionem probat in Italia et damnat in Germania." The Tetzel-Wimpina theses simply presuppose that the penitent wishes to escape penalties, and this, they go on to argue, can be done through indulgences. The reference to Thomas'

The same issue comes up again in relation to Luther's 29th thesis "On the Power of Indulgences" in which he had raised the question of whether some souls in purgatory choose to be there. Prierias responded by quoting Thomas to the effect that insofar as it results in some benefit, suffering can be freely chosen or at least willingly endured. In the case of purgatory, Prierias adds, suffering is not freely chosen but only willingly endured.[216] In his reply Luther rejects the distinction between penalties which are for our benefit and penalties which are not. All penalty and punishment is for our benefit and the contrite can therefore choose to accept it.[217] Luther's disagreement with Thomas on this point may be a real one but it is hardly of major importance. On the larger question of the contrite person's willingness to accept penalty there is no such disagreement, because for Thomas, contrition includes the willingness to make satisfaction, i.e., accept penalty.[218] For Thomas, this kind of penalty is always to the contrite person's benefit. In Prierias' response to Luther on this issue, he clearly interpreted an isolated passage in Thomas so as to maximize disagreement with Luther; and in doing so he ignored basic agreement on the more fundamental question.

On confession, the second part of penance in the scholastic schema, Luther has very little to say about Thomas' teaching. He had said in thesis 7 "On the Power of Indulgences" that remission of guilt requires submission to a priest. Prierias' response was to grudgingly acknowledge that this thesis was correct: here was a drop of truth amidst a sea of error.[219] Luther's response expresses amazement at the diversity of opinions among Thomists. Once again, an Italian Thomist approves this thesis while German Thomists detest it. This diversity, Luther says, raises for him the suspicion that Thomists misunderstand Thomas and that Thomas would not understand the Thomists.[220] Again, even at this early stage, Luther was not confident that the Thomists had understood Thomas correctly.

The later Luther of course modified his views on the necessity of confession to a priest. But Thomas' name recurs only once in this connection, in a sermon preached on 29 August 1529. Against "Augustinus, Summa, Scotus, Thomas", Luther asserts that Jesus' command to the lepers to go show themselves to the priest (Lk. 17:14) does not refer to confession.[221] Thomas in fact does not use this Scripture passage in connection with confession.[222] Luther is mistaken in using Thomas' name in this regard, though one suspects that his list of opponents ("Augustinus, Summa, Scotus, Thomas") is simply a convenient way of referring to a widely held view with which he disagrees.

On the subject of absolution Luther only once takes issue with the teaching of Thomas. For Luther at this stage, absolution was declarative and confirmative (*declarando, approbando*), whereas Prierias held that absolution was *dispositive* and *ministerialiter*, i.e., effecting what it

---

"inconsistency" seems to be a sarcastic way of pointing out disagreements among his followers.

[216] Walch 18, 325f. Prierias quotes from Thomas, IV *Sent.*, d.21, q.1, a.1, solutio IV (Vivès 10, 588). The mature Thomas did not speak to this question.

[217] WA 1, 668, 20-34.

[218] *S.T.* Suppl., q.1, a.1.

[219] Walch 18, 318.

[220] WA 1, 660, 1-10: ". . .Sed id admiror, quid acciderit vobis Thomistis, ut tam diversam sentiatis. Hanc enim meam conclusionem Thomistae et tuae sectae fratres in Germania miro zelo detestantur. An alium habeatis Thomam in Italia et alium in Germania, ignoro, Nisi forte mihi suspitionem facere vultis, quod nec Thomistae Thomam, nec Thomas Thomistas intelligat." The Tetzel-Wimpina theses had indeed condemned thesis seven, arguing that there can be forgiveness without confession to priests (Theses 26, 27 in Walch 18, 84)!

[221] WA 29, 541, 14ff.

[222] Lk. 17:14 is not cited in the *Summa Theologiae*, the *Summa Contra Gentiles*, or the *Scriptum*. A parallel passage (Mt. 8:4) is cited once in another context in *S.T.* 1a2ae, q.103, a.3.

signified.[223] Against this view, Luther argued that since contrition presupposed a state of grace, forgiveness must have already taken place; absolution declares and confirms this forgiveness.[224] Luther's understanding of Thomas' teaching on this is correct: absolution is both declarative and effective.[225] Yet the difficulty Luther points to is a real one in Thomas, for he "occasionally simply presupposes a state of grace for confession" and thus he would seem to be logically impelled to say that the remission of sins takes place before absolution.[226] Thomas' teaching is thus not as unambiguous as Prierias' presentation of it would imply.[227]

When we come to the subject of satisfaction, the "third part" of penance, we arrive finally at what Luther regarded as the *fundamentum* of Thomas' teaching on penance (and *indulgences*).

> Third, I regard Thomas' foundation as false, namely, that God requires a penalty from sinners and remits nothing without the requisite satisfaction. This is contrary to the truth that God does not despise a troubled and contrite spirit [Ps. 51:19]. What God remits, he remits totally, applying only perhaps some chastisement according to his will, and this can be remitted neither by the Church nor by heaven.[228]

Thomas' assumption that God remits nothing without satisfaction on the part of sinner is, according to Luther, the heart of the difference between them on the subject of penance. The objection Luther expresses here is indeed a fundamental one. It lies at the heart of his critique of indulgences, for the whole theory and practice of indulgences assumes that God requires in every case that the sinner make satisfaction.[229] And it also brings us close to the subject of justification and the mystery of the relation between God's justice and mercy.[230]

But again we must ask, does Thomas in fact teach that God remits no sin without requiring satisfaction on the part of man? If one read only Prierias' treatise, to which Luther was responding, one would indeed get this impression. For Prierias focuses almost entirely on the subject of human satisfaction to the exclusion of themes such as God's mercy, the gratuity of God's

---

[223] Walch 18, 318.

[224] WA 1, 659, 1-3, and 17-40.

[225] *S.T.* 3a, q.84, a.3. Cf. Thomas' Opusculum "De Forma Absolutionis," in Vivès 27, 417-423.

[226] Poschmann, *Penance*, p. 171.

[227] The related issue of the necessity of faith for receiving the sacrament comes up in relation to Thomas only once. In his 1520 "Resolutio disputationis de fide infusa et acquisita," Luther defends the thesis that "Accessuro ad Sacramentum omnino necessaria est Fides infusa." According to him, "Ista positio statuitur adversus multorum varias opiniones. Quarum ista est potissima Scoti, Thomae et aliorum his innixa verbis magistri [Lombard] dicentis: Sacramenta novae legis causantur gratiam." (WA 6, 88, 7ff). This issue had first come up in connection with penance in Luther's 1518 discussions with Cajetan at Augsburg. And Cajetan had conceded that on this point Luther was not heretical: "with a slight redefinition Luther's view might stand" (Wicks, "Roman Reactions," p. 550). The ambiguity of Thomas on the requisite disposition for absolution has already been pointed out.

[228] WA 1, 658, 6-10: "Tertio, fundamentum Thomae falsum iudicio, scilicet quod deus requirat poenas a peccatore, nec remittat nisi requisita satisfactione. Contra verum est, quod spiritum contribulatum et contritum non despicit. Et quod remittit, totum remittit, nisi forte flagella adhuc pro suo arbitrio inferat, quae nec Ecclesia nec coelum relaxare potest."

[229] This is the assumption, at least, behind Prierias' defense of indulgences. By giving the pope power to remit divinely imposed punishments, Prierias elevates the power of the pope at the expense of God's power according to Luther (WA 1, 658, 10-19).

[230] Returning to this theme in a sermon in 1531, Luther says: "Wo das vorgeht, Nicht wie die Zophisten spiritum sanctum incipere, nos perficere. Das sagt S. Thomas, furtrefflich diabolus, qui dicunt per Evangelium remitti, sed opus esse satisfaccione. Neyn, hoc non est Evangelium. . ." (WA 34 I, 466, 20ff. Cf. *ibid*., 3ff.)

forgiveness, or the "satisfaction" of the cross of Christ. One can see how, from Luther's point of view, this single-minded focus on human works of satisfaction is a denial of the Gospel.

Thomas himself does indeed have a good deal to say about penitential works of satisfaction. But in this very context there is another side to his teaching which scarcely comes to light in Prierias' representation. First, throughout his discussion of penance, Thomas understands it as a participation in the passion of Christ.[231] Thus Christ's satisfaction is primary and human satisfaction is secondary. Second, Thomas teaches that human satisfaction is *not* absolutely necessary: the grace by which sin is forgiven cannot be made contingent on some future event such as works of satisfaction: "what grace has once done endures forever."[232] And in any case, for Thomas, man cannot make satisfaction in the strict sense of the word; there can only be a "proportionate equality" between man's offence and his satisfaction, and God graciously accepts whatever man is able to pay.[233] Finally, according to Thomas, remission of guilt and eternal punishment is "from grace alone."[234] Man in no way "earns" God's forgiveness by works of satisfaction:

> ...the difference between the grace of God and the grace of man, is
> that the latter does not cause, but presupposes true or apparent
> goodness in him who is graced, whereas the grace of God causes
> goodness in the man who is graced, because the good-will of God,
> which is denoted by the word 'grace', is the cause of all created
> good.[235]

Here we see another side to Thomas' teaching on penance -- a side which Prierias ignores. In his preoccupation with defending current penitential practice and indulgences Prierias gives short shrift to what is the real *fundamentum* in Thomas' teaching. Luther undoubtedly arrived at his conclusion as to the foundation of Thomas' teaching through his reading of Prierias and other Thomists. And given the way in which Thomas' teaching was presented by these Thomists, his conclusion is understandable. But it is nevertheless mistaken: in the final analysis, for both Luther and Thomas, God's forgiveness is freely and graciously given to human beings.

With this, our survey of Luther's critique of Thomas on penance is complete. Given the centrality of penance in Luther's personal and theological development, and given the proximity of this issue to the heart of his Reformation concern, one might have expected a more persistent if not a more thoroughgoing critique. But as we have seen, the later Luther rarely returns to speak of Thomas in this regard. The actual critique as it stands is developed almost entirely in controversy with the Thomists; it points to some real though minor differences with Thomas; and in many cases it turns out to be a critique not of Thomas but of a distorted image of Thomas

---

[231] E.g. *S.T.* 3a, q.86, a.4 ad 3. Yet, for Thomas, God can forgive without the sacrament of penance (*S.T.* 3a, q.86, a.2). Cf. *S.T.* Suppl., q.5, a.1 ad 3 where Thomas distinguishes between forgiveness before God and forgiveness before the Church.

[232] *S.T.* 3a, q.88, a.1: "Si ergo absolute non fieret peccatorum remissio, sed cum quidam conditione in futurum dependente, per gratiam et gratiae sacramenta, sequetur quod gratia et gratiae sacramenta non essent sufficiens causa remissionis peccatorum. Quod est erroneum, utpote derogans gratiae Dei....gratia simpliciter tollit maculam et reatum poenae aeternae....Et quod gratia semel facit, perpetuo manet."

[233] *S.T.* Suppl., q.13, a.1.

[234] *S.T.* 3a, q.86, a.4 ad 2.

[235] *S.T.* 3a, q.86, a.2. There is a remarkable parallel between this statement and one that Luther made in thesis 28 of his 1518 Heidelberg Disputation: "The love of God does not find, but creates, that which is pleasing to it. The love of man comes into being through that which is pleasing to it." (WA 1, 354, 35-36; tr. from LW 31, 41).

mediated to Luther by his Thomist opponents. Moreover the whole critique is overshadowed by Luther's suspicion, mentioned more than once, that the Thomists had not understood Thomas correctly. The irony is that although he did not know it, this suspicion was fully justified precisely on the issue which Luther identified as the *fundamentum*.

6. The Lord's Supper

Though the evolution of Luther's eucharistic theology is a long and complex development, it will generally be conceded that it falls into two somewhat distinct phases, both of which have at their core different controversial preoccupations. Up until roughly 1524, Luther opposed those elements in the scholastic tradition which in his view wrongly understood the sacrificial character of the mass.[236] The second phase in his development was dominated by controversy with the Swiss reformers and "Schwärmer" who in his view denied the real presence.[237]

This admittedly oversimplified sketch forms the most general context within which Luther's critique of Thomas' eucharistic theology must be seen. What is immediately clear is that the dual foci of Luther's development--the mass as sacrifice and the real presence--do not figure in his critique of Thomas. Though Luther's critique of Thomas on the eucharist spans both phases in his development, and though this critique is a relatively frequent one, the issues involved are, from Luther's own point of view, relatively peripheral.

The primary theme on which Luther takes issue with Thomas' eucharistic theology has to do with transubstantiation. In 1519 Luther had to a considerable extent clarified his views on the sacraments in general.[238] The critique of Thomas following from this clarification began in his *An den christlichen Adel deutscher Nation* which appeared in June, 1520.[239] Here he argues that transubstantiation is not an article of faith: this is "a delusion of St. Thomas and the pope." The real presence, on the other hand, is an article of faith.[240] While not yet explicitly rejecting transubstantiation, Luther here asserts that Thomas was mistaken in regarding it as being *de fide*.

It is by no means clear that Luther was correct in ascribing this view to Thomas. Nowhere does Thomas state that transubstantiation is an article of faith, and it is only by a questionable inference that he can thus be interpreted. Already in his early *Sentences Commentary*, Thomas envisions three possible explanations of how the real presence comes about on the altar: these are conventionally designated by the terms annihilation, consubstantiation and transubstantiation. Thomas here rejects the annihilation theory and describes consubstantiation as "heretical."[241] Later in the *Summa Contra Gentiles* Thomas rejects these same theories as nothing more than "false."[242] Finally in his *Summa Theologiae* Thomas rejects annihilation as "false"[243] and consubstantiation as "heretical."[244] However, none of this directly implies that transubstantiation is an article of faith.

---

[236] For an extended study of this question see Francis Clark, *Eucharistic Sacrifice and the Reformation*, (London: Darton, Longman and Todd, 1960). See also James F. McCue, "Luther and Roman Catholicism on the Mass as Sacrifice," in *Journal of Ecumenical Studies*, 2(1965), 205-233. Cf. Hartmut Hilgenfeld, *Mittelalterlich-traditionelle Elemente in Luthers Abendmahlsschriften*, (Zurich: Theologischer Verlag, 1971). Hilgenfeld re-opens the old debate about whether the later Luther fell back into a "scholastic" understanding of the eucharist. But he fails to raise the crucial question of what parts of the scholastic tradition Luther knew.

[237] For an account of this controversy see Heinrich Bornkamm, *Luther in Mid-Career*, pp. 501-551. Clarification of the theological issues involved can be found in Egil Grislis, "The Manner of Christ's Eucharistic Presence According to Martin Luther," in *Consensus: A Canadian Lutheran Journal of Theology*, 7(1981), 3-15.

[238] Cf. Ursala Stock, *Die Bedeutung der Sakramente in Luthers Sermonen von 1519*, (Leiden: Brill, 1982).

[239] It would seem that in 1519, Luther still held to the view of transubstantiation. In his "Sermon von dem Hochwirdigen Sacrament" of that year Luther still applies the language of change to the sacramental elements (WA 2, 749, 10ff). Cf. McCue, "Luther and Roman Catholicism on the Mass as Sacrifice," p. 212.

[240] WA 6, 456, 34ff: ". . .den es ist nit ein artickel des glaubens, das brot und wein nicht wessenlich und naturlich sey im sacrament, wilchs ein wahn ist sancti Thome unnd des Papsts, sondern es ist ein artickel des glaubens, das in dem naturlichen brot und weyn warhafftig naturlich fleisch und blut Christi sey. . ."

[241] IV *Sent.*, d.11, a.1, sol. 1 (Vivès 10, 254).

[242] *SCG* IV, cap. 63, 5.

[243] *S.T.* 3a, q.75, a.3.

[244] *S.T.* 3a, q.75, a.2.

And in fact, the very term "article of faith" does not have the conceptual clarity in Thomas that it was later to attain. Thomas uses this term primarily in reference to the articles of the creed: those things which directly order us to eternal life are *de fide*.[245] They are known by revelation and they cannot be proven demonstratively.[246] Moreover, Thomas says explicitly that the eucharist is not a special article of faith, but rather it is, like all other miracles, included under the article on God's omnipotence.[247] Nor is there anything in Thomas to suggest that he regarded the decree on the eucharist from Lateran IV (1215) as a formal dogmatizing of transubstantiation.[248] Likewise, when Thomas sometimes labels consubstantiation as "heretical," we must recall that in his works the later conceptual clarity in regard to this term is largely absent. "Heresy" can be understood as the obstinate denial of an article of faith,[249] but it can also be understood as "inordinate speaking" or even disobedience to church discipline.[250] For all these reasons it is extremely dubious to say that Thomas regarded transubstantiation as an article of faith.

At the same time, it is highly probable that Luther's understanding of Thomas on this point was a widespread one on the eve of the Reformation. In all likelihood Luther came to this understanding through Gabriel Biel with whom he was of course thoroughly familiar. For Biel clearly held transubstantiation to be an article of faith. In arriving at this position Biel cites Thomas at great length. While Biel ultimately rejects Thomas' argumentation for transubstantiation, he reports Thomas' dismissal of consubstantiation as heretical and he sees his own affirmation of transubstantiation as an article of faith to be in full harmony with Thomas.[251] Thus Luther, in ascribing to Thomas the view that transubstantiation is an article of faith, echoes a highly questionable interpretation which was certainly widespread on the eve of the Reformation.

Later in the same year (1520), in his *De captivitate Babylonica*, Luther for the first time rejects this opinion of Thomas as a false one.[252] But more than this, it is an unfortunate one because Thomas bases it on an incorrect understanding of Aristotle:

> But this opinion of Thomas hangs so completely in the air without
> support of Scripture or reason that it seems to me he knows neither
> his philosophy nor his logic. For Aristotle speaks of subject and
> accidents so very differently from St. Thomas that it seems to me
> this great man is to be pitied not only for attempting to draw his
> opinions in matters of faith from Aristotle, but also for attempting

[245] *S.T.* 2a2ae, q.1, a.6. Cf. 2a2ae, q.1, aa.7, 8 and 9.

[246] *S.T.* 1a, q.46, a.2.

[247] *S.T.* 2a2ae, q.1, a.8 ad 6.

[248] Hilgenfeld (*Mittelalterlich-traditionelle Elemente*, p. 387) seems to think that transubstantiation was officially defined at Lateran IV. However, McCue has shown that "The anti-Albigensian confession of faith of Lateran IV was not interpreted as a dogmatic exclusion of all other theories of the real presence other than transubstantiation until eighty-five years after that Council." "The Doctrine of Transubstantiation from Berengar through the Council of Trent," in P. Empie and T. Murphy, eds., *The Eucharist as Sacrifice*, (Minneapolis: Augsburg, 1967), pp. 89-124, p. 123.

[249] *S.T.* 2a2ae, q.5, a.3.

[250] *S.T.* 2a2ae, q.11, a.2 ad 2. Cf. Jared Wicks, "Roman Reactions," p. 529, n.32.

[251] Biel argues for this position on the basis of the determination of the Church and the authoritative teaching of the saints. On Biel's understanding and use of Thomas in this matter, see John Farthing, *Thomas Aquinas and Gabriel Biel: Interpretations of St. Thomas Aquinas in German Nominalism on the Eve of the Reformation*, (Durham: Duke Univ. Press, 1988), pp. 118-120. When he speaks of the official determination of the Church, he is no doubt referring to Lateran IV (1215) and the Council of Constance (1415). When he speaks of the authority of the saints, the context leaves no doubt that he is referring to Thomas.

[252] WA 6, 508, 7ff.

48

to base them upon a man whom he did not understand, thus building an unfortunate superstructure upon an unfortunate foundation.[253]

Leif Grane has gone to great lengths to argue that Luther was correct: Thomas bases his theory of transubstantiation on a misunderstanding of Aristotle.[254] But this view is largely irrelevant when one recalls the way in which Thomas uses Aristotle in general: Aristotle's thought is placed into the service of theology, and in Thomas' hands he thus acquires a "wax nose." An historically accurate portrayal of Aristotle's thought is far from being Thomas' main concern.[255] What is important to observe in Luther's critique at this stage is the fine distinctions he makes. Transubstantiation is a theological opinion, a false one and an unfortunate one. But it is still a permissible one:

> I permit every man to hold either of these opinions as he chooses.
> My one concern at present is to remove all scruples of conscience,
> so that no one may fear being called a heretic. . .[256]

The real issue for Luther at this point is not whether transubstantiation is true or false. Rather it is that this opinion of Thomas has been made into a binding article of faith. For Luther, no theoretical explanation of the manner in which the real presence comes about can be made into dogma. By doing this the church has become "the Thomistic, that is, the Aristotelian church."[257] The authority of Thomas in church and theology is at the heart of Luther's objection here.[258] As Luther said in the following year in his work against the Thomist Ambrosius Catharinus, the Thomists "transubstantiate" Thomas himself, i.e., they raise him to the level of an infallible teacher and transform his opinions into articles of faith.[259]

In 1522 the same issue comes up again in Luther's German answer to Henry VIII's *Assertio septem sacramentorum*.[260] Here Luther says that transubstantiation has not been proven, and yet the Thomists and papists believe and teach it.[261] Moreover it is a view which was introduced to the world by Thomas.[262] If by this Luther means that Thomas was the first to devise the theory, he is technically incorrect. For the theory was represented by some theologians already in the 11th and 12th centuries.[263] The element of truth, on the other hand, is that Thomas seems to have been the first to label other theories as false or heretical.[264] Moreover, it was surely in large measure the influence of Thomas which led to the subsequent widespread acceptance of the theory.

Again in 1523, in his *Von Anbeten des Sakraments des heiligen Leichnams Christi*, Luther attacks Thomas' view of transubstantiation. But here again the major issue has to do with the fact

---

[253] WA 6, 508, 20ff. Tr. from LW 36, 29.
[254] Leif Grane, "Luthers Kritik an Thomas von Aquin in De captivitate Babylonica."
[255] On this see the section on "Aristotle" above.
[256] WA 6, 508, 27ff. Tr. from LW 36, 30.
[257] WA 6, 508, 12f.
[258] On this, see below, Ch. III.
[259] WA 7, 706, 13-19.
[260] This German work is entitled *Antwort deutsch auf König Heinrichs Buch* (WA 10 II, 227-262). It differs substantially from Luther's Latin *Contra Henricum Regem Angliae* also written in 1522 (WA 10 II, 180-222).
[261] WA 10 II, 247, 22ff.
[262] WA 10 II, 264, 3ff: "Hats doch die wellt nie sso weytt glewbt, ehe denn es durch Thomam Aquinas aussbracht ist."
[263] McCue, "The Doctrine of Transubstantiation," pp. 90f.
[264] *Ibid.* p. 100.

that it has been made into an article of faith. In the papists' view, all are heretics who do not accept this opinion of Thomas as a necessary truth.[265]

Luther remained silent on this question in relation to Thomas until 1531, when, in a table talk, Luther again credited Thomas with "inventing" transubstantiation.[266] And finally in another table talk from 1541 Luther again labels transubstantiation a "Thomist view."[267] Thus there is no reason to believe that Luther modified his view substantially after his initial full-blown critique of 1520. Nor is there reason to believe that Luther ever altered his view on the permissibility of transubstantiation. Though it was in his opinion false, one does not become a heretic by either affirming or denying it. His critique is, in the final analysis, directed against the use to which Thomas has been put by his followers. By dogmatizing his opinion, they illegitimately create new articles of faith. From Luther's perspective, Thomas may have been wrong but he was entitled to his opinion.

A secondary issue on which Luther attacked Thomas' eucharistic theology has to do with reception of the eucharist in both kinds. In article 16 of "Exsurge Domine," Leo X had censured Luther's view on the advisability of giving the sacrament in both kinds as well as his view that those who receive the sacrament in both kinds are not heretics.[268] In his German reply of 1521 (*Grund und Ursach aller Artikel*), Luther defends his position in part by quoting the famous hymn Thomas had composed for the feast of Corpus Christi, "Verbum Supernum Prodiens":

> Again in the hymn, 'Celestial Word,' the church sings how he gave
> his disciples flesh and blood under the two kinds in order to feed
> the whole man, who is twofold in nature. If the church is right in
> singing this then they certainly ought to give both kinds to all
> christians.[269]

Here we have the only direct quotation from Thomas that is to be found in Luther's writings, though Luther does not mention Thomas' name in this context. And the quotation is used by Luther to buttress his argument in favor of receiving the eucharist in both kinds.

It is interesting in this context that Luther in the following year preached a sermon on the Feast of Corpus Christi (June 4, 1522). And in this sermon he, at least tentatively, places the blame on Thomas for the practice of withholding the cup from the laity.[270] It is true of course

---

[265] WA 11, 441, 18ff: "Der Dritte yrthum ist, das ym sacrament keyn brot bleybe, sondern nur gestallt des brotts....[The papists] yderman ketzer schellten, wer nicht ihn den münchtrawm, durch Thomas Aquinas bekrefftiget, fur nöttige warheit hellt, das kein brot da bleybe." Thomas of course does teach that the opinion that "bread remains" (as Luther puts it), "is to be avoided as heretical." *S.T.* 3a, q.75, a.2. But from Luther's point of view, this in itself is merely an opinion.

[266] WATR 1, 37, 5ff. (9 Nov. 1531): "Transubstantio in sacramento altaris a Thoma reperta. Ego puto manere panem et vinum, sicut in baptismo manet aqua. . ."

[267] WABR 9, 443, 9 (June 1541).

[268] WA 7, 389, 16-19.

[269] Tr. from LW 32, 57. Luther's German version reads: "Die kirch singt auch ynn dem hymno, Verbum supernum: 'Er hat seinen iungern gebenn unter zweien gestalt sein fleisch und blut, auff das er den gantzen menschen speiset, wilcher von zweien naturn gemacht ist.' Ist die kirch ynn dieszem gesang recht, Szo sollen yhe beide gestalt geben werden allen christen. . ." WA 7, 390, 16ff. The original hymn is to be found in Thomas' "Officium de Festo Corpus Christi" (Vivès 29, 335-343). Its third stanza reads: "Quibus sub bina specie/Carnem dedit et sanguinem/Ut duplicis substantiae/Totum cibaret hominem." (Vivès 29, 340). The Weimar editors were clearly correct in regarding Luther's statement as a quotation.

[270] One version of this highly problematic sermon reads, "Man gibt die schuld Thomas von Aquin, der hat es gethon. Es ist fast gleich seinem gaist unnd geschrifft." (WA 12, 581, 23f). Another version reads, "Man gibt die schuld Thomas von Aquin, der hab es gethon, ich wayss es nicht, Es ist fast Geleich seynem gayst und schrifft." (WA 17 II, 437, 14ff).

that Thomas developed a doctrine of natural concomitance: the body and blood of Christ are present in either of the consecrated elements.[271] Yet this doctrine was of little concern to Luther; in fact he found himself in agreement with it:

> Don't pay attention to their twaddle that the whole sacrament is received in the bread. Christ knew very well that we receive everything in one kind, indeed by faith alone, without the sacrament, yet it was not without reason that he instituted both kinds.[272]

Luther's real concern in this regard lay elsewhere.

Thomas had developed his doctrine of natural concomitance to sanction and explain what was by his time an almost universal practice. And this practice had originated with the laity, not with the official Church hierarchy. But Luther was convinced that the laity now wished to receive both eucharistic elements. The problem was that the church now forbade them from doing so, and had condemned those who did (John Hus had been condemned at Constance in 1415). In Luther's mind, Thomas had in some vague way played a role in this historical development. Once again, therefore, it was Thomas' influence rather than anything Thomas said that was the object of Luther's criticism. Withholding the cup was in the final analysis a problem of authority for Luther.

Luther's central and most vehement criticism of scholastic eucharistic theology focused on the sacrificial nature of the mass. In 1520 he called this "by far the most wicked abuse of all,"[273] and in 1528 he named it "the greatest of all abominations."[274] Yet it is significant to note that on this topic Thomas was never the object of Luther's critique. Only once is Thomas' name mentioned in the context of a discussion of sacrifice, and then it is merely to recount Thomas' teaching on the *ex opere operato* efficacy of the sacrament.[275]

In summary, Luther's critique of Thomas' eucharistic theology is insubstantial. Though it comes up with relative frequency, the issues quickly dissolve upon closer examination. But though the critique is insubstantial in this sense, it is not insignificant. For the critique in all its aspects masks a deeper and more fundamental problem, namely, that of authority. It is not Thomas' views which are at issue here but rather the way in which they have been dogmatized in the church. Luther's critique of Thomas on the eucharist is merely a symptom of this larger concern.

---

[271] *S.T.* 3a, q.76, a.2 and q.80, a.12. Luther was aware of Thomas' teaching if not directly, then by way of Gabriel Biel. On this see Farthing, *Thomas Aquinas and Gabriel Biel*, p. 130.

[272] WA 7, 399, 26-30. Tr. from LW 32, 62. This is at least analogous to Thomas' teaching that God did not bind his power to the sacraments nor to the church (*S.T.* 3a, q.64, a.7).

[273] WA 6, 512, 7f. Tr. from LW 36, 35.

[274] WA 26, 508, 30f. Tr. from LW 37, 370f.

[275] WA 29, 183, 9ff. (Sermon for 23 March 1529). Luther drew his understanding of this, if not directly from Thomas, then probably through Biel who presents Thomas' doctrine in a hostile and somewhat inaccurate way. On this, see John Farthing, "Post Thomam: Images of Thomas Aquinas in the Academic Theology of Gabriel Biel," (Duke Univ. Dissertation, 1978), p. 327. I cite here Farthing's dissertation which includes an extremely valuable appendix of Thomas-citations in Biel. This was omitted from the book *Thomas Aquinas and Gabriel Biel*. For Thomas' very moderate views on the sacrificial nature of the mass, see *S.T.* 3a, q.83, a.1.

7. Monasticism

Since they were both monks, it is hardly surprising that both Luther and Thomas Aquinas devoted a good deal of reflection to the theology of the monastic life. Luther's reflection, critical of some traditional views from the outset, led gradually to a definitive critique of monasticism in his 1521 treatise *De votis monasticis iudicium*.[276] Throughout this development, it was not the abuses of monastic life that drew Luther's criticism but rather its theological foundations. And it was on these grounds that Luther finally in 1521 came to reject monasticism in general as a mistaken form of the Christian life. To be sure, Luther did not in 1521 absolutely exclude every possibility of monasticism.[277] Even in 1533, Luther could explicitly affirm such a possibility in principle.[278] But his requirements for a legitimate monasticism are so stringent that it is a matter of doubt whether anyone could meet them.[279]

It was only after the appearance of his definitive critique in 1521 that Luther began to specifically single out for criticism Thomas' theology of the monastic life. On at least fifteen occasions between 1522 and 1538, Luther attacked various aspects of Thomas' thought on this topic. The survey which follows shows that this critique has two primary themes: first Thomas' understanding of Christian perfection, and second, Thomas' view of monastic vows as a kind of second baptism. The first of these is important for Thomas' theology of the monastic life, and the frequency with which Luther returns to the second indicates that it is for him, if not a major problem, at least a significant irritant in Thomas' theology.

Luther's first allusion to Thomas' theology of monastic life occurs in his 1520 *Assertio omnium articulorum M. Lutheri per bullam Leonis X. novisimam damnatorum*. Here he concedes that John Hus may have erred in reducing the evangelical counsels to the number of twelve, by reckoning virginity and celibacy to be one and the same. In this, Luther says, Hus was deceived by the theology of Thomas and the Thomists.[280] But this is only the most minor concession in Luther's defense of John Hus (Article 30).[281]

Luther's more serious critique of Thomas on this matter begins in 1522 in a sermon preached on New Year's Day. Thomas teaches, according to Luther, that it is not necessary for Christians to be perfect. It is enough for Christians to be in the "state of perfection" (i.e. in

---

[276] WA 8, 573-669. For the best account of the gradual development of Luther's critique to 1521, see Bernhard Lohse, *Mönchtum und Reformation: Luthers Auseinandersetzung mit dem Mönchsideal des Mittelalters*, (Göttingen: Vandenhoeck und Ruprecht, 1963). For a more recent account that includes Luther's entire career, see Heinz-Meinolf Stamm, *Luthers Stellung zum Ordensleben*, (Wiesbaden: Steiner, 1980).

[277] Cf. Luther's letter to Melanchthon of 9 September 1521 (WABR 2, 382-386). While Luther says here that vows do not contradict Christian freedom, he expresses grave doubts about the practical possibility of taking them in a free and evangelical way. Cf. Stamm's discussion of this letter in *Luthers Stellung zum Ordensleben*, pp. 38-45.

[278] WA 38, 164, 16ff. (*Die Kleine antwort auff Herzog Georgen nehestes buch*, 1533).

[279] Given these requirements, Lohse asks, "Who would still become a monk?" *Mönchtum und Reformation*, pp. 354f. Otto Pesch concurs with Lohse on this: "Luthers Kritik am Mönchtum in Katholischer Sicht," in H. Schlier, E. Severus, J. Sudbrack, and A. Pereira, eds., *Strukturen Christlicher Existenz: Beiträge zur Erneuerung des Geistlichen Lebens*, (Würzburg: Echter Verlag, 1968), pp. 81-96, 371-374; pp. 89 & 95.

[280] WA 7, 136, 12-14: "Fortassis in hoc peccavit Ioannes Huss, quod duodecim Consilia Evangelica fecit, cum non sit nisi unicum virginitatis sive coelibatus. In qua tamen re deceptus est per impiam Thomae et Thomistarum Theologiam."

[281] The source of Luther's allusion to Thomas here is unclear. Thomas does not enumerate the evangelical counsels in this way, nor does he equate celibacy and virginity in the *Summa Theologiae*, in the *Summa Contra Gentiles*, or in the *Sentences Commentary*. Nor can this be found in Thomas' other writings on the monastic life: *De perfectione vitae spiritualis* (Vivès 29, 117-156); *Contra impugnantes Dei cultum et religionum* (Vivès 29, 1-116); and *Contra pestiferam doctrinam retrahentium hominis a religionis ingressu* (Vivès 29, 157-190).

religious life) and to intend to become perfect. *282* What Luther has in mind here is the law which demands perfection. Since such perfection is impossible, the law "drives us to Christ" (Luther is here preaching on Galatians 3: 23-29). For Thomas, of course, there is a sense in which Christians are not "required" to be perfect: one enters the *status perfectionis* (i.e. religious life) not because one is perfect but because this is the end intended.*283* Yet Thomas agrees that the law demands perfection (which consists fundamentally in charity). In order to avoid saying that the law prescribes something impossible, Thomas distinguishes three grades of perfection. The highest grade of perfection, loving God as much as he is lovable, is impossible for any creature. The second grade, loving God as much as is humanly possible, will be possible only in heaven. The lowest grade of perfection, the removal of obstacles to the love of God, is attainable in this life. But the removal of such obstacles (mortal sin, for instance) depends on forgiveness and thus on the grace of God.*284* This understanding of Christian perfection is the foundation for grasping Thomas' theology of the religious life, i.e., of the *status perfectionis*. There is thus a sense in which Luther's statement about Thomas is correct. And yet, as a description of Thomas' view, it is a drastic oversimplification. It is unclear from this sermon that Luther appreciates the full complexity of Thomas' teaching.

In another sermon preached on 12 July 1523 Luther returned to the related issue of the "evangelical counsels" in Matt. 5. According to Luther, Thomas teaches that these are not precepts but rather counsels pertaining to the "perfect," i.e., those living under vows. And it is sufficient for them to strive after these counsels with free will.*285* The difference between Luther and Thomas is clear on this point. Thomas does indeed teach that the statements found in Matt. 5 are to be understood as counsels and not precepts. They are moral demands which are optional, but which render the attainment of one's final end more expeditious, and they do pertain primarily to those "in status perfectionis."*286* Though Thomas rarely discusses the role of grace in relation to these evangelical counsels, he does not say that free will alone is sufficient in one's attempts to follow these counsels.*287* The basis of Luther's opposition at this point is also clear: ". . . everything in Matthew 5 is command, but they [the scholastics] say these are counsels. . .they are too burdensome to be Christian law."*288* As "Christian law" they apply to all, and precisely because they are so burdensome, they "drive us to Christ," as was said earlier.

Further, in his 1523 exposition of I Peter, Luther makes explicit another disagreement with Thomas. He disapproves of Thomas' view that "monks and priests" are in a higher state than ordinary Christians.*289* Again, this is undeniably Thomas' view: while he does not espouse a "two-

---

282 WA 10, I 1, 497, 7ff: "Auch haben sie S. Thomas von Aquino, der leret, Es sey nit nodt volkommen zu seyn, sondern sey gnug, das sie im stand der volkommenheyt seyn und gedencken, vollkommen zu werden."

283 *S.T.* 2a2ae, q.185, a.1 ad 2; q.186, a.1 ad 3 and a.2.

284 *S.T.* 2a2ae, q.184, a.2.

285 WA 12, 625, 5ff: "Nota de eis qui dixerunt, non esse praeceptum, sed consilium et ad perfectos pertinere u. et dixerunt, quod satis sit mit dem libero arbitrio darnach trachten u. Thomas der ertzketzer est causa hujus et fluxit ex, Paris u. nota conscientias conformare, libellos scripserunt." Luther is also critical of the way in which the distinction between precepts and counsels is used to form consciences and comfort afflicted consciences in the confessional. On this, see other versions of the same sermon in WA 12, 625, 14ff, and WA 11, 148, 36ff.

286 *S.T.* 1a2ae, q.108, a.4. Cf. *S.T.* Suppl., q.67, a.4 ad 3; and *SCG* III, c.130.

287 I have argued elsewhere that for the mature Thomas, no good act whatsoever is possible without the help of grace. On this complex and much disputed question, see my *Luther and Late Medieval Thomism*, pp. 45-48.

288 WA 39 II, 189, 29ff (1542); (tr. from LW 34, 306).

289 WA 12, 353, 16ff: "Es wundert mich recht seer, das solch blindheyt hat mügen unter uns auffkomen. Da hatt geschrieben Thomas, der prediger münch, und sagt unverschampt, das münch und pfaffen ynn eynem bessern stand seyen, denn gemeyne Christen."

fold" perfection, one for laity and one for religious,[290] he does hold that all the evangelical counsels are ultimately reducible to poverty, chastity and obedience, that those who vow to follow these thereby attain their final end more expeditiously[291] and therefore "should be said to be in the state of perfection."[292] Moreover, Thomas' discussion of the vows as a whole leaves no doubt that those who take them are in a "higher state" than lay people. And this Luther rejects.

In his exposition of II Peter (1523/24) Luther again blames Thomas for placing too high a value on the monastic life.[293] But here for the first time Luther attacks Thomas' view of the vows themselves. According to Luther, Thomas teaches that entry into a monastic order is the equivalent of baptism. It carries with it the promise of freedom and forgiveness of sins. In this, Thomas equates an institution of Christ with a human tradition, and freedom and forgiveness is thus attained through a human work.[294] On this point, Luther's understanding of Thomas is accurate. In several places Thomas discusses entry into the religious life in connection with baptism.[295] His view is that "by entrance into religion man obtains remission of all his sins.... Hence we read [in the *Lives of the Fathers* VI, 1] that by entering religion, one receives the same grace as by being baptized."[296]

In taking this position Thomas was appropriating a theme which had been standard throughout the entire history of monasticism, although he modified some of the more extreme statements in the tradition.[297] Luther, for his part, at no time ascribed to this view. And by the time of his "Sermon von der Taufe" of 1519 he clearly held that the baptismal vows were the highest and the best vows: all other vows (marriage, religious orders, etc.) were equal ways of "fulfilling one's baptism," but they were in no sense a "second baptism."[298] What is interesting in Luther's critique of Thomas is that Luther seizes on this detail which may well be the weakest link in Thomas' theology of the monastic life. How does Luther know that Thomas "wrote" this, as he says? Gabriel Biel can be ruled out in this case, since he does not mention Thomas' view on this question.[299]

Johann Paltz, on the other hand, did cite Thomas on this question, but according to Lohse misunderstood Thomas.[300] Perhaps the most likely possibility is that Luther actually read Thomas

---

[290] On this issue, see Otto H. Pesch, *Theologie der Rechtfertigung bei Martin Luther und Thomas von Aquin: Versuch ein systematisch-theologischen Dialogs*, (Mainz: Grünewald, 1967), p. 446, n. 22; and H. McSorley, "Thomas Aquinas, John Pupper von Goch and Martin Luther: An Essay in Ecumenical theology," in J. Deschner, L. Howe and K. Penzel, eds., *Our Common History as Christians: Essays in Honor of Albert C. Outler*, (N.Y.: Oxford Univ. Press, 1975), pp. 97-129; p. 121, n. 28.

[291] *S.T.* 1a2ae, q.108, a.4.

[292] *SCG* III, c.130.

[293] WA 14, 36, 1ff: "Es werden thumen hochschulen, Bischoff, monachi, illos intelligit certissime, ne dubitate, qui omnes certo credunt paupertatem suam, votum esse viam et vitam: quod si non crederent, in cenobio non manerent. Ita scripsit Thomas et alii. Qui tandem sunt 'Abnegantes.'"

[294] WA 14, 62, 4ff: "Thomas scripsit: si monachus ingrederetur vel monialis in cenobium, idem esset ac baptismus. Vide verbum dei et institutionem Christi equiparatur hominum traditione. . . .Sie werffen solche stenden auff, durch welch man sol selig werden, wie Thomas, der prediger münch, unverschampt geschriben hat, wenn eyner inn eynen orden gehet, das es als viel sey, als wenn er ytzt aus der tauffe keme, da verheyssen sie freyheyt und vergebunge der sund durch eygene werck."

[295] Cf. *S.T.* Suppl., q.35, a.1; *S.T.* 2a2ae, q.189, a.1 ad 4 and a.2 ad 3.

[296] *S.T.* 2a2ae, q.189, a.3 ad 3: "Rationabiliter autem dici potest quod etiam per ingressum religionis aliquis consequatur remissionem omnium peccatorum. . . .Unde legitur, quod eamdem gratiam consequuntur religionem ingredientes quam consequuntur baptizati." Thomas does not associate religious vows with baptism in his *opuscula* on the religious life (listed above, n. 281).

[297] Lohse, *Mönchtum und Reformation*, pp. 120 and 157. Cf. Pesch, "Luthers Kritik am Mönchtum," p. 87.

[298] WA 2, 735, 34ff. Cf. Pesch, "Luthers Kritik am Mönchtum," p. 88.

[299] Farthing, "Post Thomam," Appendix I.

[300] Lohse, *Mönchtum und Reformation*, p. 167.

on the subject of monastic vows shortly before 1523. This supposition would help to account for the fact that while Luther had long been critical of the *scholastic* equation between monastic vows and baptism, it was only in 1523 that he began to repeatedly attach *Thomas* on this issue--an attack which continued up until 1537.

In the following year (1524) Luther again attacks the teaching of Thomas, but this time on the wider issue of Christian perfection. Lecturing on the book of Malachi, and speaking of the perfect faith which God requires from us, Luther alleges that the wicked (*impii*) find comfort in Thomas' teaching that a lower grade of faith is sufficient.[301] While it is not perfectly clear what Luther has in mind here, Thomas does teach that faith is not equal in all.[302] If Luther is alluding to the distinction between implicit and explicit faith, then, according to Thomas, the level of explicit faith required by God depends on one's state or office.[303] Thus he can say that not all people are equally bound to have explicit faith.[304] If this is what Luther means by "perfect faith," then he is correct in saying that for Thomas, a "lower" grade of faith suffices for some.[305]

The critique of monastic vows as a second baptism is taken up again by Luther in his 1527-30 lectures on Isaiah. Twice in the course of these lectures, Luther attacks Thomas on this point: Thomas teaches that "One who enters a monastery undertakes a baptism. . ."[306] Luther now adds, however, that for Thomas it is not only entry into the monastery but also the daily renewal of vows and repentance for sins that constitute new baptisms.[307] This attack is essentially the same as the earlier one, though now it appears in what seems to be an exaggerated form.[308]

Luther's subsequent references to Thomas' teaching on this particular matter, since they add little to what has already been said, can be catalogued summarily. In 1530, in his *Vermahnung an die Geistlichen, versammelt auf dem Reichstag zu Augsburg*, Luther repeats his allegation that for Thomas, becoming a monk is the same as being baptized.[309] Melanchthon, in his 1531 *Apology of the Augsburg Confession* had accused Thomas of the same thing, and Luther added in the margin: "Blasphemia B. Thomae."[310] In Luther's 1532-34 *In Esaiam Scholia*, he again levels this complaint against Thomas, associating this now with his critique of the Anabaptists.[311] Further in 1533, in

---

[301] WA 13, 684, note 5: "Deus exigit a nobis similiter perfectam fidem. Christianos ergo orat illum quotidie in auribus dei; impii autem securi sunt ex doctrina quam docent ut Thomas et alii olim: sufficit vel unum gradum fidei etc."

[302] *S.T.* 2a2ae, q.5, a.4 ad 3.

[303] *S.T.* 2a2ae, q.2, a.7.

[304] *S.T.* 2a2ae, q.2, a.6: ". . .ita etiam superiores homines, ad quos pertinet alios erudire, tenentur habere pleniorem notitiam de credendis et magis explicite credere."

[305] One finds in these same *Praelectiones in prophetas minores* (1524ff) an even more obscure reference to Thomas' theology of the monastic life: commenting on Amos 4, Luther says: "Praedicate non lege mandate oblationes, et abundetis et decipiatis vulgus, quasi ista prosint [Am Rande: ut Thomas von frywilligen gelossen closter levent]." (WA 13, 136, note 9.) The sense of this statement is that Thomas attributes some beneficial value to the sacrifices of the monastic life.

[306] WA 31 II, 163, 12ff: "Sic Thomas Aquinas dicit: Ingrediens monasterium incipit Baptismum et quocies renovat suum votum indies, tocies renovatur baptismo. Illae sunt laqueae, quibus in suis ordinibus et erroribus permanere debent."

[307] WA 31 II, 315, 24ff: "Augustinianus et Franciscanus habent sua sculptilia, scilicet: si ego hanc regulam servo, tunc sum salvus. Accedit Thomas: quocies regulatus respirit et redit a lapsu, denuo rebaptizatur. Hic fecit perpetuum baptismum..."

[308] I cannot find Thomas saying this in *S.T., SCG*, the *Sentences Commentary*, the commentary on Isaiah, or in any of his works on the religious life (listed above, n. 281). Nor does one find this in the *Glossa Ordinaria* on Isaiah (which Luther thought Thomas had written).

[309] WA 30 II, 300, 21ff: ". . .Thomas Aquinas. . .der sagt frey, das Münch werden sey gleich so viel als getaufft werden. . ."

[310] WA 30 III, 492, 6 (col. 631).

[311] WA 25, 186, 22ff: "Sic mollissimus·viscus et blandus quidam laquens fuit ad capiendos stultos illud vulgatissimum et maxime impium Thomae dictum, quod observatio Ordinis et vita Monastica sit alter Baptismus. Ita Monachi hac sententia capti fuerunt moeri Anabaptistae." For further suggestions along these lines, see Kenneth R. Davis, *Anabaptism and Asceticism: A Study in Intellectual Origins*, (Scottdale, PA: Herald Press, 1974).

the very work in which Luther acknowledges the possibility of a reformed monastic life (*Die kleine antwort auff H. Georgen nehestes buch*),[312] Luther mistakenly names Thomas as the originator of this "monastic baptism."[313] And finally in the *Smalcald Articles* of 1537, Luther repeats the charge: to say with Thomas that monastic vows are equal to baptism is blasphemy.[314]

Luther's final statement on Thomas' theology of the monastic life, in his *Auslegung des ersten und zweiten Kapitels Johannis* (1537/38), places the entire critique in perspective. Luther finds Thomas' erroneous teaching so deplorable precisely because his influence has been so enormous. When Luther thinks of the most influential teachers on these matters, the names of St. Gregory and Thomas Aquinas come first to mind. The universal acceptance of their teaching, in Luther's view, has led to the flourishing of a monasticism which, in promoting a kind of self-salvation, implicitly denies the teaching of Christ.[315]

In summary, Luther's critique isolates in Thomas two elements in the theological foundation of monasticism: the superiority of the religious life and the equation of monastic vows with baptism. On both of these Luther's understanding of Thomas is essentially correct. And he finds both of them unacceptable: there is an intrinsic equality between lay and religious vocations. The view of religious vows as a kind of baptism undermines this equality, elevates the religious vocation over others, and implies a kind of self-salvation. It is for these reasons, too, that Luther regards the issue as being of considerable importance. The monastic life is a mistake, according to Luther, at least when it is built on such faulty premises. And Thomas was in his view largely responsible for laying these foundations.

---

[312] See above, n. 278.

[313] WA 38, 148, 13ff: "Solche schendliche, lesterliche lere von der meineidigen, trewlosen, abtrunniger Münchentauffe haben sie erstlich von Sanct Thoma Prediger ordens. . ." Lohse has shown that on this question Thomas was appropriating a traditional theme in monastic theology--one whose origins can be traced to Jerome, Cassian, etc. (*Mönchtum und Reformation*, p. 120).

[314] WA 50, 251, 26ff: "Und sie rhumen aus ihrem S. Thoma, das closter gelubde der Taufe gleich sey, Das ist eine Gottslesterunge."

[315] WA 46, 769, 19ff: "Dieweil wir bisher solcher Lere Christi nicht gefolgt haben, so ist alles recht gewesen, was S. Gregorius und der Thomas Aquinas und andere gesaget haben, und daher sind alle Mönche und Nonnen kommen. . ." Cf. Luther's statement on monastic vows in the *Smalcald Articles* (WA 50, 251, 15-29).

8. Justification

The single, central, controlling idea in Luther's theology was undoubtedly his understanding of justification. This was for him "the hinge on which all else turns,"[316] "the article on which the Church stands or falls."[317] His general critique of "the scholastics" reflects the centrality of this issue for Luther. It was the heart of his critique at the very beginning in his 1517 "Disputatio contra scholasticam theologiam" and it persisted right through to his "Disputatio de Homine" of 1536.[318] "The scholastics," he insisted, were Pelagians.[319]

It is, however, Luther's critique of *Thomas* on this issue that is of interest here. In the following analysis of that critique, two considerations must be kept in mind. First, because of the systematic centrality of justification in Luther's thought, his critique of Thomas on this issue is related to his critique of Thomas on almost every other issue. Thus, for example, Luther's critique of Thomas on penance is related to his critique of Thomas on justification. While this is important to bear in mind, the following analysis is restricted to only those issues which fall more or less directly under the rubric of justification. Second, systematic comparisons of Luther and Thomas on justification have proliferated in recent years and have analyzed a variety of differences. Whatever the differences between Luther and Thomas on justification may be, the present focus is exclusively on the differences as *Luther* saw them. The following documentation of this critique reveals it to be astonishingly limited in its range and intensity.

It began in 1521 in Luther's reply to his Thomist opponent, Ambrosius Catharinus. Here Luther says that it is through the study of Thomas (in conjunction with Aristotle) that free will, moral virtue and natural philosophy have been revived in theology.[320] These three are the foundational elements in the misguided "scholastic" theology of nature and grace, as Luther understands it. From his point of view, the renewed emphasis on free will has undermined the Pauline *sola gratia*, moral virtue has displaced faith in the process of justification, and natural reason has usurped the place of revelation in theology.[321] All this is due to the baneful influence of Thomas.

Luther further elucidates this critique in two sermons preached in 1522. First, Luther attacks what he understands to be Thomas' teaching on acquired virtue: Thomas errs in saying that one becomes virtuous through practice, just as a harpist becomes proficient by long practice. Thus one becomes charitable, chaste, humble, etc., by exercising these virtues. Luther opposes this view to that of St. Paul, according to which the law is fulfilled through faith alone (i.e. through love).[322] Thus in Luther's view, one becomes righteous through faith whereas for Thomas one becomes righteous by doing righteous acts. Another sermon from the same year (on Titus 3: 4-7) spells out how Thomas conceives of the role of grace in producing these righteous acts: grace

---

[316] WA 18, 786, 30 (1525).

[317] WA 40 III, 352, 1-3, (1540); cf. WA 40 III, 335, 5-10.

[318] On these critiques see Janz, *Luther and Late Medieval Thomism*, pp. 24-30.

[319] WA 2, 394, 31ff (1519).

[320] WA 7, 739, 26-30: "Diximus enim, Angelum significare doctorem in Ecclesia. Et certum est, Aristotelem mortuum et damnatum esse doctorem hodie omnium universitatum magis quam Christum. Quia autoritate et studio Thomae elevatus regnat, resuscitans liberum arbitrium, docens virtutes Morales et philosophiam naturalem, et triceps scilicet Cerberus, immo tricorpor Gerion."

[321] WA 7, 737, 25ff.

[322] WA 10 III, 92, 17ff: "Paulus sagt: Niemand erfullet die gebott dann alleine der glaube. Die liebe ist nichts denn der glaube. Do irret Thomas mit den seinen, Das ist mit dem Aristoteli, die do sagen, durch ubung wirt einer virtuosus, wie ein Harpffen spyler durch lange ubung wirt ein gut Harpffen spyler, so meinen die narren, die tugende, lieb, keuscheit, demut durch ubung zu erlangen, est ist nit war, gleyssner und des teuffels merterer werden drauss. . . .Derhalben haben sie geirret, als ich hab gesagt, Aristoteles und Thomas, das durch ubung tugentsam einer solt werden."

only helps to complete and embellish such works. Thomas (and others) thus belittle the role of grace and lead the people astray.[323]

Here we do well to pause and inquire into the accuracy of Luther's understanding of Thomas on these particular issues.[324] First, does one according to Thomas, become righteous (justified) by performing righteous acts? At first sight it would appear that this is the case, since justification is treated in the *Summa Theologiae* within the systematic context of human acts by which human beings move toward their *telos* (i.e. in the *Secunda Pars*). Yet, one can cite an abundance of sources, especially from Thomas' Pauline commentaries, in which he speaks of justification *sola gratia*.[325] What this indicates is that for Thomas, human beings are not justified by their acts if "justification" means what it sometimes means for Luther, i.e., the forgiveness of sins. This first step and *sine qua non* presupposition for progress toward one's final end, the *initium fidei*, is "from God moving inwardly through grace."[326] On the other hand, if "justification" refers to the entire process by which one reaches the final goal, then human actions are of course part of the process. As Thomas puts it in his commentary on Romans, justification is *sola gratia sine operibus precedentibus*, but not *sola gratia sine operibus subsequentibus*.[327] Or, as he says in the *Summa Theologiae*, the grace of God does not presuppose goodness in human beings but creates it.[328] In view of all this, it is a misunderstanding or at least an oversimplification to say as Luther does that for Thomas, one is justified through one's good acts.

Second, is it correct to say as Luther does, that for Thomas grace only serves to complete and embellish the works accomplished by human beings? Here too we must say that Luther misunderstands the relation of grace, good works and merit in Thomas. For Thomas in the *Summa* teaches that grace is the principle for all good works: no good act whatsoever is possible without grace.[329] If Luther is alluding here, as he well may be, to the scholastic distinction between fulfilling the law according to the substance of the act or according to the intention of the lawgiver, then Thomas' teaching is that man cannot even fulfill the law according to the substance of the act without the help of grace.[330] Finally, it will be recalled that Luther makes this particular critique in a sermon on Titus 3: 4-7. Thomas' commentary on this same passage makes it clear how far he is from belittling the role of grace as Luther alleges:

---

[323] WA 10 I 1, 115, 7ff: "Darumb wirtt zu wenig und zu gering von ihr [Gnade] gepredigt, so man ihr nitt mehr gibt, denn das sie die werck schmucke und helffe vollnbringen, wie die Sophisten Thomas, Scotus und das volck irren und vorfuren. . ."

[324] The fullest systematic comparison of Luther and Thomas on justification is that of Otto H. Pesch, *Theologie der Rechtfertigung*. For a comparison of Luther and Thomas on the relationship of justification to the sacraments, see Horst Kasten, *Taufe und Rechtfertigung bei Thomas von Aquin und Martin Luther*, (Munich: Kaiser Verlag, 1970). For a full comparison on the issue of free will, see Harry J. McSorley, *Luther: Right or Wrong? An Ecumenical-Theological Study of Luther's Major Work, 'The Bondage of the Will'*, (N.Y. - Minneapolis: Newman-Augsburg, 1969). Much has been written on the related issue of the certainty of salvation. See for example Stephanus Pfürtner, *Luther and Aquinas--A Conversation: Our Salvation, Its Certainty and Peril*, (London: Darton, Longman and Todd, 1964). Yet one finds in Luther only one reference to Thomas on this issue, and there Luther explicitly *exempts* Thomas from his attack on other scholastics. See WA 1, 290, 38ff (1518).

[325] See for example Janz, *Luther and Late Medieval Thomism*, p. 58, n. 120.

[326] *S.T.* 2a2ae, q.6, a.1.

[327] *In Epistolam ad Romanos*, cap. 3, lect. 4 (Vivès 20, 434).

[328] *S.T.* 3a, q.86, a.2.

[329] *S.T.* 1a2ae, q.109, a.2. On the interpretation of this problematic passage see my *Luther and Late Medieval Thomism*, pp. 45-48.

[330] *S.T.* 1a2ae, q.109, a.4. Cf. Janz, *Luther and Late Medieval Thomism*, pp. 52-55.

> When he [Paul] says 'Not by works, etc.' he posits the basis of
> salvation: and he first excludes the presumed basis and secondly he
> shows the true basis. The presumed basis is that we are saved on
> account of our merits, which he excludes. . . .But the true basis is
> the mercy of God alone....[331]

Clearly Luther's understanding of Thomas on this issue is far from accurate.[332]

What then can be said of Luther's more general complaint that free will, moral virtue and natural philosophy have been "revived" and are being given undue weight in theology. Further, was this revival the direct result of what Luther saw as the reigning authority of Thomas? Recent research leaves little doubt that there was in fact such a revival in some late medieval theological circles. About this Luther was correct. The semi-pelagian tendencies of his mentor, Gabriel Biel, are a vivid illustration of this.[333] But was the blame for this, as Luther contends, to be placed on the shoulders of Thomas? The simple fact is that Thomas' theology of nature and grace was interpreted in two very different ways on the eve of the Reformation: on the one hand, some such as Gabriel Biel (d. 1495) and John Pupper of Goch (d. 1475) understood Thomas in much the same way that Luther understands him.[334] But on the other hand, Thomists such as Capreolus (d. 1444) vehemently rejected such an interpretation of Thomas and saw him rather as a champion of a thoroughly Augustinian theology of nature and grace[335] On which side then does the "real" Thomas stand? Here we can say unequivocally that he sides with those who understood him to be teaching a fundamentally Augustinian theology of nature and grace. The blame for the late medieval rejuvenation of Pelagian tendencies cannot justly be placed on his shoulders.

It was not until 1528 that Luther returned to his critique of Thomas on issues pertaining to justification. In a sermon preached on 1 June of that year, Luther briefly took issue with Thomas' understanding of faith. For Thomas, faith is "some infused quality" which has to do with the assent of the intellect.[336] For Luther, on the other hand, faith is a far more comprehensive

---

[331] *In Titus* cap. 3, lect. 1 (Vivès 21, 550): "Deinde cum dicit: 'Non ex operibus. . .', ponit rationem salvandi; et primo excluditur ratio praesumpta; secundo, ostenditur ratio vera. Ratio praesumpta est quod propter merita nostra simus salvati, quod excludit. . . .Sed vera ratio est sola misericordia Dei. . ." Tr. from H. McSorley, "Thomas Aquinas, John Pupper von Goch, and Martin Luther," p. 121, n.29.

[332] Harry McSorley has pointed out that, like Luther, the 15th century nominalist John Pupper von Goch contrasted this same passage (Titus 3:4-5) with Thomas' teaching. "Thomas Aquinas, John Pupper von Goch, and Martin Luther," p. 121, n. 29. Luther was familiar with Goch's *Fragmenta* (he wrote a preface to this work in 1522; WA 10 II, 329-330). But it is not known whether Luther read Goch's *De libertate christiana* in which he bids his reader to choose between St. Paul and Thomas on these issues. For more on Goch's critique of Thomas, see David Steinmetz, "'Libertas Christiana': Studies in the Theology of John Pupper of Goch (d. 1475)," in *Harvard Theological Review* 65 (1972), 191-230.

[333] Despite the wealth of recent literature on Biel, Heiko Oberman's treatment is still fundamental: *The Harvest of Medieval Theology*. Cf. my article "A Reinterpretation of Gabriel Biel on Nature and Grace," in *The Sixteenth Century Journal* 8(1977), 104-108.

[334] On Biel's understanding of Thomas, see Farthing, *Thomas Aquinas and Gabriel Biel*, pp. 150-180. Farthing has shown that Biel systematically misrepresents Thomas' teaching on nature and grace. On Goch's understanding of Thomas, see H. McSorley, "Thomas Aquinas, John Pupper von Goch, and Martin Luther"; and D. Steinmetz, "'Libertas Christiana'."

[335] Janz, *Luther and Late Medieval Thomism*, pp. 60-91.

[336] WA 27, 173, 6ff: "Inspiciunt [the Schwärmer] fidem ut opus, da wir sind, et sommium et cogitationem cogitant. Et quando audiunt vocem fides, ist in frigida vox. Nos dicimus: Non respicienda cogitatio, sed quid fides capere possit. Thomas: est qualitas quidem infusa." Note that Luther's statement here that "they [the Schwärmer] regard faith as a work" does not refer to Thomas. Luther could well have said the same thing about Biel, given the importance of the concept of *fides acquisita* in his theology. On this, see Heiko Oberman, *The Harvest of Medieval Theology*, pp. 72ff. One does not find in Thomas a similar concept of a *fides acquisita*. On this see Roger Aubert, *Le Problème de l'Acte de Foi: Données Traditionnelles et Résultats des Controverses Récentes*, (Louvain: Publications Universitaires de Louvain, 1950), p. 69. The final sentence in the quotation above seems to acknowledge the difference between Thomas and those who

term referring to the entire act by which one accepts salvation. Faith in Thomas' sense is only one element in this act of acceptance. Luther, therefore, sees correctly that he and Thomas use the term in very different ways. It is noteworthy, however, that Luther does not carry this particular insight any further, though it clearly has implications for other issues.

Luther came back to this subject in two table conversations in the early part of 1533. Again, Luther says that Thomas understands faith as some infused gift or quality. And this infused faith can exist together with mortal sin, in fornicators for instance.[337] Luther repeated this in a second table conversation from about the same period, adding here that this is Thomas' "impious" teaching in the *Summa Contra Gentiles*.[338]

On the factual matter involved here, Luther is correct. Thomas does indeed teach in the *Summa Contra Gentiles* that infused faith and mortal sin can co-exist in the same person.[339] Here we have an accurate citation of what must be seen as a minor point in the *Summa Contra Gentiles*: only one sentence in this entire work deals with the issue! What this may imply is that Luther possessed far more than a passing familiarity with this work. And it may also be significant that the passage Luther refers to occurs in the heart of the section on grace which is, as a whole, a polemic against Pelagianism.[340] While we do not have enough evidence to say that Luther read this section it remains a possibility--perhaps even a probability.

On the substantive issue involved in Luther's critique--the co-existence of faith and mortal sin--it is readily understandable from Luther's perspective why he would find this objectionable. For him faith is the act of accepting God's forgiveness, and therefore to say that it can co-exist with mortal sin is nonsense. Within Thomas' systematic context, on the other hand, it is quite understandable for him to say that they can co-exist. For him, faith is first and foremost an infused intellectual habit which can become lifeless when it is not formed by charity. Thus faith is only one moment in the process by which one is made righteous. And not every mortal sin implies disbelief. The entire difference on this issue, therefore, hinges upon different understandings of the meaning of "faith."[341]

The above survey exhausts Luther's critique of Thomas on the subject of justification. What is immediately clear is how astonishingly limited this critique is, in its scope, in its duration and in its intensity. Out of the hundreds of critical remarks made on Thomas' theology, only six bear directly on the issue which most would acknowledge as the central and decisive idea in Luther's theology. While numbers do not tell the whole story, one cannot ignore the fact that

see faith as a work.

[337] WATR 3, 104, 18-22 (early 1533): "Thomas Aquinas ist ein grosser wescher gewest, qui pro varietate verborum diversitatem finxit rerum: fidem formatam, informem, infusam. Infusam fidem donum vocat et qualitatem, quas potest esse in scortatore et stare cum peccato mortali, a quo eriperemur fide acquisita."

[338] WATR 1, 191, 11-13, (early 1533): "Summa Thomae contra gentiles, dies ist sein catechismus, ibi dicit fidem infusam posse stare cum peccato mortali. Quo quid potest magis dici impium?"

[339] SCG III, cap. 154, (Vivès 12, 461): "Unde, fides et spes et alia quae ad fidem ordinantur possunt esse in peccatoribus, qui non sunt Deo grati. . ." There is greater ambiguity on this issue in the *Summa Theologiae*. Here, on the one hand, Thomas teaches that those in a state of mortal sin are without the grace of God (*S.T.* 3a, q.87, a.4); and infused faith is clearly to be categorized under "grace." Yet elsewhere Thomas sees even "lifeless faith" (i.e., faith unformed by charity) as a gift of God (*S.T.* 2a2ae, q.6, a.2). Not every mortal sin, he says, destroys the infused habit of faith (*S.T.* 2a2ae, q.24, a.12 ad 5).

[340] SCG III, cap. 147-163 (Vivès 12, 449-468).

[341] This issue, however, is complicated by a doctrine which Luther does not mention in relation to Thomas, namely the *simul iustus et peccator*. Perhaps Thomas' teaching on the coexistence of faith and mortal sin should be the systematic point of departure for approaching Luther's *simul iustus et peccator*. For a different analysis, see O. Pesch, *Theologie der Rechtfertigung*, pp. 109-122, 526-552.

Luther criticizes Thomas' teaching on penance, the eucharist, purgatory, baptism, etc., far more frequently.

Moreover, one cannot help but notice what Luther does *not* criticize in Thomas' theology of nature and grace. While Luther attacks "the scholastics" as Pelagians, and while he specifically names scholastics such as Scotus, Biel and Prierias[342] in this connection, he never accuses Thomas, whom he acknowledges as the greatest of the scholastics, of Pelagianism. Nor does he attack Thomas on the issue of the cooperation between grace and free will. Thomas' understanding of merit is never directly attacked by Luther. Luther's understanding of the Christian as *simul iustus et peccator* is not mentioned in relation to Thomas. Thomas' formula *fides caritate formate* is not criticized by Luther. Luther's silence on these issues in regard to Thomas is hardly what one would have expected, given the centrality of justification for Luther and his view of Thomas as the greatest of the scholastics. It is a silence which calls into question the general assumption of Luther-scholarship, namely, that justification was the issue on which Luther most bitterly opposed Thomas Aquinas. Rather, the evidence suggests that in Luther's critique of Thomas' theology, justification was a relatively insignificant issue.

Some would immediately object that there is an *implicit* critique of Thomas' theology of justification running throughout almost everything that Luther said. In assessing the validity of this objection, two considerations must be born in mind. First to posit such an implicit critique in Luther is to make an assumption which is based on centuries of Protestant-Catholic polemic in which both sides were convinced that there were fundamental, unbridgeable, and church-dividing differences between Luther's and Thomas' theologies of justification. But when we set aside this polemical tradition and look at Luther and Thomas themselves, this assumption no longer seems obvious and self-evident. The systematic comparisons produced in the last several decades most pointedly call this assumption into question.[343] But whether or not this assumption is ultimately warranted, the crucial question here is whether Luther himself saw it that way. The evidence suggests that he did not.

The second important consideration is this: if there is such an implicit critique of Thomas' theology of justification running throughout Luther, why does it not become explicit? To argue that such a critique remained implicit in Luther is surely to accuse him of a reticence totally foreign to his character. After all, on many other issues Luther makes his critique of Thomas all too explicit. The fact that on this issue he did not calls into question the legitimacy of positing such an implicit critique.

Admittedly, Luther's critique of Thomas has here been isolated from his general critique of "the scholastics." But, as has already been pointed out, this general critique is highly problematic.[344] Luther sometimes accuses "the scholastics" of teaching something when he is fully aware that there are exceptions. And he is not reluctant to specifically name those he is attacking. Moreover, he is aware that the Thomists themselves do not in all cases faithfully represent the teaching of Thomas.[345] In other words, Luther does not have an undifferentiated view of scholasticism. His critique of "scholastic theology" is not identical with his critique of Thomas. The fact remains that while Luther spent energy attacking some other scholastics on the issue of justification, he did not do so in the case of Thomas.

---

[342] In WA 1, 684, 13ff. Luther accuses Prierias of holding a semi-pelagian view of the *praeparatio ad gratiam*. In 1520 Luther accused the Louvain Scotists and the Cologne Thomists of being Pelagians (WA 6, 193, 4ff).

[343] Among such comparisons, the most important is O. Pesch's *Theologie der Rechtfertigung*.

[344] See the introduction to this chapter above.

[345] See below, Ch. III.

How then can one account for this? A tentative hypothesis can be suggested. Though the young Luther lacked a profound understanding of Thomas' theology of nature and grace, he was deeply suspicious of it, perhaps because of the way in which Biel had called on the authority of Thomas to support his own semi-pelagian teaching.[346] Yet Luther never explicitly mentioned Thomas in this connection until 1521-22 when he accuses Thomas of belittling the role of grace. After an interval of six years Luther returned to Thomas' doctrine of justification, but now he no longer accused Thomas of minimizing the role of grace. Rather, now, from 1528 to 1533 Luther's focus was exclusively on Thomas' understanding of faith. And even in subsequent years Luther never returned to his earlier critique. What this may mean is that in the interval (1522-28) Luther was in some way exposed to Thomas' teaching on grace. Perhaps he read the section on grace in the *Summa Contra Gentiles*: his accurate reference to a minor detail in this work makes this plausible. There Luther would have found a theology of justification very different from his own, but one which in no way could be construed as Pelagian or as minimizing the role of grace.[347] Thus his earlier deep suspicion of Thomas' theology of justification was somewhat allayed. And for this reason, Luther never repeated his earlier accusations against Thomas. While Luther continued to dislike Thomas' theology as a whole, he could not indict Thomas' theology of justification in the same way that he could indict other scholastic theologies of justification.

This hypothesis is an attempt to make sense of the evidence, i.e., it is an attempt to explain why Luther's critique of Thomas on justification is so limited. But whether or not one accepts this hypothesis, the evidence clearly suggests that in Luther's view, justification was far from being the most important issue on which he wished to confront Thomas' theology. Whatever theologians and historians may say about the most basic and fundamental differences between Luther and Thomas, *this* difference does not seem to have been a very important one for Luther himself.

---

[346] On this, see Farthing, *Thomas Aquinas and Gabriel Biel*, pp. 150-180.

[347] Cf. *SCG* III, cap. 147-163 (Vivès 12, 449-468), where Thomas teaches that grace is necessary for man to reach his goal, that grace cannot be merited, that grace is the cause of one's turning towards God, that grace is what enables one to avoid sin, that grace is necessary for freeing people from bondage to sin, that grace enables people to *persevere* in the good, that it is the cause of faith, hope, and love in us, etc.

9. Law

One of the most serious tasks of theology, according to Luther, was to distinguish correctly between law and Gospel. In fact the heart of his theology can be explained exclusively on the basis of this distinction. Here scholastic theology came under heavy criticism. Already in his 1517 *Disputation Against Scholastic Theology*, almost one-third of the theses attacked the understanding of law which Luther found in "the scholastics."[348] If we inquire into the identity of these "scholastics," there is good reason to agree with Leif Grane that they were first and foremost Luther's nominalist teachers.[349] In the light of all of this there still remains a remarkable and admittedly somewhat puzzling fact: only *once* in the course of his entire career did Luther criticize the teaching of the person whom he acknowledged to be the greatest of the scholastics--Thomas Aquinas--on this issue.[350]

This single albeit relatively substantial critique occurs in Luther's 1531 lectures on Galatians. In his comments on Gal. 4:27 Luther raises the issue of the abrogation of the old law after Christ.

> When Thomas and other scholastics speak about the abrogation of the Law, they say that after Christ the civil and ceremonial laws are fatal, and that therefore they have now been abrogated, but not the moral laws. These men do not know what they are saying. When you want to speak about the abrogation of the law, discuss chiefly the law in the proper sense of the word--the Law in the spiritual sense. Include the entire Law, without distinguishing between the civil, the ceremonial, and the moral. For when Paul says that through Christ we have been set free from the curse of the Law (Gal. 3:13), he is certainly speaking about the entire Law, and especially about the Moral Law. . . .[351]

The difference therefore between himself and Thomas, as Luther sees it, is that for him "the entire Law has been abrogated for believers in Christ,"[352] whereas for Thomas the moral law remains in effect.

How accurate, we must ask, was Luther's perception in this case? First Luther is correct in reporting that Thomas makes this threefold distinction in speaking of the old law: civil or

---

[348] WA 1, 224-228. Theses 57-89 deal with the subject of law.

[349] Grane thus sees this disputation as the culmination of Luther's break with his nominalist teachers. *Contra Gabrielem: Luthers Anseinandersetzung mit Gabriel Biel in der Disputatio Contra Scholasticam Theologiam, 1517* (Copenhagen: Gyldendal, 1962) pp. 369 ff.

[350] Among the scholastics, Luther acknowledged Thomas to be the "teacher of all teachers." See below Ch. IV, n. 102.

[351] WA 40 I, 671, 28ff: "Thomas et alii Scholastici de abrogatione legis loquentes dicunt Iudicialia et Caeremonialia post Christum mortifera ideoque iam abrogata esse, non item moralia. Hi ignorant, quid loquuntur. Tu vero cum voles de abrogatione legis loqui, disputa praecipue de lege proprie dicta ac spirituali et complectere simul totam legem, nihil distinguens inter Iudicialem, caeremonialem et moralem. Nam cum Paulus ait nos per Christum a maledicto legis liberatos esse, certa de tota lege loquitur, ac praecipue de morali. . ." Tr. from LW 26, 446f. Cf. George Rörer's version of this in WA 40 I, 671, 14ff.

[352] WA 40 I, 672, 27f: "Quare credentibus in Christum tota lex abrogata est."

judicial, ceremonial and moral.[353] He is also accurate in his view that for Thomas the civil and ceremonial law have been abrogated.[354] On the question of the abrogation of the moral law, it would appear at first sight that here too Luther is right. For Thomas does indeed say that the moral precepts are eternal.[355] Yet Thomas can say that when St. Paul speaks of Christians being set free from the curse of the law (Gal. 3) this means not only the ceremonial percepts but also the moral percepts.[356] And when St. Paul says that Christians are not under the law (Gal. 5), this refers to the moral law.[357] The old law, including its moral percepts, is in fact a "law that kills."[358] Thus there is for Thomas a sense in which the moral law *is* abrogated by the advent of Christ.[359]

It is also important to ask what abrogation of the moral law meant for Luther. Without attempting to describe the full richness of Luther's theology of the law, we can say that what "abrogation of the moral law" manifestly does *not* mean is that the law is without significance for the lives of Christians. In his 1537/38 sermons on the Gospel of John, Luther can say that after justification, ". . .I discover that the law is precious and good, that it is given to me for my life; and now it is pleasing to me."[360] He can also say in a disputation against the antinomians in 1539 that one of the functions of the new law is "to order that sort of new life which those who have become saints and new men ought to enter upon."[361] Abrogation of the moral law for Luther does not mean that it is in every sense absolutely null and utterly void. What it *does* mean becomes clear in the very passage of his Galatians commentary where he criticizes Thomas' view: "Therefore the Law, with all its children, must be cast out that is, cursed be any doctrine, life, or religion that strives to achieve righteousness in the sight of God by means of the Law or works."[362] In short, abrogation of the moral law means that it does not justify. If this is correct, then it is difficult to see a real difference here between Luther and Thomas. For Thomas also teaches that

---

[353] *S.T.* 1a2ae, q.99, aa. 1-5. Thomas discusses the moral precepts in q.100, the ceremonial precepts in qq. 101-103, and the civil precepts in qq. 104-105. For an interpretation, see Ulrich Kühn, *Via Caritatis: Theologie des Gesetzes bei Thomas von Aquin*, (Göttingen: Vandenhoeck & Ruprecht, 1965), pp. 173-191.

[354] On the abrogation of the civil law, see *S.T.* 1a2ae, q.104, a.3. On the abrogation of the ceremonial law, see *S.T.* 1a2ae, q.103, a.3. Cf. the further discussion of these below.

[355] *S.T.* 1a2ae, q.103, a.3 ad 1: "Ad primum ergo dicendum quod lex vetus dicitur esse in aeternum, secundum moralia quidem, simpliciter et absolute."

[356] *In Gal.* 3:12, lect. 4 (Vivès 21, 206f).

[357] *In Gal.* 5:18, lect. 5 (Vivès 21, 244).

[358] *S.T.* 1a2ae, q.98, a.6. For an interpretation of the "law that kills" in Thomas, see Otto Pesch, "Paul as Professor of Theology," pp. 599ff.

[359] The entire question is complicated by Thomas' use of the term (which Luther prefers not to use) "nova lex Evangelii." This "law of the New Testament" is the grace of the Holy Spirit (*S.T.* 1a2ae, q.108, a.1), and it justified only insofar as it is grace (*S.T.* 1a2ae, q.106, a.2). This "new law" is thus a "law of freedom" (*S.T.* 1a2ae, q.108, a.1). Misunderstanding of this can lead to its becoming more burdensome than the old law (*S.T.* 1a2ae, q.107, a.4). Ulrich Kühn (*Via Caritatis*) used all this evidence and more to show that Thomas' "nova lex Evangelii" is not the proper object of Luther's attack.

[360] WA 46, 662, 18ff: ". . .aber hie ist nu das Gesetz köstlich und gut und mir gegeben zum leben und gefellet mir." Tr. from LW 22, 144.

[361] WA 39 I, 542, 16ff: ". . .sed utitur officio legis, insectari et arguere vitia et instituere vitam, quomodo iam novi homines sancti novam vitam ingredi debeant." For more statements such as these, see the citations given by Paul Althaus, *The Theology of Martin Luther*, (Philadelphia: Fortress, 1966), p. 266-273.

[362] WA 40 I, 671, 25ff: "Eiicienda est igitur omnis Lex cum sua prole, Hoc est maledicta sit igitur omnis doctrina, vita, religio, quae conatur lege aut operibus parare iustitiam coram Deo." Tr. from LW 26, 446.

the moral law did not justify even before the advent of Christ.[363] Much less then do the works of the law make one righteous after the coming of Christ.[364]

The crux of Luther's disagreement with Thomas on this issue seems to come down to a problem of language. By "abrogation" of the law, Luther means that the law does not justify. What Thomas means by "abrogation" is that it becomes utterly null and void--without significance for Christians. Thus Luther can say that the moral law is abrogated, and Thomas can hold that it is not abrogated without any real contradiction. Luther's objection to Thomas' teaching on this issue is therefore a matter of linguistic misunderstanding. This in turn suggests that Luther's critique was not based in this instance on a study of Thomas himself.[365]

The source of Luther's misunderstanding is in all likelihood to be found in Gabriel Biel. For Biel cites Thomas' view of the law in support of his own position, without describing Thomas' full teaching.[366] And yet there is little doubt that Biel's teaching differs substantially from that of Thomas.[367] Moreover, Biel's disciple, and Luther's own teacher Bartholomaeus von Usingen, reflects Biel's teaching: Christ has abrogated the civil and ceremonial law but retained the moral law as "necessary for salvation."[368] Thus it is quite understandable that Luther should attribute this view of the moral law to Thomas.

In the same passage of his Galations commentary which has been discussed here, Luther goes on to criticize Thomas' view of the abrogation of the civil law of Moses. According to Luther, these precepts have been abrogated in the sense that "the political laws of Moses do not apply to us at all."[369] Yet, Luther continues, it would not "be a sin if the emperor used some of the civil laws of Moses; in fact, it would be a good idea if he did. Therefore the sophists are in error when they imagine that after Christ the civil laws of Moses are fatal to us."[370] Since the immediate context of this passage is a critique of Thomas, Luther probably means to include Thomas under this term, "the sophists." Yet, while other scholastics may have held the position Luther criticizes, Thomas clearly did not. He in fact ascribes to precisely the view which Luther advocates: the civil precepts were annulled by the coming of Christ. Yet, though they have no binding force, it would not be sinful for a ruler to require their observance. Thus, Thomas holds,

---

[363] S.T. 1a2ae, q.100, a.12.

[364] Indeed, it is difficult to see how St. Paul could be interpreted differently. Commenting on Paul's statement that we are justified by faith without the works of the law (Romans 3:28), Thomas says "Non autem solum sine operibus caeremonialibus, quae gratiam non conferebant sed solum significabant, sed etiam sine operibus moralium praeceptorum..." In Rom cap. 3, lect. 4 (Vivès 20, 434). This is only one out of an abundance of references that could be cited. Cf. Janz, Luther and Late Medieval Thomism, p. 58, n. 120.

[365] A reading of the treatise on law in the S.T. or a reading of the Pauline commentaries would in all likelihood have resulted in the abandonment of this critique, or at least a more cautious statement of it. There is likewise no evidence that Luther read Thomas' Sentences Commentary on this topic, and in any case the treatment there differs considerably with that of the mature Thomas. Pesch (Theologie der Rechtfertigung p. 449, n. 40) speaks of Thomas' "deepened" understanding of the new law in the S.T. where "grace and the new law are identical." While Luther may have read the treatise on law in the Summa Contra Gentiles(Bk. III, cap.114-138), Thomas does not discuss there the subject of the law's abrogation in Christ. Kühn (Via Caritatis, pp. 126f.) contrasts the teaching on law in the SCG with that found in the S.T. On this, see also Pesch, Theologie der Rechtfertigung p. 406, n. 27.

[366] On this, see Farthing, Thomas Aquinas and Gabriel Biel, pp. 95f. In this connection Biel refers only to Thomas' early Sentences Commentary.

[367] Heiko Oberman, The Harvest of Medieval Theology pp. 112-119.

[368] Ibid., p. 118

[369] WA 40 I, 673, 14f. Tr. from LW 26, 448.

[370] WA 40 I, 673, 22ff. Tr. from LW 26, 448.

they are abrogated but not "fatal" to us, i.e., it would not be sinful to observe them.[371] Again, in this case, Luther was clearly unaware of Thomas' teachings.

Finally, in this same context, Luther comes to speak of the ceremonial law. This part of the Mosaic law has been abrogated as well. But it is not true, he adds,

> that after Christ has been revealed, the ceremonies of Moses are fatal; otherwise Christians would sin when they observe the festivals of Easter and Pentecost, which the ancient church established on the basis of the example of the Law of Moses, although in a far different manner and for a different purpose.[372]

In this case, Thomas clearly does teach that the ceremonial law was not only abrogated, but its observance by Christians is mortally sinful.[373] Obviously though, this would not apply to the observance of Easter and Pentecost. And Luther would have to admit that the ceremonial law of Moses is only related in the most remote sense to these Christian festivals. Thus, all significant disagreement on this point evaporates.

Recent systematic comparisons of Luther and Thomas on the topic of law have argued persuasively that there are no major and fundamental differences: while their understandings are not identical, neither are they mutually contradictory.[374] This, as we have seen, was not Luther's view of the matter. Yet on only one occasion in his career did he make an attempt to specify what this difference was. And in doing so he based himself on an understanding of Thomas which, it seems safe to say, Thomas would not have recognized as his own. Traditional Protestant attacks on Thomas' "legalism" thus can scarcely be grounded in Luther's critique of Thomas.

---

[371] *S.T.* la2ae, q. 104, a.3. Thomas teaches that it would only be sinful to observe these laws if we did so under the illusion that such observance would make us righteous in the sight of God.

[372] WA 40 I, 673, 35ff. Tr. from LW 26, 448.

[373] *S.T.* la2ae, q. 103, a.4. Biel refers to Thomas' understanding of the ceremonial law, citing *S.T.* la2a, q. 99, a.3. On this, see Farthing, *Thomas Aquinas and Gabriel Biel*, p. 95.

[374] O. Pesch, *Theologie der Rechtfertigung*, pp. 399-467. U.Kühn, *Via Caritatis*.

10. Baptism

This study has already touched on baptism in an ancillary way in connection with Luther's attack on Thomas' theology of the monastic life. Yet when we broach the subject itself, it is immediately clear that scholastic understandings of baptism are not a major concern for Luther. Rather it was the Anabaptist view which bore the brunt of Luther's polemical energies in this case. This does not mean of course that baptism and its place in the economy of salvation are understood precisely in the same way by Luther and the scholastics. What it does suggest is that Luther attached little importance to the differences.[375]

Up until 1532 in fact, Luther never commented on Thomas' theology of baptism in itself. But in that year, or shortly before, Luther evidently found something he disliked in Thomas' theology of baptism. And this "flaw" he kept coming back to until the end of his life.

The first instance of this complaint is found in a table talk from 18 August 1532. According to Luther, Thomas teaches that there is a "heavenly power" in the water of baptism which imprints a character on the soul.[376] That the problem persisted in Luther's mind is clear from the fact that five years later it resurfaced in a much more important, carefully written and definitive work--the Smalcald Articles (1537). Here Luther's objection is to some extent clarified:

> Therefore we do not agree with Thomas and the Dominicans who
> forget the Word (God's institution) and say that God has joined to
> the water a spiritual power, which, through the water, washes away
> sin.[377]

Luther's protest is against separating the "word" from the element and unduly emphasizing the power in the water itself.

In the following years the issue again emerged in a sermon on baptism (10 February 1538). Here Luther begins with Augustine's famous statement that "the water touches the body and washes the soul." Thomas explains this, he continues, by saying that the Holy Spirit infuses a "heavenly, divine power" into the water, and it is this which washes the soul.[378] According to another report of this same sermon, Luther recognizes that for Thomas, water itself cannot wash away sin, but rather it is the power of the Holy Spirit in it which does this.[379]

It is not implausible that in preparation for this sermon, Luther consulted Thomas himself. The parallels between Luther's statement about Thomas' teaching and the article in the *Summa Theologiae* which treats this question are notable.[380] Luther accurately paraphrases the starting

---

[375] Horst Kasten, in his study *Taufe und Rechtfertigung*, undertakes a systematic and quite ahistorical comparison. He argues that because of the scholastic understanding of grace as habit, baptism and justification are related in a certain way in Thomas' theology. Because Luther rejects the *habitus* theory, he must redefine this relationshp (p. 12). While this study may be helpful as a systematic clarification, it is not grounded on any explicit critique to be found in Luther. Kasten does not raise the question of what Luther knew about Thomas; for Thomas' views he relies solely on the *Summa Theologiae*; and he treats Luther only up to 1529 (p. 240), i.e., before Luther began to explicitly criticize Thomas on the subject of baptism.

[376] WATR 2, 202, 21ff (18 Aug. 1532): "Thomas dixit, quod in baptismate im wasser soll ein heimliche kraft sein; ibi coepta est disputatio, et deinde imprimitur character..."

[377] WA 50, 241, 12ff. Tr. from T.G. Tappert, ed. *The Book of Concord* (Philadelphia: Fortress, 1959) p. 310.

[378] WA 46, 168, 18ff: "Augustinus dicit: ːrifft den leib et lavat seel. Quomodo hoc fit? Ibi disputant praedicatores Monachi, Thomas, quod in aqua sit heimliche göttliche krafft, quam spiritus sanctus hin ein gelegt, qua lavat animam."

[379] WA 46, 168, 30ff: "Thomas de Aquin dicit: Aquam quidem non posse abluere peccatum, sed aliquam virtutem spiritus sancti esse in ea."

[380] Cf. *S.T.* 3a, q.62, a.4; and WA 46, 168, 18ff, quoted above, n. 378.

point of Thomas' discussion, namely the quotation from Augustine given by Thomas in the *Sed contra*: "Whence hath water so great power, that it touches the body and cleanses the heart?" Luther then goes on to give his own summary of Thomas' answer to this question, as we have seen. Luther's statement about Thomas' teaching thus seems to be a summary of this particular article in the *Summa*. The parallels are too great to argue that the way in which Luther sets up the question is mere coincidence, and especially so since he claims to be giving an account of Thomas' view. This article in the *Summa* could of course be a distant memory in Luther's mind from his student days, but it seems unlikely that it would suddenly be recalled in 1538. And of course we cannot rule out the possibility that Luther's knowledge of this article was mediated to him through some Wittenberg colleague or through some other scholastic theologian whom he had recently read. Thus, it is plausible that Luther consulted Thomas himself on this question.

Meanwhile, in his lectures on Genesis from this same period (1535-45) Luther returns to the dispute over how baptism justifies. He again takes issue with the view (this time ascribed to Thomas and Bonaventure) that God infuses a power into the water and therefore that it is the baptismal water itself which brings about justification. In Luther's opinion the water remains water, and in itself it is no better, as he puts it, than the water which cows drink.[381]

Finally, Luther brings the topic up again in one of his last sermons, and in fact, in his last recorded reference to Thomas Aquinas (10 January 1546). It is not, as Thomas thinks, the power in the water which purifies, but rather it is the cleansing of the Holy Ghost which results in a re-birth.[382]

In evaluating Luther's critique, we should first note that Luther does not dispute Thomas' view of the effect of this sacrament. Rather the question is one of sacramental causality: how does baptism produce its effect? Does Luther correctly understand Thomas' views on this question?

First, Luther is technically correct in saying that for Thomas there is a certain divine power in the water. But to simply leave it at that amounts to a rather serious distortion of Thomas' view because it ignores all the subtle qualifications which Thomas insists on. Thomas holds that though the principal cause of grace is God himself, the sacraments are instrumental causes of grace.[383] But is this instrumental power in the water? It is, Thomas says, "insofar as a body can be moved by a particular spiritual substance so as to produce a particular spiritual effect."[384] Thus it can be said that there is spiritual power in the water in the same way that a voice perceived by the senses can bear within it a spiritual power.[385] Properly speaking though, "instrumental power is not in any genus."[386] Moreover, the sacramental power is strictly speaking in both words and things as they combine to form one sacrament.[387]

---

[381] WA 42, 170, 8ff: "Sicut Sophistae quoque nugantur, cum disputant, Quomodo Baptismus iustificet. Nam Thomas et Bonaventura sentiunt quandam virtutem efficiendi a Deo aquae inditam, cum baptisatur Infans, ut ita aqua Baptismi sua virtute creet iustificationem. Contra nos dicimus Aquam esse aquam, nihilo meliorem in sua substantia quam eam, quam vacca bibit." Note that Biel aligns Bonaventure, Scotus and Occam on this question, and contrasts them with Thomas. On this see Farthing, *Thomas Aquinas and Gabriel Biel*, pp. 106ff. Biel's presentation of Thomas' teaching does not seem to reflect the precise position which Luther criticizes.

[382] WA 51, 122, 25ff: "Ideo non mera Aqua, ut Sophistae disputarunt, nesciunt, quomodo Aqua purificat. Non est krafft, ut Thomas. Sed Bad, da der heilige Geist badet, Non ut Bader in der stuben, Sed sic, ut homo renascatur."

[383] *S.T,* 3a, q. 62, a.4.

[384] *S.T.* 3a, q. 62, a.4. ad 1.

[385] *Ibid.*

[386] *S.T.* 3a, q. 62, a.4 ad 2.

[387] *S.T.* 3a, q. 62, a.4 ad 4.

Elsewhere Thomas explicitly rejects the view that there is some kind of permanent power or presence of the Holy Spirit in the water itself.[388] This view, which he ascribes to Hugh of St. Victor, reduces baptism to its material element, water. For Thomas, the water of baptism is not miraculous water.[389] Water remains water: "...the power of the sacraments which is ordained unto the remission of sins is derived principally from faith in Christ's passion."[390] Thus, while Thomas does say that there is spiritual power in the water, his view is not as crudely materialistic as Luther represents it.

Luther's second objection to Thomas' teaching is directly related to this first one: since for Thomas the power inheres in the water, the sacrament is in effect reduced to water and the words of institution are forgotten. Is this a fair characterization of Thomas' position? It is difficult to find a basis for this accusation in Thomas' writings. Rather Thomas teaches that the words and the material element are inseparable.[391] In the *Summa Theologiae*, his first question on the sacrament of baptism devotes two articles to a consideration of the water and two articles to a consideration of the "word."[392] Both are needed for there to be a sacrament. Forgetting of the words invalidates the sacrament.[393] It is noteworthy that in this connection, Luther refers not only to Thomas but also to the Dominicans.[394] Luther's understanding could well be attributable to a one-sided and distorted presentation of Thomas' teaching among Thomists.

In the final analysis, Luther's complaint against Thomas' theology of baptism is just that-- a complaint. In comparison to Luther's attack on the Anabaptist view, this one fades into insignificance. The fact that the older Luther kept coming back to it until the end of his life indicates at the most that Thomas' teaching, as he (mis)understood it, was a significant irritant for him.

---

[388] *S.T.* 3a, q. 66, a.1 ad 2.
[389] The blessing of the water does not change the water, nor is it necessary except for arousing the devotion of the people. *S.T.* 3a, q. 66, a.3 ad 5.
[390] *S.T.* 3a, q. 62. a.5 ad 2.
[391] *S.T.* 3a, q. 62, a.4 ad 4.
[392] *S.T.* 3a, q. 66, aa.2 and 3 on water; aa.4 and 5 on " the word."
[393] *S.T.* 3a, q. 66, a.6.
[394] Cf. above, n. 377.

11. Angels

One of the striking differences between Luther and Thomas Aquinas is what could be called their contrasting preoccupations--Luther with the devil and Thomas with angels. Luther acknowledged that he had "by the grace of God...learned to know a great deal about Satan."[395] Thomas could well have said the same about angels: so unusual, in fact, was the scope of his angelological writings that he came to be known as the "angelic doctor."[396]

Luther was aware of Thomas' extraordinary interest in angels and, on some five occasions during his career, took the opportunity to comment on his teaching. The first occurs in a sermon preached on 26 December 1529. Commenting on the song of the angels to the shepherds announcing Christ's birth (Lk.2:14), Luther asserts that there is more wisdom here than in "Thomas' on the substance of the angels." For it teaches us that God is to be praised.[397] The implication of course is that Thomas does not teach this.

What is interesting here is the possibility that Luther, when he speaks of "...Thomae de substantia angelorum," is referring directly to an *opusculum* on the angels which Thomas had written ca. 1270-72. This work appeared under two titles: "De Substantiis Separatis" and "De Angelis."[398] Is it possible that Luther, in speaking of Thomas' "de substantia angelorum," inadvertently conflates the two titles? If so, we have here in Luther a direct reference to one of the less well-known works of Thomas in the early 16th century.

The likelihood of this interpretation is enhanced by a consideration of Luther's critique. Luther implies that Thomas ignores this particular function of the angels, i.e. praising God. This is not the case if one is referring to Thomas' teaching in the *Summa Theologiae*: here he argues that not all the angels are sent to minister to human beings. Some remain in heaven to give glory to God.[399] But on the other hand, if Luther is referring to Thomas' *opusculum* "De Substantiis Separatis," he is correct. For in this work Thomas does not speak of the angels honoring God (except e.g. when he quotes passages such as Ps. 148:5).[400] Thus it would seem at least probable that this is the work Luther is referring to. And if it is the case that Luther was familiar with this relatively obscure work of Thomas, the received opinion about Luther's knowledge of Thomas may have to undergo some revision.

Luther's next references to Thomas' teaching on angels occur in two sermons, both preached on 29 September 1531. In his morning sermon of that day, Luther took up the text which had since Jerome become the classical locus for the belief in guardian angels, Mt. 18:10.[401] Luther pointed out here that Dionysius, unlike Thomas, thinks that the angels do not concern

---

[395] WA 26, 500, 6f (1528); tr. from LW 37, 361. Thomas also knew something of what Luther reports as one of his most troubling experiences, the assaults of the demons. On this see *S.T.* la, q. 114, a.1.

[396] The main sources for Thomas' teaching on the angels are *S.T.* la, qq. 50-64, 106-113; " De Spiritualibus Creaturis" (Vivès 14, 1-61); und "De Substantiis Separatis" (Vivès 27, 273-310). On Thomas' title of "angelic doctor," see P. Mandonnet, "Les titres doctoraux de saint Thomas d'Aquin," in *Revue Thomiste*, 17 (1909), 597-608.

[397] WA 29, 673, 17-20: "Hoc est canticum angelorum: qui intelligeret ista verba, in his inveniret magnam sapientiam. Certe plus sthet drinne quam in omnium gentilium libris et Thomae de substantia angelorum. . .das got sein ehre habe."

[398] On this see F.J. Lescoe, ed., *Saint Thomas Aquinas Treatise on Separate Substances*, (West Hartford: St. Joseph College, 1963), p. 2.

[399] E.g. *S.T.* la, q. 112, a. 2.

[400] Cf. Lescoe, *Treatise on Separate Substances*, p. 134.

[401] The belief had its origin with Jerome but was systematized in the 12th century by Honorius of Autun. On this, see Jaroslav Pelikan, *The Growth of Medieval Theology* (Chicago: Univ. of Chicago Press, 1978), p. 297.

themselves with human beings. But, according to Luther, Scripture does not speak of angels in this way.[402] In his concern to have guardian angels, Luther clearly sides with Thomas.[403]

In his afternoon sermon of that same day, Luther's theme is the same. Here, however, his judgment sounds more negative: Thomas does not take into account the guardianship of the angels spoken of in Ps. 91:11-12 (Vulgate Ps. 90:11-12).[404] Again, it is worth noting that Luther is incorrect if he has the *Summa Theologiae* in mind.[405] But if Luther again has in mind Thomas' "De Substantiis Separatis," he is correct: Thomas does not refer to this particular Psalm in this work. This is perhaps another indication of Luther's familiarity with this *opusculum*.

In the following year (1532-33), Thomas' name comes up again in connection with angels, this time in a purely incidental reference. Commenting on Ps. 121:1 and referring to faith as the knowledge of invisible things, Luther adds that it is nevertheless not pure speculation, like Thomas' "de angelis."[406] Here again we have a likely reference to Thomas' *opusculum* on the angels, but this time Luther names it by the other title under which it went. If it is indeed this *opusculum* which Luther is referring to, it is held up here by him with disapprobation as an example of an excessively speculative theological method which proceeds far beyond the scriptural data.[407] Even though Luther only makes this objection explicitly in this one incidental reference, it is clearly the heart of his critique of Thomas' theology of the angels.

Luther's final reference to Thomas' angelology occurred on 26 December 1537. On this day Luther again preached on the song of the angels (Lk. 2:14), and once again the Angelic Doctor came under criticism. According to Luther, Thomas wrote and speculated much on how the angels converse, but here in this scriptural passage the angels converse in ordinary human language.[408] With a kind of gentle irony Luther chides Thomas for positing a special angelic system of communication when Scripture has a simpler answer to the perplexing problem of how the angels converse.[409] It should also be noted that in this case Luther is not referring to Thomas' *opusculum* since this question does not arise in that work. In all probability Luther has in mind here the *Summa Theologiae* where Thomas devotes a question to this topic. Luther's reference to this single question in the *Summa* in itself suggests that Luther possessed more than a passing acquaintance with the book. A detailed and specific reference such as this is unlikely in one who had merely a cursory overview of the work.

Taken as a whole, Luther's critique of Thomas' teaching on the angels could hardly be called an impassioned one. Far more wide-ranging assaults on Thomas' angelology can be found

---

[402] WA 34 II, 257, 4ff: "Dionysius et alii doctores aliter scripserunt de angelis ut Thomas, quomodo angeli coram deo et kummern sich unser nicht. Sic non scriptura loquitur de eis." Cf. the parallel record of this sermon in WA 34 II, 257, 21-30.

[403] Cf. Thomas' teaching on guardian angels in *S.T.* 1a, q. 113.

[404] WA 34 II, 279, 6f: "... multi scripserunt philosophi de angelis, Thomas, Dionysius, sed haben den schweis geschrieben, nemo hat angerurt, quod hic in ps...." Cf. the parallel record in WA 34 II, 279, 23f.

[405] See *S.T.* 1a, q. 57, a. 2; q. 113, a. 1; q. 113, a. 3.

[406] WA 40 III, 50, 19ff: "Haec igitur sententia est huius versus, quod fides sit notitia rerum invisibilium, et tamen exspectandarum, ne scilicet existimemus eam esse puram speculationem, qualis est Thomae de Angelis..."

[407] Thomas' *opusculum* on the angels is particularly vulnerable to this critique, referring as it does to Aristotle and Dionysius twice as often as to Scripture.

[408] WA 45, 351, 20ff: "S. Thomas scripsit magnum librum und seer speculirt, quomodo angeli colloquantur und gestalt, sed non assecutus. Sed seipsos relevant non in sua angelica substantia et voce, sed in menschlicher sprach, rede, gesang..."

[409] Thomas treats this question in *S.T.* 1a, q. 107, without referring to the Scripture passage Luther was commenting on. The question is not discussed in the *Summa Contra Gentiles* nor in the *Sentences Commentary*. It is treated in *De Veritate* q. 9, aa. 4-7 (Vivès 14, 533-537), and less extensively in *In I Cor.* cap. 13, lect. 1 (Vivès 21, 24) and in *In Job* cap. 1, lect. 1 (Vivès 18, 3-5). Biel does not mention Thomas' views on this question, nor does he refer to Thomas' *opusculum* "De Substantiis Separatis." See Farthing, *Thomas Aquinas and Gabriel Biel*, pp. 27-29.

within the scholastic schools themselves.[410] Yet the issue, for Luther, points beyond itself to more fundamental methodological differences: for him, it is not the business of theology to elaborate a purely speculative angelology which goes far beyond the data of revelation. Nor, in the final analysis, was Luther's extensive "knowledge" about devils comparable to Thomas' extensive "knowledge" about angels. For far from being a speculative construct, Luther's demonology was based on experience.

[410] E.g. in the condemnation of 1277, 37 out of the 219 condemned theses bear on Thomas' angelology, and the "correctoria" literature too pays much attention to this aspect of Thomas' theology. On this, see James Collins, *The Thomistic Philosophy of the Angels*, (Washington: Catholic Univ. Press, 1947), p. xii.

12. Papal Authority

Judging by the enormous effort Luther devoted to this subject, the papacy can safely be called a major element in his Reformation protest.[411] To a large extent, this issue was brought into the forefront of Luther's consciousness by his early opponents. And many of these early opponents were Thomists--Tetzel, Prierias, Catharinus, etc.--who by the standards of their own time represented an extreme papalist position.[412] It is hardly surprising then that by 1521 Luther was identifying such an exaggerated papalist position with Thomism as such.[413] Luther's counterattack against the Thomist school was in large measure directed against their papalist ecclesiology.

However, this was not an attack on Thomas. The position which Luther confronted in this controversy with the Thomist school was far more extreme than anything Thomas had ever said about the papacy. Thomas had after all made only a handful of comments on the subject which taken together amount to a rather modest position on papal authority. Ideas such as infallibility and papal absolutism find no place in his writings.[414] Thus the subject of the papacy is one of the clearest areas on which Luther's Thomist opponents went far beyond their master.[415] Luther's attack on *their* idea of papal authority scarcely implicates Thomas Aquinas.[416]

Even more significant is the fact that Luther shows virtually no interest whatsoever in Thomas' views on this matter. Only in a very few places in Luther's writings does one find Thomas' name mentioned in connection with the subject of papal authority. And even these few references to Thomas are only related to the subject of papal authority in a remote and ancillary way.

The earliest of these references are to be found in Luther's *Ad Prieratis* of 1518. In relation to indulgences, Prierias had said that the power of the keys (Mt.16:19) had been given to Peter alone, and had claimed Thomas' authority for this view.[417] And Thomas, though he makes many distinctions in regard to the keys, does indeed teach that only the pope can grant indulgences.[418] Luther agrees that this is Thomas' view and objects that the keys have been given to all priests and to the whole church. This objection to Thomas' teaching is made three times in *Ad Prieratis*.[419]

In Luther's 1521 reply to Catharinus, Thomas' name comes up again in relation to the same "Petrine" passage in Matthew. This time the question is what the word "rock" in Mt.16:18

---

[411] For the best recent account of Luther's views, see Scott Hendrix, *Luther and the Papacy: Stages in a Reformation Conflict*, (Philadelphia: Fortress, 1981).

[412] E.g. Prierias, who in his *Dialogue de potestatae papae* against Luther, asserts that the authority of the popes is superior to that of Scripture (Walch 18, 334). Other papalists such as Cajetan represent a more cautious position.

[413] In his *Ad librum eximii magistri nostri magistri Ambrosii Catharini, defensoris Silvestri Prieratis acerrimi, responsio(1521); WA 7, 705-778.*

[414] A representative contemporary interpretation of Thomas on this issue can be found in Yves Congar, "St. Thomas and the Infallibility of the Papal Magisterium," in *The Thomist*, 38(1974), 81-105.

[415] Even the most moderate and judicious Thomist among Luther's opponents, Cajetan, went well beyond Thomas' teaching. As Otto Pesch has said, "The papalist ecclesiology of Cajetan is not to be simply identified with the thought of St. Thomas." ("Existential and Sapiential Theology," p. 184, n.3).

[416] According to Martin Brecht, when Luther asserted against Prierias that popes and councils can err, he "was directly rejecting Thomas, Prierias' chief authority" (*Luther*, p. 244). This is clearly incorrect.

[417] Walch, 18, 317f.

[418] *S.T.* Suppl. , q. 26, aa. 1 and 3; cf. *S.T.* Suppl., q. 19, a. 3.

[419] WA 1, 655, 9ff: "Nam ego non capio, quomodo in isto verbo Christi: Quodcunque solveris etc. Petro sit datum privilegium. Non enim privilegium, sed lex generalis et irrefragabilis data est non Petro tantum, sed omnibus prorsus sacerdotibus et toti ecclesiae. Cur ergo tu cum Thoma tuo id soli Petro arrogas, ut privilegium appelles?" Cf. WA 1, 657, 14ff. and 665, 9ff.

refers to. According to Catharinus it refers to Peter and his successors, while according to Luther it refers to Christ or to Peter's confession in Mt.16:16. And Luther, taking it for granted that Catharinus' view is also that of Thomas, criticizes both of them on these grounds several times throughout this work.[420] In point of fact, Thomas agrees with Luther that the "rock" of Mt.16:18 can be understood as the confession of Peter.[421]

Taken together, these remarks can scarcely be seen as constituting a substantial critique of Thomas' views on papal authority. Though Luther identified Thomism with extreme papalism and devoted much effort to refuting it, he does not seem to have surmised Thomas to be the source of this view. While on many other issues Luther offered substantive critiques of Thomas, on this one he did not. It was rather the exaggeration of papal authority among his contemporaries that concerned him. And as he pointed out in his exposition of John 1 and 2 (1537/38), such exaggeration went hand in hand with the exaggeration of Thomas' authority: those who confer infallibility on the pope also see Thomas as inerrant, since the pope has approved his writings.[422] It was this strange logic of "creeping infallibalism" among his opponents that was of far more concern to Luther than Thomas' view of papal authority.

[420] WA 7, 716, 26ff: "Te autem rogo, accutissimum dialectum, qui scias extra propositum esse dandum exemplum aliud, profer mihi locum scripturae, in quo idem vocabulum simul significet hominum in totum impium et simul pium ac sanctum, sicut hic insanis in vocabulo 'Petra', quod Petrum sanctum et successorem impium simul tibi significat. Ubi didicisti haec sacrilegia et haeretica monstra, nisi in Magistro tuo S. Thoma?" Cf. WA 7, 717, 1ff; 710, 14ff.

[421] S.T. 2a2ae, q. 174, a. 6: "Ita etiam in tempore gratiae, super revelatione facta Apostolis de fide unitatis et trinitatis fundatur tota fides Ecclesiae: secundum illud Matth. 16, 18: 'Super hanc petram', scilicet confessionis tuae, 'aedificabo Ecclesiam meam'." Harry McSorley has pointed out that neither Augustine, nor Gregory I, nor the medieval canonists identified the "rock" with Peter. See McSorley's article, "Some Forgotten Truths about the Petrine Ministry," in Journal of Ecumenical Studies, 11 (1974), 208-237, p. 211, n.11.

[422] WA 46, 768, 32ff: "Non ergo posthac dicendum: Papa non errat, Patres non errant, Thomas vera scripsit, quia approbantur a papa..." Cf. 768, 12ff. See the discussion of Luther on the authority of Thomas below, Ch. III.

13. Purgatory

The doctrine of purgatory, which came to full flower in the fertile Christian imagination of the 12th century,[423] was by Luther's time a standard feature of the theological landscape. It was natural therefore that the young Luther received this part of the theological tradition without protest. When however he became embroiled in the controversy over indulgences, the doctrine of purgatory began to capture more and more of his attention. And it was then that Luther began to be increasingly critical of what he took to be the standard view. This, along with the fact that his early opponents were primarily Thomists, explains why Luther, on this subject too, critically engaged the thought of Thomas Aquinas, albeit in a limited way.

His critique began in early June of 1518, in his reply to Tetzel's attack on his earlier "Sermon von Ablass und Gnade." Here he was critical of Thomas' teaching that masses can benefit souls in purgatory, and of the popes' confirmation of Thomas' teaching on this matter.[424] Luther's understanding of Thomas was correct: Thomas (at least the early Thomas) did indeed hold that the celebration of the eucharist can benefit souls in purgatory.[425] In this matter though, it is unlikely that Luther was relying on his personal reading of Thomas. The more likely sources for Luther's knowledge in this instance are first, "common knowledge"; second, his Thomist opponents; and third, Gabriel Biel's accurate and sympathetic account of Thomas' view.[426]

In August of 1518, in his "Resolutiones" on the 95 theses, Luther returned to Thomas, this time attacking his view of the location of purgatory. Thomas holds, according to Luther, that purgatory is beneath the earth. Though Luther still firmly believes in its reality, he asserts that he does not know where it is.[427] The implication is that Thomas "knows" too much about such obscure inessentials. Again Luther correctly reports Thomas' view: unlike Dante, Thomas locates purgatory beneath the earth, though, he adds, "Nothing is clearly stated in Scripture about the situation of purgatory, nor is it possible to offer convincing arguments on this question."[428] In this case too Thomas' opinion was widely known and accurately reported by Biel.[429] There is nothing here to suggest that Luther resorted to a reading of Thomas himself.

Almost at the same time (August 1518), Luther published his *Ad Prieratis*. Here in replying to the Thomist Prierias, he confronted Thomas' teaching on several particular questions. First, in reaction to Luther's view that the fear of those in purgatory approaches despair, Prierias had cited Thomas to the affect that their fear is rather a "filial" one. Luther's only comment is that Thomas' view does not concern him.[430] Second, Prierias had, by citing Thomas, attacked Luther on the

---

[423] Jacques Le Goff, *The Birth of Purgatory*, (Chicago: Univ. of Chicago Press, 1984).

[424] WA 1, 389, 35ff: "Der funffte grund ist von den altar und kirchen zu Rom, in welchen man seelen erlosst mit messen, und die H. bebste das dulden und darzu sanct Thomas in sulcher lere von bebsten bestetiget..." I follow here the chronology by Brecht, *Martin Luther*.

[425] *S.T.* Suppl., q. 71, a.9 (based on IV *Sent.*, d. 45, q. 2, a. 3; Vivès 11, 374-377).

[426] On Biel, see Farthing, *Thomas Aquinas and Gabriel Biel*, pp. 183f.

[427] WA 1, 555, 29ff: "Nihil de igne et loco purgatorii loquor, quod non ea negem, sed quod alia est illa disputatio nec a me nunc instituta, deinde quod nesciam, ubi sit locus purgatorii, licet B. Thomas illum sub terra esse putet...." The "Resolutiones" had been in preparation since February of 1518.

[428] *S.T.* Suppl., Appendix II, a.2 (this material was taken from IV *Sent.*, d. 21, q. 1, a. 1; Vives 10, 587). Le Goff correctly senses that Thomas deals with these questions with some reluctance (*The Birth of Purgatory*, p. 268). Unlike some of his followers, "There is no doubt that he wished to avoid establishing any sort of vulgar arithmetical accounting of time spent in purgatory." (*Ibid.*, p. 274).

[429] Farthing, *Thomas Aquinas and Gabriel Biel*, pp. 42f.

[430] WA 1, 663, 15ff: "Respondeo: tuo te gladio peto. Temeritas est, in iis, quae nos ratio naturalis non docet, velle aliquid diffinire nostra auctoritate. Elue hanc temeritatem tuam, qui sine autoritate tanta fiducia pronuncias, non esse in purgatorio nisi filialem timorem: Thomas enim non audio."

question of whether souls in purgatory have a certain hope of salvation. Luther again responds that the bare authority of Thomas is unconvincing.[431] Third, on the question of whether the church has power over souls in purgatory, Prierias had cited "the saints" to the effect that it does. Luther interprets this to mean Thomas, and he simply denies Thomas' view.[432] Fourth, against Luther's view that some souls in purgatory suffer willingly, Prierias had cited Thomas to prove that this view was "foolish and ridiculous." Luther again replies to the effect that Thomas' words need not be taken as divine oracles.[433] Thus on all four of these particular questions, Luther does not dispute what Thomas' teaching is, nor does he care to argue at length against it. These particular facets of purgatory are not the real issue here. Rather the real issue for Luther once again is the authority of Thomas: the mere citation of Thomas in support of a position is simply unconvincing.[434]

In 1520 we find one indirect reference to Thomas in connection with purgatory in Luther's reply to Leo X's "Exsurge Domine." Though Luther still firmly believes in the existence of a purgatory,[435] he argues that it cannot be proven from Scripture. For this reason, the denial of purgatory is not heretical, just as, Luther adds, the denial of Thomas' sainthood is not heretical even though he has been canonized.[436] Here Thomas' name (and another issue) is brought up in connection with the heretical nature of the denial of purgatory. This is in an incidental way appropriate since Thomas does teach that the denial of purgatory is a heresy.[437] Yet the real issue is whether something which is not provable from Scripture can be made into an article of faith.

It was not long before the logic of Luther's basic position led him to an outright denial of the existence of purgatory. By the time he wrote the "Smalcald Articles" in 1537, he could characterize purgatory as "an illusion of the devil" because it is "contrary to the fundamental article that Christ alone, and not the work of man, can help souls."[438] Thus what had been for Luther an issue which fell into the gray area of *adiaphora* now seems to have become more fundamental: affirmation of purgatory, it would seem, is now for Luther a heresy.

It is hardly surprising then that Thomas' teaching on purgatory was no longer of interest to Luther. Only once does it come up again, in his late lectures on Genesis. There, in the context of a polemic against "papal teaching" on the afterlife, Luther recalls that for Thomas, hell is surrounded by purgatory.[439] And the "sophists" assent to the papal teaching on the existence

---

[431] WA 1, 664, 6ff: "Ad decimam sextam conclusionem, ubi purgatorium dixi videri prope desperationem, tu contra certam spem salutis in purgatorium ponis, et hoc non nisi nuda Thomae auctoritate, quod remitto ad fundamentum meum secundum."

[432] WA 1, 667, 11ff: "Ad vicesimam sextam dicis, ecclesiam habere potestatem in purgatorium secundum sanctos (id est S. Thomam) et hoc per applicationem meritorum Christi. Respondeo ut supra: S. Thomam nego."

[433] WA 1, 668, 12ff: "Ad vicesimam nonam primum somnia mea vocas, deinde ex S. Thoma de poena voluntaria longum trahis sermonem, et in fine dicis, contrarium siquis asserat, stultus et ridiculus sit.... Respondeo: Ita loqueris sine iudicio, ac si necesse sit verbum B. Thoma oraculum haberi."

[434] See the extended treatment of this crucial topic below, Ch. III.

[435] In his German response (*Grund und Ursach aller Artikel*) Luther says: "Ich hab das fegfewr noch nie geleucknet, halt es auch noch..."(WA 7, 451, 11f).

[436] WA 7, 149, 27ff: "Et quae necessitas est pro purgatorio sic tumultuari. ....Suo quisque periculo hic credat vel non credat, non est haereticus, si purgatorium non credit, nec ideo Christianus, si credit....Sicut si non credam Thomam Aquinatem esse sanctum, licet a Papa canonisatum, non sum Haereticus..."

[437] *S.T.* Suppl., Appendix II, a. 1 (taken from IV *Sent.*, d. 21, q. 1, a. 1; Vivès 10, 586).

[438] Tappert, ed., *Book of Concord*, p. 295, par. 12.

[439] WA 44, 812, 4ff: "Papa fingit quatuor ordines mortuorum. Primus est infernus damnatorum, secundus purgatorium, et dicit Thomas Aquinas infernum esse velut medium centrum, quod ambiat purgatorium..." This is essentially correct. Cf. Thomas *S.T.* Suppl., q.69, a.7; taken from IV *Sent.*, d.45, q.1, a.1 (Vivès 11, 356-360).

of purgatory because of Thomas' influence. But, Luther adds, Thomas is of no importance.[440] Because of the way in which Luther's views had developed, Thomas' teaching on the particulars of purgatory now seemed irrelevant.

[440] WA 44, 812, 13ff: "De purgatorio nulla mentio est in sacris leteris. ... Sophistae Papae assentiuntur propter Thomam. Verum nihil ad nos Thomas."

14. Veneration of Images

A minor issue on which Luther criticized the theology of Thomas has to do with Thomas' distinction between three kinds of worship or adoration: *latria* (the kind of worship owed to God), *hyperdulia* (the kind of veneration owed to Mary, for example), and *dulia* (the kind of devotion owed to the saints). Luther first broaches this subject in a sermon from 14 September 1522. Here, speaking of paintings (presumably of Christ), Luther refers to Thomas' distinction and ascribes to him the view that one should "worship" such paintings but only insofar as they represent Christ. This teaching of Thomas has led to "abuse," as Luther calls it.[441] Though Thomas was by no means the first to make such distinctions, he did indeed hold that images of Christ deserve the worship of *latria* insofar as they point beyond themselves to Christ.[442]

Luther brought this issue up again in his lectures on Isaiah in the years 1527-30. Commenting on the author's polemic against the use of wood for idols (Isaiah 44:15), Luther mentions Thomas' teaching on the adoration of the cross. He teaches, according to Luther, that it is to be adored with *hyperdulia*, i.e., with a lesser form of *latria*, and thus he avoids the charge of idolatry.[443] Again, Thomas does seem to teach this, at least in the *Scriptum*.[444] But, by the time he wrote the *Summa* all mention of *hyperdulia* is dropped from this question and all adoration of the cross is to take the form of *latria*.[445] Luther is unaware of this because he is in reliance on Biel who summarizes only Thomas' treatment in the *Scriptum*.[446] Be this as it may, from Luther's vantage point, Thomas' teaching on the veneration of images is clearly reprehensible, at least insofar as it has led to abuses in popular piety.

---

[441] WA 10 III, 335, 9ff: "Darnach is noch ain ander missbrauch kommen durch Thomam Aquinatem, dem man die tauben jnss or maldt (ja ich mayn es sey ain junger teüfel gewesst) das manss sol anbeten und hat grosse klughait für geben mit Dulia, Hyperdulia: der sagt man solss anbeten, aber doch so ferr, das man zusamen knüpf den der in himel ist mit dem, das der maler gemalt hat."

[442] III *Sent.*, d. 9, q. 1, a. 2, q1a. 2 (Vivès 9, 155); and *S.T.* 3a, q. 25, a. 3. In this case Luther was in all probability familiar with Thomas' view from this reading of Biel, who accurately and sympathetically summarized this question from Thomas' *Sentences Commentary*. On this, see Farthing, *Thomas Aquinas and Gabriel Biel*, p. 101; and "Post Thomam", p. 325.

[443] WA 31 II, 349, 19ff: "Descripsio ligni. Ists nicht eyn plage, quod hanc materiam sumunt ad idolum, quae prodest ad inferiores usus....Thomas scribit Crucis lignum esse adorandum hyperdoulia i.e. minori latria. Ideo has idolatras confutat."

[444] III *Sent.*, d. 9, q. 1, a. 2, q1a. 4 (Vivès 9, 455f).

[445] *S.T.* 3a, q. 25, a. 4.

[446] See above, n. 442.

15. Conclusion

Luther's critique of Thomas' theology has now been documented and analyzed in all its particulars. We have here witnessed in detail the first and most important encounter and disengagement between Luther's world of thought and that of Thomas Aquinas. It remains now to make a few more general remarks on the scope and nature of this confrontation.

On the one hand, the dimensions of Luther's critique should not be exaggerated. Luther did not daily have Thomas Aquinas on his mind. And he did not, in the case of every Christian doctrine, ponder the relation of his views to those of Thomas. The Angelic Doctor was not the starting point for his theological reflection. But on the other hand, it would be quite mistaken to think that Luther was disinterested in Thomas. It is not the case that the young Luther simply dismissed Thomas as hopelessly mistaken and insignificant. Rather the evidence indicates that at different stages of his career and for various reasons Luther paid considerable attention to Thomas' theology. At times he used Thomas' theology as a foil over against which to define his own views; at times he devoted considerable energies to refuting Thomas' position; and at times he simply reminds his readers of Thomas' teaching on a particular issue. This perduring interest in Thomas is perfectly understandable in light of the fact that Thomas was, in Luther's view, a major spokesman for the theological tradition which he had abandoned.

The limitations in the scope of Luther's critique are illustrated by what he does *not* criticize in Thomas. Here one could mention the doctrines of God, creation, trinity, christology, etc. But perhaps the most striking silence of Luther is on the topic of Thomas' social ethics. This is of particular interest, first, because Luther showed a lively interest in the general topic of social ethics, and second, because on this topic we know that Luther possessed a thorough knowledge of Thomas' teaching. Gabriel Biel, whom Luther studied assiduously, had accurately and at great length summarized the whole range of Thomas' views: more than fifty questions in Biel's *Collectorium* are devoted to this topic.[447] Yet Luther never mentions, let alone criticizes, Thomas' social ethics. What one is to make of this silence remains an open question, but it can hardly be without significance that Luther, while he criticized many aspects of Thomas' thought, remained silent on this one which he was thoroughly familiar with.

Be this as it may, it is Luther's actual critique which is of concern here. Our treatment has ordered this subject matter under various doctrinal rubrics, and these in turn have been arranged according to their significance for Luther. This last step of course is a matter of judgment, and it should be understood more as a tentative suggestion than a definitive assertion.

First, there can be no doubt that Luther perceived at the heart of his many differences with Thomas important methodological considerations. Recent interpreters have recognized that for Luther the way in which theology is done is a matter of the highest concern.[448] Their emphasis is to some extent reflected in Luther's actual critique of Thomas: faulty theological method, while it may not inevitably lead to error, at least diminishes the possibility of avoiding it. Luther's most important methodological critique, I suggest, has to do with the role of experience in theology. Without fully developing this line of though, and without using the modern terminology, Luther shows a clear awareness of the difference between what modern interpreters have called "existential" and "sapiential" theology.

[447] Farthing, *Thomas Aquinas and Gabriel Biel*, pp. 71-87; and "Post Thomam", pp. 317-321.

[448] E.g. Leif Grane, *Modus Loquendi Theologicus*; and Reinhold Weier, *Das Theologieverständnis Martin Luthers*, (Paderborn: Bonifacius-Verlag, 1976).

Luther's concern for the manner in which the theological enterprise is carried out is also reflected, in a secondary way, in his attack on Thomas' use of Aristotle. Though this critique is an impassioned one, I have argued that Luther-scholarship has traditionally overestimated its significance. Further, the role of Scripture in the theological task is clearly of the highest importance to Luther. But his critique of Thomas on the authority of Scripture is a limited one. And though exegetical issues are involved in all other theological differences, we find in Luther no sustained and thoroughgoing critique of Thomas' exegetical method. The concrete results of exegesis seem to have been of far greater interest to Luther than Thomas' exegetical method itself.

As we have seen, the vast majority of Luther's critical energies were focused on individual doctrinal issues. Among these issues there are some which must be categorized as major grievances, issues on which one finds in Luther a vehement criticism of Thomas. First in this category comes the issue of penance and indulgences. This critique, occasioned by controversy with Thomist opponents, turns out to be in large measure a critique of a distorted image of Thomas mediated to Luther by these opponents. Thomas' teaching on the Lord's Supper also falls into this category of major grievances. Here, however, the issue, upon closer examination, dissolves into the larger issue of the authority of Thomas' teaching. Luther's attack on Thomas' theology of the monastic life is likewise a relatively impassioned one: Luther fastens upon real differences here and deplores Thomas' teaching precisely because it had been, in his view, so enormously influential.

Other doctrinal issues, in my view, must be categorized as less significant: perhaps "serious complaints" would characterize them best. Though the criticisms in this case are serious, they are relatively infrequent and unemphatic. His critique of Thomas on justification is astonishingly limited, and, as I have argued, relatively unimportant. So too is his critique of Thomas on the issue of the law, and furthermore, in this case Luther's critique is based on a misunderstanding. And on the subject of baptism, Luther fastens upon a minor aspect of Thomas' teaching, interpreted in a way which is scarcely consonant with Thomas' intention.

A final set of doctrinal issues must, in my view, be categorized as no more than grumblings, lamentable shortcomings in Thomas' theology. Some of these topics such as Thomas' teaching on angels and Thomas' view of papal authority point beyond themselves to larger issues. Yet, in themselves, they are in no way central to Luther's concerns. Thus Thomas' teaching on purgatory, while it initially came under attack, quickly became irrelevant to Luther. And Thomas' view of the veneration of images, while it had led to abuses in popular piety, was only a minor irritant for Luther.

This then is the scope and general shape of Luther's attack on the theology of Thomas. In all its detail and complexity, it is our only access to Luther's perception of the theological differences between himself and the person he took to be the greatest among the scholastics. It is the accurate and comprehensive description of this which has been the first and most important task of this study.

But obviously this study has also gone far beyond description, into the more hazardous area of analysis. In the case of each doctrine, a brief analysis has sought to assess the veracity, cogency and significance of Luther's critique. And unlike the description, no claim can be made that the analysis is comprehensive or definitive. Indeed an entire analytic study could be devoted to many of these topics. The brief analyses given here should therefore be understood as starting points, as suggestive rather than definitive.

Moreover, an entire book could be written on the significance of the material presented here for what has come to be known as the "fundamental-difference" issue: what is the single most basic disagreement between Luther's theology and that of Thomas Aquinas? Is there one difference which lies at the heart of all their other differences? And would an answer to this long-disputed question provide the key to understanding Protestant/Catholic differences? A glance at only the most recent discussion of these issues shows that they are far from being settled. Among recently suggested "fundamental differences" we could list Christology (Congar, Baur); anthropology (Muhlen); epistemology and linguistics (the Wurzburg Synod of Catholic Dioceses); ecclesiology (Ebeling, Brandenburg, Muller, Jüngel, Frieling, Lehmann); Aristolelean scholasticism vs. Platonic Augustinianism (Beineart); faith (Herms, Ratzinger); etc.[449] Which if any of these suggestions finds support in Luther's critique of Thomas? This enormously complex question will, for the time being, remain an open one.

In fact, the debate over important issues such as these may be interminable. The fact is that we do not have from Luther's hand a treatise *Contra Thomam*. Such a treatise would of course have given Luther's view of the matter, but even then some would no doubt argue that Luther's perception was inadequate. We are left in the final analysis, therefore, with Luther's critique of individual doctrines. And comparisons on this level, it must be pointed out, do not tell the whole story.

This is illustrated, on the one hand, by the fact that different doctrinal statements in Luther and Thomas sometimes are attempts to describe one and the same reality. Pesch has convincingly shown how vast differences in theological method (existential vs. sapiential) can lead in Luther and Thomas to varying and even contradictory formulations of identical perceptions of the truth.[450] Thus apparent doctrinal contradictions are not always real ones.

And on the other hand, the opposite is also true. Verbal agreement on a specific doctrine need not always signify real and fundamental agreement. For not only are differences in theological language to be considered, but also the fact that individual doctrines have different intra-systemic functions in the theologies of Luther and Thomas. Thus apparent doctrinal consensus is not always real.

All of this enormously complicates the general comparative study of Luther and Thomas. Nevertheless, the indispensible groundwork for such study, it is hoped, has been laid in this chapter.

In his most general statement on Thomas' theology, Luther, in 1524, characterized Thomas as "the source and foundation (grundsuppe) of all heresy, error and obliteration of the Gospel."[451] It is of course open to question whether this statement is an exaggeration tossed out in the heat of controversy or whether it is to be taken with absolute seriousness as expressing Luther's definitive view. But in any case, the statement is certainly emphatic.

In comparison, many will find Luther's criticism of individual doctrines in Thomas curiously unemphatic. The reason for this, I suggest, is that Luther was far more concerned with Thomas' influence than with Thomas himself. We have seen that many of Luther's attacks on Thomas are in the final analysis attacks on Thomas' influence. In Luther's view, though Thomas' teaching is at many points in error and therefore deplorable, this is not in itself disastrous for the church and the Gospel. What *is* disastrous is the way in which Thomas' views have been given authoritative status and therefore universal influence in the church. For this reason, as we shall see, Luther's

---

[449] From the vast literature on this topic, I cite here only the summary of Harding Meyer, "Fundamental Difference-
-Fundamental Consensus", in *Ecumenical Trends*, 15 (1986), 38-41.

[450] Pesch, "Existential and Sapiential Theology."

[451] WA 15, 184, 29ff: "...Thomas von Aquin, der born und grundsuppe aller ketzerey, irthum und vertilgung des Evangelii (wie seyne bucher beweysen)..." In the treatise, *Wider den neuen Abgott und alten Teufel, der zu Meissen soll erhoben werden* (1524).

most passionate, trenchant and unrelenting critique is directed against the authority of Thomas in church and theology. In other words, for Luther, the real problem with Thomas is not Thomas, but his followers. And it is to this critique that we now turn.

CHAPTER III

LUTHER ON THE AUTHORITY OF THOMAS

The issue of authority was a major one in the academic world of the late Middle Ages. Social and political developments, for one thing, gave new urgency to the debate over the relation between secular and ecclesiastical authority. Conciliarists and papalists debated the locus of doctrinal authority within the church itself. The authority of Scripture was a hotly controverted issue among theologians and canonists.[1] Humanism and scholasticism clashed, at least to a degree, over the question of authority.[2] And within scholasticism itself, the conflict between the *via antiqua* and *via moderna*, whatever else it may have been, was a dispute over authority. Even within these *viae*, members of religious orders and representatives of theological schools vigorously debated their allegiances to different authorities. Thus it is not surprising that questions of social, ecclesiastical and theological authority loomed large on Luther's reform program. And his opponents agreed: the issue of authority was close to the heart of the entire controversy.[3]

The problem of the authority of Thomas Aquinas, therefore, was only part of the much larger problem. Its close relation to this broader issue can be witnessed in the fact that Luther's attempt to assess and redefine the authority of Thomas went hand-in-hand with his attempted redefinition of all authority in church and theology. The attempt to limit the authority of Thomas carried within it the implicit enhancement of other loci of authority.

The depth of Luther's concern with the topic is astonishing. When Luther speaks of Thomas Aquinas, it is the question of his authority which comes up with by far the greatest frequency. By comparison, it is raised roughly three times as often as the next most frequently raised issue (namely penance). This statistic alone suggests that the issue of Thomas' authority is a significant, if not *the* most significant one for Luther.

It goes without saying that the historical circumstances had something to do with this. The majority of references to the authority of Thomas occur in Luther's writings between the years 1518 and 1521. And it was of course precisely during these years that Luther most vigorously engaged the Thomist school in controversy--a school which, as we shall see, had a very different view of the authority of Thomas in theological matters. Prierias, Cajetan, Hochstraten, Catharinus, etc., again and again, in their assaults on the "new" teaching, raised this issue for Luther. The fact that in this case the polemical agenda was set for him clearly helps to account for the frequency with which it comes up in his writings. But even after the front of controversy had shifted away from the Thomists in the 1520's, the question still persisted in Luther's mind: up until 1538 Luther continued to occasionally raise this issue.

---

[1] On this, see the important work of Hermann Schuessler, *Der Primat der Heiligen Schrift*.

[2] James Overfield, *Humanism and Scholasticism*. Overfield argues convincingly that there was no titanic struggle between humanism and scholasticism in Germany. Yet, when they did clash, the question of authority was involved. See for instance P. Kristeller's description of Lorenzo Valla's view in his essay "Thomism and the Italian Thought of the Renaissance," in E. Mahoney, ed, *Medieval Aspects of Renaissance Learning*, pp. 29-91, especially pp. 63ff.

[3] As J. Pelikan has rightly said, "At every stage and on every issue of the defense of the Roman Catholic faith against the Reformers...it became evident to all that, just as in the fifteenth century, there was one issue implicit within all the other issues: the doctrine of authority." *Reformation of Church and Dogma*, (Chicago: Univ. of Chicago Press, 1983), p. 262. Cf. Pontien Polman, *L'Élément Historique dans la Controverse religieuses du XIVe Siecle*, (Gembloux: Duculot, 1932). Polman argued that for Luther, the emphasis on the exclusive authority of the Bible undermines the importance of history in his theology. Thus in controversy with his opponents, arguments from history (or tradition) are devalued and in fact his historical arguments, insofar as they are used, are largely opportunistic (pp. 5-31). In the light of more recent studies, and as this Chapter will show, Polman's view now appears to be an over simplification. For more along these lines, see John Headley, *Luther's View of Church History*, (New Haven: Yale Univ. Press, 1963).

When we speak of Luther's critique of the authority of Thomas, it will immediately be clear that this is not a critique of Thomas himself. Obviously Thomas had no control over the way in which his work was used or abused after his death, and the same unfortunately can be said of Luther. When Luther therefore criticizes the authority of Thomas, he is in fact criticizing what he considers to be an abuse of Thomas' work. Thus the single issue on which Thomas' name comes up most frequently in Luther's writings does not involve a critique of Thomas, but rather of his late medieval followers - the Thomist school.

The context, therefore, indispensable for understanding Luther's view of the authority of Thomas, is the late medieval "Wegestreit." Recent scholarship has made it increasingly clear that late medieval theology was deeply divided not only into a *via antiqua* and *via moderna* but also into more narrowly defined "schools" such as the *via Thomae, via Albertistae, via Scotistae, via Gregorii*, etc.[4] This pluralism in late medieval theology has not yet been fully investigated, but it can safely be said that it involved much more than the old debate between *realistae* and *terministae* or *nominales*, as they were sometimes called. It also involved, for one thing, the question of the relative authority of these different masters (Thomas, Albert, Scotus, etc.) To be appointed to a late medieval university to lecture "in via Santi Thomae," for instance, meant that the professor was expected to resolve all questions along the lines laid down by Thomas. What was at stake, therefore, in the debates between the various *viae* was the relative authority of Thomas or Albert or Scotus, etc.

Such debates in the late 15th and early 16th century universities were frequent and impassioned. In fact they often reached acrimonious if not absurd levels. Thus students in the *via moderna* at Heidelberg in 1503 defended the thesis, "A Thomist is more stupid than any man," and even defended their *via* with violence.[5] Though perhaps more sober, professors too commonly attacked the reigning authorities in rival *viae*. Thus it is not unusual to find in the late medieval "Wegestreit" challenges to the authority of Thomas Aquinas.

This is the immediate context for understanding Luther's critique of the authority of Thomas. As a scholastic theologian in the early 16th century Luther was part of this "Wegestreit." Trained at Erfurt in the *via moderna* Luther began his theological career as an Occamist. At the fledgling University of Wittenberg, only the *via Thomae* and the *via Scoti* were taught until 1507 when one of Luther's teachers, Jodocus Trutvetter, was hired to represent the *via moderna* there. In 1510 Trutvetter returned to Erfurt and in the following year Luther was appointed to represent the *via moderna* in Wittenberg. He was thus the second appointment in the *via moderna* to a faculty heavily dominated by the *via antiqua*. An attack on the master of a rival *via* was to a degree expected from such a new appointee. And such an attack *in itself* would not have set Luther apart from his scholastic milieu.

Nevertheless, by the time Luther's attack on the authority of Thomas began in 1518, he had already, in theory at least, distanced himself from the scholastic "Wegestreit." He had broken definitively with the *via moderna* in 1517 in his "Disputatio contra scholasticam theologiam."[6] But rather than allying himself with another of the scholastic *viae*, Luther had in this disputation been

---

[4] An older work which is still of fundamental importance is Gerhard Ritter, *Via Antiqua und Via Moderna auf den deutschen Universitäten des XV. Jahrhunderts*, (Heidelberg: C. Winter, 1922). More recently Heiko Oberman has paid close attention to these divisions in his *Werden und Wertung der Reformation: Vom Wegestreit zum Glaubenskampf*, (Tübingen: Mohr, 1977). James Overfield summarizes the most recent literature in *Humanism and Scholasticism*, pp. 49-60.

[5] Cited in Overfield, *Humanism and Scholasticism*, p. 59. Other examples adduced by Overfield (pp. 181 and 183) allow one to say categorically that there were no insults hurled by Luther at Thomists that did not have parallels elsewhere in the academic life of the early 16th century.

[6] WA 1, 221-228. For the literature on this see my *Luther and Late Medieval Thomism*, pp. 24ff.

critical of all of them. In this sense Luther ceased, in principle, to be a scholastic theologian. Yet, as we shall see, he rightly continued to understand himself as a Roman Catholic theologian. It was only in the following years that he gradually abandoned this latter self-definition, and in this process of re-defining himself, certain developments in his understanding of the authority of Thomas played a crucial role. It is these developments which will be examined in detail in what follows.

Luther's critique of the authority of Thomas began in 1518, and not unexpectedly in controversy with a Thomist. Silvester Prierias had attacked Luther's 95 theses "On the Power and Efficacy of Indulgences" in June of that year in his hastily compiled treatise *De Potestatae Papae Dialogus*.[7] There, in his introduction, Prierias spelled out the foundational principles according to which Luther's theses were to be evaluated. First, the pope is the head of the universal church. Second, just as the church cannot err, so too the pope cannot err in defining doctrine. Third, those who disagree with the church and the pope are heretics. Fourth, the church can infallibly establish something either through its statements or by its action. Those, therefore, who disagree with what the church *does* are heretics. Thus, in relation to indulgences, those who say that the church cannot do what it in fact does, are heretics.[8]

In his reply (August 1518), *Ad dialogum Silvestri Prieratis de potestatae papae responsio*,[9] Luther too begins by laying down his foundational principles and thus his general understanding of authority in church and theology at this stage of his career. The first principle is St. Paul's admonition to the Thessalonians to "test all things, and hold to that which is good." The second is Augustine's statement that only the canonical writings are to be regarded as free of error. The third is canon law's stipulation that indulgence preachers are not permitted to preach anything but what is in their letter of authorization.[10] Here, in these foundational principles, according to Luther, Prierias' argument is already destroyed. For in support of his argument he adduces only the opinions of Thomas Aquinas, "without Scripture, the Fathers, canons or reason."[11] This then is the heart of Luther's treatise: his authorities (Scripture, the Fathers, canon law and reason) are marshalled against Prierias' authority (Thomas Aquinas). And thus this work, which is ostensibly about the power of the pope, is to a large degree about the authority of Thomas. It could well have been published under the title, "Test all things--even Thomas."

The elaboration of this theme, to a large extent, occupies Luther throughout the remainder of his treatise. Prierias is identified from the beginning and throughout with Thomism.[12] Yet, in what must have been a stinging blow to this eminent Thomist, Luther judges the crude indulgence preacher Tetzel to be "sharper" and "more learned."[13] As a Thomist, Prierias has not only immersed himself in Thomas' commentaries but he has, Luther says, submerged in them: he has failed to keep any kind of critical distance.[14]

Moreover, Thomism has become more of a "peripatetic" theology than a Pauline theology.[15] Luther, for his part, does not want to have only Thomas (and Prierias) as teachers when it comes

---

[7] In *Lutheri opera Latina var. arg.* 1, 344-377. German tr. in Walch 18, 310-345.

[8] Walch 18, 314f.

[9] WA 1, 647-686.

[10] WA 1, 647, 19-28. It should be noted here that Thomas too ascribes to Augustine's principle that only the canonical writings are inerrant. On this, see *S.T.* 1a, q.1, a.8 ad 2.

[11] WA 1, 647, 29ff: "His fundamentis, si me intelligis, simul intelligis, totum tuum Dialogum funditus eversum. Nam tu perpetuo verborum textu non nisi nuda verba ponis aut solas opiniones Divi Thomae mihi nunc demem decantas, qui aeque (ut tu) nudis verbis incedit, sine scriptura, sine patribus, sine Canonibus, denique sine ullis rationibus..."

[12] E.g. WA 1, 647, 6; 663, 36ff; 668, 17.

[13] WA 1, 650, 13ff.

[14] WA 1, 651, 1ff.

[15] WA 1, 652, 31ff.

to these matters pertaining to the soul. Scripture, the Fathers, canon law and reason are better teachers than Aristotle. The word of God, spoken by the one and only teacher Jesus Christ, is a more reliable teacher than Thomas.[16]

Prierias, according to Luther, simply identifies Thomas' opinion with what he calls "the opinion of the saints," and he reminds Luther that Thomas' teaching has been approved by the Church. But Luther wonders why, among all the doctors of the Church, Prierias does not cite another one, or a text from Scripture. Ecclesiastical approval of an author, according to Luther's second *fundamentum*, does not mean freedom from error. And moreover, the Chruch's approbation of Augustine (who said that only the canonical books are free of error) is higher than that of Thomas. But the Church's highest approbation goes to Paul (who said "test all things"). This then is Luther's first *fundamentum*.[17] "...I fear Thomas," Luther says, "not as much as St. Paul or Augustine."[18]

It is perhaps Prierias' mode of theological argumentation which Luther finds most frustrating. Again and again Prierias tries to prove his point simply by citing Thomas. But, according to Luther, the bare opinion of Thomas proves nothing. Without substantiation from Scripture, the Fathers, canon law and reason the opinion of Thomas is unconvincing.[19] Luther thinks this is characteristic of Thomists: by citing only Thomas they offer no evidence and therefore prove nothing.[20] In fact, Luther says, when one adduces only the opinion of Thomas without also adducing evidence from Scripture, the Fathers, the Church and reason, one ceases to speak as a theologian.[21]

Luther also has reservations about another aspect of the scholastic method, namely, to proceed in theological argumentation by way of distinctions. Though this is "the laudable practice of the Thomists," and though Luther himself occasionally proceeds in this way,[22] it seems to him that the Thomists have carried this too far. Who gives them the authority to divide the "most simple words of the most simple and only teacher, Christ" into various senses? Is this interpreting Scripture or is it tearing Scripture apart? Even such distinctions must themselves be grounded in Scripture, the Fathers and reason.[23] Moreover it is typical of "holy scholastic theology" to defend each distinction with seven new distinctions,[24] and then to persuade people that the teaching of

---

[16] WA 1, 648, 32ff: Speaking of penance as a habit in the soul, Luther says, "Secundum, habitualis illa poenitentia, nec a vobis intelligibilis nec vulgo tradibilis, nulla est apud me, sed a vobis conficta ex Aristotele, praesertim si qualitatem quandam in anima perpetuam et ociosam intelligitis: aut doce eam ex Scriptura, Patribus, Canonibus, rationibus. Nolo (ut scias) te aut S. Thomam nudos habere magistros in his rebus, quae ad animam pertinent, quae solo verbo dei vivit et pascitur, ideoque unus est eius magister Christus..."

[17] WA 1, 662, 17ff: "Primo auctoritatem B. Thomae inducis, cuius sententiam sanctorum vocas numero plurali, forte reverentiae causa, Et ut huic credam, dicis a Romana Ecclesia, regula fidei, probatum. Miror, quod inter tot Ecclesiae doctores non aliquando alium quoque aut textum scripturae inducas: ideo per fundamentum secundum iterum tam te quam Thomam reiicio. Quia et Augustinus receptus est ab Ecclesia magis quam S. Thomas, Paulus autem maxime, qui fundamentum meum primum est."

[18] WA 1, 674, 3.

[19] WA 1, 648, 18 and 648, 32.

[20] WA 1, 656, 20ff.

[21] WA 1, 664, 39-665, 2: "...Et hac tua professione obstrictum te volo, ut, quoties mihi divum Thomam adducis sine scriptura, sine patribus, sine ecclesia, sine ratione loquentem, memor sis te dialecticum, non theologum agere..."

[22] WA 1, 670, 9ff.

[23] WA 1, 650, 18ff: "Primo, quid dedit tibi aut Divi Thomae hanc potestatem, ut verbum simplicissimum simplicissimi et unici doctoris Christi in tres divideres sectas? Hoccine est Scripturam interpretari, an potius dilacerare? Qua Scriptura, quibus patribus, quibus rationibus hanc distinctionem stabilis, quaeso? Thomae non credo: Sylvestrum, etsi Palatii Magistrum, nego."

[24] Luther's judgement on this is quite correct in regard to the Thomist school from Capreolus to Cajetan. On this, see my *Luther and Late Medieval Thomism*.

Christ cannot be understood without them, that Christ cannot be understood without Thomas.[25] For Luther, the authority of Thomas alone is insufficient grounds for such distinctions: other authorities (Scripture, the Fathers, reason) must warrant them as well.

Thus throughout the treatise Luther's strategy is to oppose the authority of Thomas to that of Scripture, the Fathers, canon law and reason. For instance, where Prierias cites only the teaching of Thomas in support of his argument, Luther responds by citing a text from Scripture, one from canon law, the teaching of Gerson and others.[26] Elsewhere, he is simply content to cite the opinion of the Fathers against that of Thomas.[27] The authorities he cites, he is convinced, outweigh the authority cited by Prierias: in the future, he says, Prierias should bring Thomas onto the battlefield in better armor,[28] i.e., not "in the nude,"[29] but protected by the greater authority of Scripture, the Fathers, canons and reason.

Without the support of these greater authorities Thomas' teaching is in fact merely a theological opinion, in Luther's view. Its truth is as "probable" as other opinions.[30] And as a "probable" opinion, it is in fact a "doubtful" one which does not require the assent of faith.[31] The problem with the followers of Thomas is that they take these mere opinions and make them into articles of faith:

> You Thomists are to be strongly censured for daring to impose
> on us the opinions and frequently false ruminations of this holy man
> as though they were articles of faith...you think nothing except
> Thomas is worth reading and you want to see nothing false in
> him...[32]

Yet, Luther asserts, Thomas presented his views as opinions--not articles of faith: he disputes everything. Even in dealing with articles of faith Thomas begins with an "Utrum?" Why then do the Thomists not allow Luther to dispute doubtful matters that have not yet been determined? "Am I the Church," Luther says, "...that my disputations will be taken for definitions?" But because the Thomists dogmatize all that Thomas said, they brand as heretical everyone who does not follow Thomas' opinions.[33] For his part, Luther wishes to continue to dispute these things on which there has been no official decision by the Church: he rejects Prierias' accusation

---

[25] WA 1, 651, 6ff: "Haec ideo impugno, ut hanc tuam distinctionem denuo septem aliis nove conficitis distinctionibus defendas, more sacrae scholasticae Theologiae, Et tum dicas omnes nihilominus in verbo Christi intellectas, ut persuadeas mihi, doctrinam Christi sine Thomae et Sylvestri distinctionibus intellegi non posse: id enim opus est ut persuadear, qui Christum nisi sine Thoma intellegi vix credo."

[26] WA 1, 655, 37-656, 12.

[27] WA 1, 657, 14ff.

[28] WA 1, 686, 28ff.

[29] Luther refers frequently to the "nude" opinions of Thomas: E.g. WA 1, 647, 29ff; 656, 4ff; 664, 6ff; etc.

[30] WA 1, 656, 4-12.

[31] WA 1, 664, 38ff: "Concedo, esse argumentum probabile, id est dubium et dialecticum, cui non sit necessarium accedere fidei."

[32] WA 1, 658, 1ff: "Vos Thomistae graviter estis reprehendendi, qui sancti huius viri opiniones et saepius falsas meditationes nobis pro articulis fidei audetis statuere, et id unice curatis, ut, sicut nihil praeter Thomam dignamini vestra lectione, ita nihil vultis in eo falsum videre..."

[33] WA 1, 661, 29ff: "Quisdem criminis reus mecum es et tu et S. Thomas, immo Thomas omnium maxime, qui per omnia ferme sua scripta aliud nihil facit quam disputat et, quod grande est, etiam ea quae fidei sunt in quaestiones vocat et fidem vertit in 'utrum?' ut nosti. Cur ergo mihi, quaeso, non permittis disputare de iis rebus, quae sunt dubiosissimae et non determinatae? Nunquid ego Ecclesia sum, immo plus quam Ecclesia, ut meae disputationes pro diffinitionibus accipiantur?..."

of heresy and, as he frequently says in this treatise, awaits the decision of a council of the Church.[34] Until then, the right of Christian freedom prevails in these matters.[35]

The same understanding of authority pertains to what Prierias had referred to as "facts of the Church." According to Prierias, we recall, those who say that the Church cannot do what it in fact does, are heretics. For Luther, "facts of the Church" cannot simply be identified with Thomas' opinion.[36] The "fact" that St. Gregory offered indulgences is not a proof for Thomas' teaching on the treasury of merit.[37] Moreover, Luther says, Thomas and his followers disagree with a "fact" of the Church, the immaculate conception. Though this had not been officially defined as a dogma, the Church gave expression in its worship and devotion to this widely accepted belief. Yet the followers of Thomas were still disputing this "fact of the Church."[38] Why then did they not extend the same freedom to Luther on the subject of indulgences?

One of the major irritants for Luther in Prierias' attack has already been alluded to: the accusation of heresy. The Thomists, in Luther's estimation, are too hasty in their use of this term.

> As I said, it is their custom...to call one a 'heretic' in almost every second syllable. The Thomists have learned to say nothing but 'heretic, heretic, heretic'. And yet they prove nothing except to show that something has been said against their completely cold and naked opinions.[39]

Thus, in the final analysis, for the Thomists, 'heretics' are those who do not follow the opinions of Thomas.[40] Luther of course disagrees: there are many subjects on which Thomas has given his opinion but on which the Church has not yet officially spoken. Once the Church has made such a determination, Luther will be in heresy if he disagrees.[41] Elsewhere in his treatise Luther puts the matter in another way. Mimicking the scholastic style, he distinguishes between two kinds of heresy: if heresy is taken to be that which is contrary to Thomist opinion, then he is indeed a 'heretic'; if it is taken to be that which is contrary to the teaching of the Church, then he is Catholic.[42] In short Luther refuses to follow the Thomists in making a simple identification between the teaching of Thomas and the teaching of the Church.

This uncritical identification is the Thomist school's fundamental mistake. What Thomas held forth as opinions are transformed by his followers into articles of faith.[43] What Thomas

---

[34] E.g. WA 1, 658, 6ff; 661, 29ff; 665, 9ff; 680, 36.

[35] WA 1, 647, 29ff.

[36] WA 1, 667, 23ff.

[37] WA 1, 680, 36ff.

[38] WA 1, 655, 37ff.

[39] WA 1, 672, 1ff: "Sicut dixi, vester iste mos est, si mos vocari posset tanta cholera aestuare, ut altera pene syllaba 'haereticum' dicatis: nil nisi 'haereticum, haereticum, haereticum' Thomistae loqui didicerunt, et tamen nihil prorsus efficitis, nisi quod contra vestras frigidissimas et nudissimas opiniones dictum aliquid esse probatus." On prierias' global use of the term "heresy," see Jared Wicks, "Roman Reactions," p. 529. For the literature describing the progressive narrowing of this term, see Wicks, *ibid*, p. 529, n. 32.

[40] WA 1, 662, 3ff: "Ideo ignosco tibi, quod me haereticum vocas, sciens hunc esse morem Thomistarum, ut haereticus esse, velit nolit, cogatur (dumtaxat apud Thomistas) qui opiniones Thomae non fuerit secutus..." Cf. WA 1, 655, 7ff.

[41] WA 1, 665, 9ff: "...Haereticus autem ero, si, postquam Ecclesia determinaverit, non tenuero."

[42] WA 1, 670, 27ff: "Respondeo et ego per distinctionem: Haeresis accipitur uno modo pro ut est contra opiniones nudas Thomistarum, et sic est haeretica, alio modo pro ut est contra doctrinam fidei et ecclesiae, et sic est catholica." Cf. WA 1, 671, 27.

[43] WA 1, 658, 1ff. (Quoted above, n. 32.)

approached in disputation is now made mandatory by the Thomists,[44] as though it is necessary to take Thomas' words as divine oracles.[45] The Thomist approach to the authority of Thomas is therefore a misunderstanding and a distortion, part of the "miserable fate" which Thomas has suffered at the hands of his followers.[46] In this way too the Thomists have failed to understand Thomas correctly.[47]

The 1518 treatise *Ad Prieratis* which has been examined here represents Luther's first major statement giving his view of the authority of Thomas. This early understanding of Luther bears within it heavy traces of the late medieval "Wegestreit." For like representatives of alternate *viae*, Luther sees Thomas as only one among many theologians and his teaching as nothing more than theological opinion. He strongly resists, as did others in the "Wegestreit," the Thomist propensity to identify Thomas' teaching with the teaching of the Church. But he also has begun to move beyond the conflict between the *viae*: he opposes the authority of Thomas not to some other scholastic master, but to the higher authority of "Scripture, the Fathers, canon law and reason." It is against this higher authority that all things--even Thomas--must be tested.

Other writings from the year 1518 confirm the view of Thomas' authority established in *Ad Prieratis*. In a letter to Staupitz, Luther makes the point that no scholastic "sect" or doctor can be authoritative because they all disagree with one another. Scripture must be the final authority.[48] Cajetan, in his confrontation with Luther at Augsburg, had appealed to the authority of Thomas much in the same way that Prierias had.[49] And Luther told Cajetan himself that "the stories of St. Thomas" were not enough to satisfy him in this regard.[50] Even Cajetan's reference to the bull "Extravagante" proves nothing since in that bull "only the teaching of Thomas is trotted out and retold."[51]

This theme--papal teaching in reliance only upon the authority of Thomas--is raised again in Luther's "Eine Freiheit des Sermons päpstlichen Ablass and Gnade belangend" of that same year. Even the pope cannot prove his view by citing such authority. Besides, Luther adds, the pope sometimes misunderstands such authorities.[52] On some issues the pope tolerates Thomas' teaching and thus tacitly approves it.[53] Yet the Church's approval of Thomas' teaching is not total. He is indeed "approved," but the limited extent of this approval is evident in all the universities. For his part Luther will accept those opinions of Thomas which are proven by the Fathers with the help of Scripture or reason.[54]

In his "Resolutiones" on the 95 theses of 1518, Luther adds that preference must be given to the authority of the pope and the Church over Thomas. For even the scholastics contend that

---

[44] WA 1, 661, 35ff: "Sed consuetudo ista est Thomistica, qua omnia asserere soletis, etiam quae disputative proponitis aut in Thoma legitis: ideo et me assertorem credis, non disputatorem."

[45] WA 1, 668, 20ff.

[46] Cf. WA 1, 674, 24ff. Leif Grane is correct when he says: "Mehrere Male verteidigt er [Luther] deshalb die grossen Scholastiker, wie z.B. Thomas und Bonaventura gegenüber ihrer Verwendung durch die Anhänger zu Luthers Zeit. Sie hatten damals *opiniones* geäussert, die *nun* als Wahrheit ausgegeben werden." *Modus Loquendi Theologicus*, p. 167.

[47] Cf. WA 1, 660, 5ff.

[48] WABR 1, 160, 20ff (31 March 1518).

[49] Letter to Spalatin (14 October 1518). WABR 1, 214, 23ff.

[50] Letter of Cajetan (17 October 1518). WABR 1, 221, 39ff.

[51] "Acta Augustana" (1518). WA 2, 8, 7ff. Tr. from LW 31, 262.

[52] WA 1, 384, 14ff.

[53] WA 1, 389, 35ff.

[54] WA 1, 390, 29ff: "Zum vierden, das sanct Thomas bestetigit ist, lass ich seyn. Man weyss aber in allen universiteten, wie weyt die bestetigung sich erstrecket. Darum was der heylig vatter mit schrifft odder vornunfft beweret, num ich an, das ander lass ich seynen guten gewessen seyn."

such great men as Thomas have erred.[55] The Thomists, for their part, have received some of their ideas from Thomas, but they have also added some of their own.[56] Thus even the Thomists at certain points contradict Thomas, though unintentionally.[57]

On all these doubtful matters, therefore, disputation is permissible. Luther feels free to reject Thomas' opinions if he can give better reasons for his own views from Scripture and canon law.[58] Though the Thomists *want* Thomas to be approved by the Church in all things, this is in fact not the case. Therefore Christian liberty prevails and Christians must "test all things, holding to that which is good."[59] And this same freedom Luther is willing to extend to Thomas himself: the Church does not err in its failure to condemn Thomas' false opinions![60]

In his writings of the following year, 1519, the issue of the authority of Thomas is less prominent. Still Luther continues to challenge the way in which the Thomists (this time Jacob Hochstraten) appeal to this authority.[61] And Luther seems to be more aware than before of Thomas' celebrated status in the Church.[62] He now goes so far as to identify a council of the Church with Thomism: the Council of Constance is referred to as the "Council of the Thomists."[63] Moreover, rather than emphasizing as he did in 1518 the disagreements between scholastic schools, he now increasingly emphasizes their similarities. He remarks more than once on Karlstadt's rejection of both Scotism and Thomism,[64] and he himself asserts that the Thomists, Scotists and *moderni* agree on the central issue of free will and grace.[65]

These new emphases in 1519 presage a more significant development in Luther's understanding of the authority of Thomas in the following years, 1520-21. As we have seen, Luther had by 1518 already arrived at a clear position on what degree of authority Thomas *ought* to have in Church and theology. And on this point there is no significant development in later years. But on the question of what authority Thomas does *in fact* have in Church and theology, Luther significantly revised his earlier assessment.

Already in his *Operationes in Psalmos*, begun in 1519 and finally completed in 1521, Luther's language suggests that such a revision was underway. Fewer distinctions were now made between Thomism and other theological schools. Thomas, the Thomists and all scholastic doctors are lumped together,[66] and classified as sects.[67] Moreover, they are spoken of as being at one

---

[55] WA 1, 611, 21ff: "Et si S. Thomas, B. Bonaventura, Alexander Ales sint insignes viri...tamen iustum est eis praeferre veritatem primo, deinde et auctoritatem Papae et Ecclesiae. Nec mirum est, tantos viros in hoc errasse. Nam in quantis, quaeso, B. Thomam etiam Scholastici errasse arguunt!"

[56] WA 1, 568, 1ff.

[57] WA 1, 609, 9ff. Note that here Luther cites Thomas *against* the Thomists!

[58] WA 1, 570, 6ff.

[59] WA 1, 530, 4ff: "Unum illud addo et mihi vendico iure Christianae libertatis, quod opiniones B. Thomae, Bonaventurae aut aliorum Scholasticorum vel Canonistarum nudas sine textu et probatione positas volo pro meo arbitrio refutare vel acceptare secundum consilium Pauli 'omnia probate, quod bonum est tenete', Etsi scio quorundam Thomistarum sententiam volentium, B. Thomam ab Ecclesia esse approbatum in omnibus. Constat satis, quantum B. Thomae valet autoritas. Hac mea protestatione credo satis manifestum fieri, quod errare quidem potero, sed haereticus non ero, quantumlibet fremant et tabescant ii qui aliter sentiunt vel cupiunt."

[60] WA 1, 555, 26ff.

[61] "Scheda adversus Iacobum Hochstraten" (1519). WA 2, 386, 35ff.

[62] E.g. letter to Staupitz (3 October 1519). WABR 1, 514, 57ff.

[63] "Resolutiones Lutheraniae super propositionibus suis Lipsiae disputatis" (1519). WA 2, 421, 1ff.

[64] WA 2, 394, 22ff. Cf. his letter to Spalatin (20 July 1519), WABR 1, 422, 54ff.

[65] WA 2, 394, 31ff: "Certum est enim, Modernos (quos vocant) cum Schotistis et Thomistis in hac re (id est libero arbitrio et gratia) consentire..."

[66] E.g. WA 5, 664, 19ff.

[67] E.g. WA 5, 371, 34ff.

with priests, bishops and religious.[68] Perhaps most significantly, the pope is now identified with the Thomists.[69]

The trend continued in late June of 1520 when Luther published Prierias' latest treatise, accompanied by his own biting marginal comments. In these comments one hears again Luther's old complaints against the Thomists. For instance, Prierias makes the *via Thomae* the arbiter of heresy,[70] the Thomists have their own "truth,"[71] etc. But one also hears in these comments something new. For the first time Luther speaks of the Church as the "Church of the Thomists."[72] And he identifies for the first time "Thomist and Romanist theology."[73] Later, in early October of the same year in his *De captivitate Babylonica* Luther again explicitly calls the Church "the Thomistic Church."[74] Clearly, Luther now no longer regards Thomism as merely one voice among many in the Church.

At about the same time, Leo X's "Exsurge Domine" reached Wittenberg and Luther replied to the bull in December in his "Assertio omnium articulorum M. Lutheri per bullam Leonis X novissimam damnatorum." In this work, Luther continued his reassessment of the actual authority of Thomas in the Church. Now it is no longer only the Thomists who abuse the authority of Thomas. The pope in his bull likewise fails to cite Scripture in support of his opinion. Like the Thomists, he simply cites Clement VI's "Extravagante," which was itself based on the mere opinion of Thomas.[75] Moreover the pope, Luther mentions again, has approved Thomas' books.[76] It has now become clear to Luther, that, as he mentions in passing, "Thomas Aquinas reigns."[77]

After the bull of excommunication was issued on 3 January 1521, Luther again found himself in controversy with the Thomists, this time in the person of Ambrosius Catharinus. In his reply to Catharinus, which he completed on April 1 of that year, Luther again raises all the old charges in regard to Thomist misuse of Thomas' authority. The Thomists, he says, read only Thomas, devour him, and as it were "transubstantiate" him, raising him to the level of an infallible teacher.[78] Moreover, the Thomists vacillate in their opinions.[79] Yet, Luther treats the various *viae* as substantially identical,[80] especially on the subject of free will.[81] This last point is perhaps part of the reason why in this treatise Luther's negative judgment of Thomism reaches a new extreme.[82]

But another reason why Luther's judgment is more extreme here has to do with his new understanding of the authority which Thomas in fact has in the Church: the authority of Thomas and the study of Thomas reigns, and the result is that the Church has embraced false teaching.[83]

---

68 WA 5, 263, 6ff.
69 WA 5, 645, 34ff.
70 WA 6, 339, 35ff.
71 WA 6, 340, 30ff.
72 *Ibid.*
73 *Ibid.*
74 WA 6, 508, 11f.
75 WA 7, 124, 26ff: "Praeter haec, nullis scripturis sua probant, sed sola impia illa extravagante Cle. VI. ex opinionibus Thomae insulsissimus et meris figmentis concepta."
76 WA 7, 149, 35ff.
77 WA 7, 96, 31ff.
78 WA 7, 706, 18f: "Et quid aliud fierent, qui non nisi unum Thomam legunt, vorant et in se (quod dicunt) transubstantiant?"
79 WA 7, 710, 34f.
80 E.g. WA 7, 739, 1f.
81 WA 7, 707, 17ff.
82 Cf. WA 7, 718, 28-31; 7, 715, 11-16.
83 WA 7, 739, 28ff: "Quia autoritate et studio Thomae elevatus regnat, resuscitans liberum arbitrium, docens virtutes Morales et philosophiam naturalem, et triceps scilicet Cerberus, immo tricorpor Gerion."

Thomism has become the judge of all things.[84] Over and over again, throughout this work, papal teaching and Thomist teaching are identified: Luther refers to the blasphemies of "the papists and the Thomists";[85] he argues that the Thomists have contributed to the papacy's extinction of the Gospel;[86] he speaks of the Thomists, papists and Romanists as a single entity.[87] The Church has thus become for him the "synagogue of the Papists and the Thomists,"[88] or, as he puts it elsewhere, the "synagogue of Satan."[89] This extreme language is prompted not only by what Luther regards as erroneous teaching, but also by what he regards as the subversion of Christian freedom by a tyranny in the Church, namely, the joint tyranny of pope and Thomism.[90] The two are identical.[91]

The contrast between this and Luther's earlier understanding of the authority of Thomas is unmistakable. Now, in 1520 and 1521, he no longer argued that the teaching of Thomas was only one among many opinions. He no longer argued that the Church has not approved all that Thomas taught. And he no longer argued that the Thomists were wrong in making a simple identification between the teaching of Thomas and the teaching of the Church. He was now of the opinion that Thomism was not merely one faction among the late medieval theological schools. It was rather, as he now saw it, the preeminent one, and the Church as he now saw it was in fact a "Thomist Church." It was clear to him that the authority of Thomas reigned supreme in the Church.

There can be no doubt that Luther's revised opinion of the actual authority of Thomas in the Church was closely related to the papal bull "Exsurge Domine." For in this bull, many of the theses condemned as "heretical or scandalous or false, or offensive to pious ears, or dangerous to simple minds, or subversive of catholic truth,"[92] were in fact theses on which he had previously been attacked by his Thomist opponents. Here it became clear to Luther that the official Church in the person of the pope was taking the side of these Thomists. Yet it should not be forgotten that the development in Luther's view which has been described here was already well underway before the issuance of "Exsurge Domine," and thus it was not the bull in itself which made him change his mind. Rather it confirmed what he already believed.

At least part of the explanation for why Luther came to the conclusion he did on the authority of Thomas must lie in the massive opposition of the Thomist school in these years (1518-21). The united front presented by Wimpina, Tetzel, Prierias, Cajetan, Hochstraten, Catharinus and Dungersheim against the early Luther eventually helped to convince him that Prierias had been right from the start: Thomas was *the* authority in the Church. The combined weight of this opposition pointed to a Thomist hegemony in the Church.

Luther's polemic against Thomism reached a new height in 1522, for in the previous year another "Thomist," almost equal to the pope in eminence, had entered the lists against him. Henry VIII of England had attacked Luther in His *Assertio Septem Sacramentorum* hoping to win from Leo X the title "Fidei Defensor." In his bull awarding the title, Leo had characterized the book

---

[84] WA 7, 706, 7ff.
[85] WA 7, 717, 18.
[86] WA 7, 721, 15ff.
[87] WA 7, 777, 23f.
[88] WA 7, 721, 5.
[89] WA 7, 710, 19.
[90] WA 7, 719, 7ff.
[91] Luther refers to this joint tyranny again in his 1521 "Responsio Extemporaria" to the proceedings at Worms. WA 7, 613, 22ff.
[92] Quoted in LW 32, 5.

as being filled with "most admirable doctrine, sprinkled with the dew of divine grace."[93] While the true authorship of the work has not been settled, Luther was convinced that Edward Lee had written it.[94] Luther's reply in 1522, *Contra Henricum Regem Angliae*,[95] identified Henry throughout as a Thomist. In fact, if frequency of references to Thomism is any indication, Luther's opposition to Thomism reached its pinnacle in this work. For one finds there over a hundred references to Thomism, all of them unfavorable, most of them insulting, and few of them having to do with substantive issues. This is something of a mystery given the fact that one finds in Henry's work only one reference to Thomas! (His most frequently cited scholastic authority is Hugh of St. Victor.) Whatever the explanation, it is clear that in this work, Luther's opposition to Thomism and thus to the misuse of Thomas' authority had reached a new level of acrimony. Now, in Luther's mind at least, it was not only the pope but even secular rulers entering the lists against him under the banner of Thomism.

There is, furthermore, no evidence that in the succeeding years Luther abandoned his new understanding of the authority of Thomas in the Church. Whereas the Thomists had initially made Thomas the arbiter of orthodoxy, now the whole Church seems to have done the same. In his 1523 treatise *Von Anbeten des Sakraments des heiligen Leichnams Christi*, Luther says that the Papists call everyone a heretic who does not hold to Thomas' "fantasies" as the absolute truth.[96] And once again, in 1524, Luther refers to the "elevation" of Thomas Aquinas that took place at the Council of Constance.[97] Yet the issue of Thomas' authority now begins to fade into the background. In 1523 Luther reports that he has advised his followers to leave Thomas behind.[98] And this he himself appears to do, for between 1524 and 1530 we find no statements from him on the authority of Thomas. Preoccupation with new opponents meant that for him, at least this aspect of the controversy with Thomism had come to an end--temporarily.

It was not until 1530 that the issue was again raised by Luther in his treatise *Widerruf vom Fegefeuer*. Here Luther explains that the Dominicans have imposed their Thomas Aquinas on Christendom so that now every letter in his writings must be taken as an article of faith. Yet there were so many errors in his writings that the scholastics themselves could not tolerate it but had to condemn some of them.[99] Despite this it has now come to the point where we are expected to regard it as an article of faith when his stomach growled or when he broke wind. All his errors are now forgotten.[100] Thomas, Luther complains, has been raised to the level of an infallible teacher. Yet since the scholastics themselves held that this "approved teacher" could err,

---

[93] Quoted in Louis O'Donovan, ed., *Henry VIII's Assertio Septem Sacramentorum, 1521*, (N.Y.: Benzinger, 1908), p. 168.

[94] J. J. Scarisbrick, *Henry VIII*, (Los Angeles: Univ. of California Press, 1968), p. 112.

[95] WA 10 II, 180-222. Luther's "Antwort Deutsch auf König Heinrichs Buch" of 1522 (WA 10 II, 227-262) is not a translation of the Latin work.

[96] WA 11, 441, 18ff.

[97] "Wider den neuen Abgott und alten Teufel;" WA 15, 184, 29ff.

[98] "Wider der Verkehrter und Fälscher kaiserlichs Mandats"; WA 12, 64, 9ff.

[99] Luther refers here no doubt to the condemnations of 1277.

[100] WA 30 II, 383, 20ff: "Also haben auch die prediger münch ihren Thomam von Aquino der Christenheit auffgeladen, das alle buchstaben müssen artickel sein, der doch vol irthum stickt, bis das die hohen schulen selbs nicht haben leiden können, und etliche stück an ihm verdamnen müssen, Und war schier dahin komen, das wir musten lassen artickel des glaubens sein, wenn einen vollen Münch der bauch kurret odder einen faulen wind faren lies. Aber nu ists alles vergessen, haben nie nichts ubels gethan."

it is now a contradiction for the Church to make new articles of faith on the basis of what Thomas said.[101]

It is also significant that in 1530 Luther explicitly acknowledges his previous misjudgment of the actual authority of Thomas in the Church. In 1518, we recall, Luther had argued that Thomas was only one scholastic teacher among many: the Thomists were wrong in elevating the authority of Thomas above the rest. Now, in his *Vermahnung an die Geistlichen, versammelt auf dem Reichstag zu Augsburg*, Luther acknowledges that the Thomists had been right all along: the authority of Thomas does in fact transcend that of all other scholastic teachers. He is, Luther acknowledges, the "teacher of all teachers."[102]

Finally, Luther returns for the last time to the subject of Thomas' "infallibility" in his 1537/38 *Auslegung des ersten und zweiten Kapitels Johannis in Predigten*. In Luther's polemic here, papal infallibility and the infallibility of Thomas are related. The inerrant Pope approves Thomas who then also is regarded as inerrant.[103] This shared infallibility means that in Luther's view, the teaching of the Church is in fact the teaching of Thomas.

This examination of Luther's view of the authority of Thomas has uncovered a significant evolution of his thought. More precisely, on the question of what authority Thomas in fact has in the Church and in theology, Luther initially took the view that it was a limited authority confined primarily to one of the many scholastic schools. We have seen how his view on this question evolved to the point where he could speak of "the Thomist Church." His final assessment was that Thomism reigned supreme in the Roman Church and its theology.

At the same time, on the related question of what authoritative status Thomas *ought* to have in the church and in theology, we have seen no such development in his view. From the beginning Luther held that Thomas was one theologian among many and that as such his teachings were theological opinions--open, as are all theological opinions, to criticism. Thus, in principle, the authority of Thomas should be no greater than that of other theologians. On this, there is no evidence that Luther ever changed his mind.

It has already been pointed out that while this view of what Thomas' authority ought to be set Luther at odds with Thomism, it did not automatically estrange him from the general Catholic theological milieu from which he came. Other voices in the "Wegestreit" were also wary of according too much authority to Thomas. A number of examples illustrate this resistance.

First, Pierre D'Ailly (1350-1420), whom Luther knew well,[104] wrote a treatise against John of Montosono O.P. in relation to the immaculate conception controversy.[105] And the entire third part of this treatise is a critique of excessive estimates of Thomas' authority. D'Ailly recognizes that Thomas' teaching has been "approved" by the Church, but he argues that such approval can be understood in three ways: first, in the sense that Thomas' teaching is "useful" and "probable";

---

[101] WA 30 II, 385, 34ff: "...So halten sich auch selbs nicht, Das alles recht sey was inn einen bestettigten lerer funden wird. Exemplum de Thoma Aquinate, So ist das auch ein Zusatz, das die kirche artickel des glaubens mache mit ihrem bestetigen, Die Sophisten ertichten solchs."

[102] WA 30 II, 300, 21ff: Speaking of the scholastic teachers, Luther says, "...Uber diese alle gehet Thomas Aquinas, Lerer aller lerer (sagen anders die Prediger Münche recht)..."

[103] WA 46, 768, 32ff: "Non ergo posthac dicendum: Papa non errat, Patres non errant,Thomas vera scripsit, quia approbantur a papa, sed Coticula sumenda, papa, Christus et eius Evangelium..." Cf. the parallel passage in WA 46, 768, 12ff. where Luther says the same not only of Thomas but of others. Luther criticizes here what he sees as a kind of "creeping infallibilism." Cf. WA 46, 769, 19ff.

[104] Heinrich Boehmer asserted that Luther knew D'Ailly "almost by heart." *Luther and the Reformation in the Light of Modern Research*, (London: G. Bell, 1930), p. 160. According to Grane, Luther read D'Ailly's Sentences commentary in 1520 ("Luthers Kritik an Thomas von Aquin," p. 12, n. 41).

[105] *Apologia Facultatis Theologiae Parisiensis Circa damnationem Joannis de Montesono*, in E. du Pin, ed., *Joannis Gersonii Opera Omnia*, (Antwerp: Sumptibus Societatis, 1706), vol. 1, cols. 709-722.

second, in the sense that it ought to be believed in all its parts; and third, in the sense that it is in no part heretical or erroneous in things pertaining to the faith.[106] Thomas' teaching (and that of many other doctors) has been approved by the Church *only* in the first sense, i.e., as "useful" or "probable."[107] Then, quoting one of Luther's favorite passages, "Test all things" (I Thess. 5:21), D'Ailly goes on to argue that this applies even to the saints.[108] To illustrate, he then enumerates six examples of contradictions in Thomas and six examples of errors in Thomas.[109] Obviously, in D'Ailly's view, Thomists such as John of Montosono wildly exaggerate the authority of Thomas in Church and theology. While it is not known whether Luther ever read this treatise, it is safe to say that he would have concurred had he done so.

A second example is to be found in the person of Baptista Mantuanus, or Battista Spagnoli as he is sometimes known, a 15th century Carmelite friar who was later beatified.[110] Though of humanist orientation, Mantuanus wrote an *Opus auream in Thomistas* in which he accused the Dominicans of blindly following Thomas, and more seriously, of believing that he never erred. Mantuanus argued that the Church's approval of Thomas' teaching was not as complete as his followers claim. And in matters of faith, "he insists, as does Valla, on the superiority of the Bible and the Fathers to Saint Thomas and the other medieval doctors."[111] Even among these medieval doctors, Mantuanus insists that Thomas is not to be regarded as superior to the rest.

So too, in the humanist circles on the periphery of the "Wegestreit" there was also an acute consciousness of the danger of granting too much authority to Thomas. Lorenzo Valla, invited by the Dominicans in Rome in 1457 to deliver a eulogy on St. Thomas, was remarkably candid in this regard.[112] As his famous *Encomium S. Thomae Aquinatis* shows, Valla refused to place Thomas above other doctors of the Church. And he names no less than eight of the Fathers whom he prefers over Thomas. It is hardly surprising then, that according to reports the speech was poorly received by the Dominicans.

These examples from Luther's theological milieu indicate that there were others who were critical of the Dominican/Thomist exaggeration of Thomas' authority. Luther's early position on how the authority of Thomas ought to be regarded, therefore, did not place him outside of this milieu. His view on this question differed in no fundamental way with what we may reasonably surmise to have been a legitimate view in late 15th and early 16th century Catholic theology.

What did help to set Luther apart from the world of Roman Catholic theology in the early 16th century was his developing view on the authority which Thomas in fact had in the Church. The prime catalysts for this development were those representatives of the Thomist school who formed a more or less unified phalanx in opposition to him: Wimpina, Tetzel, Prierias, Cajetan, Dungersheim, Catharinus, and Hochstraten. In a perceptive moment, Erasmus already in 1519 explained Luther's increasingly critical views as a reaction to Dominican exaggerations of Thomas'

[106] *Ibid.*, col. 715.
[107] *Ibid.*, col. 716.
[108] *Ibid.*, col. 719.
[109] *Ibid.*, cols. 720f, and 716f.
[110] For what follows I rely on Paul Kristeller's account in "Thomism and the Italian Thought of the Renaissance," in E.P. Mahoney, ed., *Medieval Aspects of Renaissance Learning*, pp. 29-91, pp. 69-71.
[111] *Ibid.*, p. 71. Luther had read the poetry of Mantuanus (WATR 1, 107, 31). The striking similarity between Luther's critique and the critique in Mantuanus' *Opus auream in Thomistas* suggests that Luther may have read this work as well. The work is edited and printed in P. Kristeller's *Le Thomisme et la pensée italienne de la Renaissance*, (Montreal: Inst. d'Études Médiévales, 1967), pp. 137-185.
[112] I again rely here on Kristeller's account in "Thomism and the Italian Thought of the Renaissance," pp. 63f.

authority.[113] While Luther was initially highly critical of those exaggerations, he eventually came to see them as accurate descriptions of the actual state of affairs in the Church: the Church in his view had now become the "Thomistic Church."

Thus in Luther's view, the movement of Roman Catholic theology in the late 15th and early 16th centuries was from a situation of theological pluralism to the triumph of Thomism. In his view the "Wegestreit" had now in fact been decisively resolved: the *via Thomae* had emerged supreme in the Church. The other *viae*, once vibrant and creative, now had faded into subordinate positions: they had lost their viability as theological schools. Thomism now exercised a hegemony, indeed a tyranny, in the Church.

It is important in this context to raise the question of the accuracy of Luther's view. Was Luther's view of the triumph of Thomism a perceptive reading of the theological situation in which he found himself? The present state of scholarship precludes any definitive answer to this question. While some scholars point to the apparent decline of Thomism in centers such as Cologne,[114] others point to the apparent triumph of Thomism at the Council of Trent, where, as legend has it, a copy of the *Summa Theologiae* lay on the altar beside the Bible.[115] Such contrary indications, along with a host of others and indeed the whole of Roman Catholic theology in the 16th century, must be carefully reexamined before any consensus will emerge as to the accuracy of Luther's view.

Be this as it may, however, there can be no question that Luther's conviction in this regard was of decisive significance for himself. In relation to Thomas, this is the issue which Luther raises with by far the greatest frequency. No single theological difference with Thomas receives so great a share of Luther's attention. And this is not surprising when we bear in mind the major importance which the entire issue of authority had for Luther. For the question of Thomas' authority was intimately related to that larger question. Thus, as his view of the actual authority of Thomas in the Roman Church evolved, so did his progressive disillusionment with, and estrangement from, that Church.

Already in 1518, as we have seen, Luther laid the groundwork for this evolution by distinguishing between two kinds of heresy: if heresy is taken to be that which is contrary to Thomist opinion, then he acknowledged himself to be a heretic. But if heresy is taken to be that which is contrary to the teaching of the Church, then he claimed the title of "Catholic." By 1521 the implications of this distinction had already been worked out with inexorable logic. Since, as he now thought, the Church had become the "Thomistic Church," it was no longer "Catholic." His alienation from it was inevitable.

---

[113] In his letter to Albert of Brandenburg, 19 October 1519. P.S. Allen, ed., *Opus Epistolarum Des. Erasmi Roterdami*, (Oxford: Oxford Univ. Press, 1922), vol. 4, p. 105. Cited in Wicks, "Roman Reactions," p. 531, n. 42.

[114] E.g. Gabriel Löhr, *Die Kölner Dominikanerschule vom 14. bis zum 16. Jahrhundert, mit eine Übersicht über die Gesamtentwicklung*, (Cologne: Kölner Universitätsverlag, 1948), p. 18.

[115] James A. Weisheipl, "Thomism," in *New Catholic Encyclopedia*, vol. 14, pp. 126-135, p. 134.

CHAPTER IV

LUTHER'S KNOWLEDGE OF THOMAS

Throughout the foregoing chapters we have paid close attention to the question of Luther's familiarity with Thomas Aquinas. In analyzing each critique, we have asked what light it sheds on the question of what Luther knew. It now remains for us to broach the question in a more systematic and comprehensive way: Did Luther know anything about Thomas? If so, what did he know? Did he understand Thomas with any depth? How did he come to know what he knew? Did he read any of Thomas' works, or did he rely on secondary sources? And how did his knowledge compare with that of contemporary theologians in the early 16th century? This entire complex of questions must now be squarely faced.

Yet it would be foolhardy to approach these questions without a great deal of caution. Determining with any precision Luther's knowledge of one facet of the theological tradition is an enormously difficult undertaking.[1] The first problem is of course the historical gap between him and ourselves: it is troublesome enough for us to assess the knowledge of our contemporaries, let alone someone who lived four and one-half centuries ago. A second obstacle is the three-century gap that separates Luther and Thomas. For the thought of Thomas did not lie dormant during this period. Almost all theologians in the interval commented in one way or another on his teachings; thus Thomas' theology was the subject of an intricate history of interpretation which deeply affected the way in which he was read in the 16th century. Then too, the vast scope of Luther's authorship complicates the undertaking. His references to Thomas are scattered throughout an enormous literary *corpus* and all of them must be taken into account. Finally, to mention only one more of the many stumbling blocks, Luther was never in the habit of accurately quoting anyone, nor was it his custom to cite his sources precisely (except Scripture). Though this was by no means unusual for his time, it renders our task much more complex.

Nevertheless, this question, difficult as it is, demands an answer. Already in the 16th century, Luther's opponents accused him of not knowing and understanding the scholastics. As a consequence, they argued, his critique of this kind of theology rested on an extremely dubious foundation. Moreover, Luther acknowledged Thomas to be the most important and influential representative of scholasticism. Thus Luther's abandonment of this tradition cannot be adequately comprehended without taking into account his critique of Thomas. And that critique cannot be assessed without raising the question of Luther's knowledge of Thomas. The issue is therefore a central one for all who would understand Luther's break with the wider theological tradition he inherited.

The vast body of 20th century Luther-scholarship has at least tacitly acknowledged the importance of this issue. Almost every modern interpreter of Luther has offered an opinion, some heavily colored by confessional polemic, and many others totally unburdened by the evidence. It would serve no purpose to recount all these positions here. A few, however, are significant, and taken together they represent a loose consensus.

The modern discussion was inaugurated by Heinrich Denifle. In his *Luther und Luthertum in der ersten Entwicklung* of 1904, he argued that when it came to the scholastic tradition, Luther was a "Halbwisser," indeed an "Ignorant." As a student Luther had studied Thomas not at all; the later Luther had read bits and pieces for polemical reasons only.[2] Denifle's attack was almost

---

[1] With regard to Augustine, a foundation has been laid by Hans-Ulrich Delius, *Augustin als Quelle Luthers: Eine Materialsammlung*, (Berlin: Evangelische Verlagsanstalt, 1984).

[2] Heinrich Denifle, *Luther und Luthertum in der ersten Entwicklung*, 2 vols., Mainz: F. Kirchheim, 1904-09), I, pp.

immediately countered by Heinrich Boehmer. In his view, Luther had read not only Thomas' commentary on the *Sentences*, but also the *Summa Theologiae* and the *Summa Contra Gentiles*.[3] However, the evidence marshalled by Boehmer was slim and few found it convincing. Hartmann Grisar's vituperative study of 1911 reiterated Denifle's position: Luther was utterly ignorant of Thomas Aquinas.[4]

The discussion of the question remained mired in this context of extreme confessional polemic for almost thirty years. The work of Joseph Lortz then appeared in 1939 and shifted the focus of the debate, influencing an entire generation of Roman Catholic Luther-scholarship. Lortz argued that Luther reacted against a Catholicism that was not fully Catholic. Taking it for granted that Luther did not know Thomas, Lortz suggested that this lack of knowledge had tragic dimensions. For had he known Thomas, he would not have felt obliged to reject the entire scholastic tradition and the Church itself as heretical.[5]

While the Lortz-thesis was and remains controversial, his assumption about Luther's lack of knowledge of Thomas was not. Since Lortz, the vast majority of Luther-scholars have acquiesced in the view that Luther's knowledge of Thomas was minimal. In 1940, for instance, Wilhelm Link conceded that it was impossible to determine whether Luther ever read Thomas. At most, Link held, Luther may have come into contact with Thomist teaching through Aegidius Romanus and Johann Staupitz.[6] Others such as Meissinger (1952) reiterated this generally held view without adding anything more to the discussion.[7]

More significantly, in 1961 M. van Rhijn re-opened the question. Yet, after assessing the evidence available to him, he too arrived at what was by then the conventional judgement: Luther possessed only the most limited knowledge of Thomas.[8] And, meanwhile others such as Watson, Gerrish, McDonough, Vorster, etc. expressed similar opinions.[9] In 1969 Harry McSorley thoroughly reviewed the state of the question and correctly saw that the vast majority of Luther-scholars were in substantial agreement. While a few, such as F. Lau, have asserted the opposite point of view, no convincing evidence has been adduced to change the dominant opinion.[10]

Since McSorley's summation appeared in 1969, there has been no substantial change in the state of the question. Most scholars such as Walter Mostert[11] and Alister McGrath[12] repeat the conventional wisdom on this issue. And a few such as Martin Brecht, basing their view on slim evidence, continue to assert the opposite.[13] Nevertheless, the general consensus is that Luther's knowledge of Thomas was minimal.

522-590.

[3] Heinrich Boehmer, *Luther and the Reformation*, pp. 159ff. Boehmer's work first appeared in 1904.

[4] Hartmann Grisar, *Luther*, 3 vols., (Freiburg: Herder, 1911), I, p. 103.

[5] Joseph Lortz, *Die Reformation in Deutschland*, 2 vols., (Freiburg: Herder, 1962). First published in 1939.

[6] Wilhelm Link, *Das Ringen Luthers um die Freiheit der Theologie von der Philosophie*, (Munich: C. Kaiser, 1955), pp. 191ff. First published in 1940.

[7] K. A. Meissinger, *Der katholische Luther*, (Munich: Lehnen, 1952), p. 109.

[8] M. van Rhijn, "Kende Luther Thomas?", in *Nederlands Archief voor Kerkgeschiedenis*, 44 (1961), 153-156.

[9] The views of these scholars are summarized by Harry McSorley, *Luther: Right or Wrong?*, p. 140.

[10] *Ibid.*, pp. 139-141. Another minority opinion is that of Grane who follows R. Hermann in denying the importance of the question, since in Luther's view the differences between Thomas and the late scholastics are inconsequential. (*Ibid.*, p. 140).

[11] Walter Mostert, "Luther's Verhältnis zur theologischen und philosophischen Überlieferung," in H. Junghans, ed., *Martin Luther von 1526 bis 1546*, 2 vols., (Göttingen: Vandenhoeck und Ruprecht, 1983), I, pp. 347-368, p. 360.

[12] Alister McGrath, *Luther's Theology of the Cross: Martin Luther's Theological Breakthrough*, (Oxford: Blackwell, 1985), pp. 72f.

[13] Martin Brecht, *Martin Luther*, p. 94.

Given this virtual scholarly unanimity, what reason is there for a re-opening of the question? First, throughout the entire discussion some of the evidence has been clearly misinterpreted, while other evidence has been given a highly questionable interpretation. Second, and more importantly, the evidence adduced throughout the whole course of the debate has been piecemeal: none of the opinions in the discussion have been based on a thorough examination of all the evidence. In light of Luther's enormous literary output, this is perfectly understandable. But the recent compilation of complete indices to Luther's works now makes feasible for the first time a comprehensive treatment of the question. As this task is undertaken here, it should be understood from the outset that because of the nature of the case, the demand for absolutely conclusive evidence will go largely unfulfilled. In the absence of such conclusive evidence, the attempt here rather is to arrive at fair-minded and judicious assessments of the probabilities.

It would be a grave error to assume from the outset that Luther knew nothing at all of Thomas. The fact is that Luther was an intellectual, and in the world of ideas which surrounded him, those of Thomas Aquinas held a prominent place. Though Luther was trained in Occamism, this school by no means monopolized intellectual life in Germany in the early 16th century. The Thomist school, centered at Cologne, was also a vigorous and influential force. At Erfurt, where Luther studied, there were Thomists on the theological faculty. At Wittenberg too we know that in 1505, for instance, there were four Thomists, four Scotists and no Occamists on the theological faculty. And in 1508 the University of Wittenberg officially established three *viae* in the theological faculty: the *via Thomae*, the *via Scoti*, and the *via Gregorii*.[14] All of this clearly indicates that Thomism was an important element in Luther's intellectual milieu. This, coupled with Luther's "untiring intellectual curiosity,"[15] makes it implausible to suppose that Luther simply remained oblivious to Thomas' ideas.

Before inquiring into Luther's direct knowledge of Thomas, we must pay some attention to the possibility that Luther acquired at least some knowledge of Thomas through secondary sources. In order to do justice to this line of inquiry, one would have to survey the entire range of Luther's reading with a view to discerning what he could have learned about Thomas from it. Here we can only focus on what would appear to be the most likely sources.

On the face of it, the most obvious candidates would appear to be those who claimed to follow and represent the teaching of Thomas, members of the late medieval Thomist school.[16] The "father" of this school, Johannes Capreolus (d. 1444), was in all probability known to Luther only by name. Though Luther refers to him occasionally, there is no evidence that he had any first-hand knowledge of this eminent late medieval Thomist.[17] Henry of Gorkum (d. 1431), the founder of the 15th century Thomist school in Cologne, was also known to the early Luther, but only in an indirect way. Though Luther read one of his works in 1511, it does not seem to have left a lasting impression on him.[18] Conrad Koellin (d. 1536), the most important of the Cologne Thomists, was likewise virtually ignored by Luther. There is no evidence that Luther ever read his works.[19] Karlstadt, Luther's early Thomist colleague at Wittenberg, also scarcely qualifies as a transmitter of Thomas' ideas to Luther. There is much evidence to suggest, in fact, that after Karlstadt joined the cause of the Reformation, he presented a seriously distorted version of

---

[14] On this, see my *Luther and Late Medieval Thomism*, p. 8.
[15] Joseph Lortz, "The Basic Elements of Luther's Intellectual Style," p. 8.
[16] In what follows I summarize some of the conclusions of my earlier study, *Luther and Late Medieval Thomism*.
[17] *Ibid.*, pp. 88-91.
[18] *Ibid.*, pp. 92-99.
[19] *Ibid.*, pp. 100-110.

Thomas' teaching.[20] Nor was it through Cajetan that Luther encountered the teaching of Thomas. After his 1518 confrontation with Cajetan, Luther seems to have dismissed him as a theological opponent to be reckoned with. And even if he had read Cajetan's later works, he would have found there a serious distortion of Thomas' views on some crucial topics.[21] Luther, in short, did not encounter "the real Thomas" in any significant way in these eminent representatives of the late medieval Thomist school.

It is highly unlikely that other lesser Thomists transmitted Thomas' thought to Luther. Among his early Thomist colleagues at Wittenberg (besides Karlstadt), Petrus Lupinus (d. 1521) and Martin Pollich of Mellerstadt (d. 1513) could be considered. Luther perhaps had a vague idea of what went on in the lectures of such Thomist colleagues, but he certainly was not deeply impressed. Among his early Thomist opponents (besides Cajetan), Johann Tetzel, Silvester Prierias, Hieronymus Dungersheim, Ambrosius Catharinus, Jacob Hochstraten, and others could be mentioned. Luther's contempt for these opponents largely prevented him from reading their literary attacks. And when he occasionally did, he inevitably found there a presentation of Thomas' teaching which even he rightly suspected was a distortion. We have already seen ample evidence of this in the cases of Tetzel and Prierias. Luther's lesser Thomist opponents can in no way be seen as the link between him and the thought of Thomas Aquinas. If Luther ever seriously encountered the teaching of Thomas, it was not through the late medieval Thomist school.

The late medieval Augustinian school is another possibility. One of the most likely representatives of this *schola moderna Augustiniana* is Johannes von Paltz (1445-1511). Paltz was Professor of theology at Erfurt until 1505, the very year that Luther began his studies there. Thus Paltz may have briefly taught Luther in 1505. Bernd Hamm concedes that there is no proof that Luther ever read Paltz's works. Nevertheless, Hamm argues, he was certainly influenced by Paltz.[22] Paltz is significant in this context because his works are a relatively rich source for encountering the thought of Thomas Aquinas. Paltz cites Thomas "many hundreds of times," sometimes freely and sometimes word for word.[23] The fourth book of the *Sentences Commentary* is the work he cites most frequently, and citations of the *Summa Theologiae* are relatively few. Yet, in general, Thomas is Paltz's foremost scholastic authority: Thomas is cited more frequently than anyone else.[24] Though we have little indication of the reliability of Paltz's interpretation of Thomas, and though the lines of connection with Luther are not proven, we have here nevertheless at least a possibility for real encounter between Luther and the teaching of Thomas.

Another Augustinian that must be considered is Johannes von Staupitz. Unlike Paltz, Staupitz's influence on Luther is unquestionable. Already in 1927, Ernst Wolf described Staupitz as an "Augustinian Thomist" and suggested that Luther came to a good acquaintance with Thomas through Staupitz.[25] This view was reiterated by Wilhelm Link in 1940,[26] and then again by M. von Rhijn in 1961.[27] More recent scholarship, however, has called this view into question. David Steinmetz, while he acknowledges that Staupitz frequently cites Thomas, argues that Staupitz can

---

[20] *Ibid.*, pp. 111-122.

[21] *Ibid.*, pp. 123-153.

[22] Berndt Hamm, *Frömmigkeitstheologie am Anfang des 16. Jahrhunderts: Studien zu Johannes von Paltz und seinem Umkreis*, (Tübingen: Mohr, 1982), p. 332.

[23] *Ibid.*, p. 196.

[24] *Ibid.*, pp. 195f. Hamm points out that Johannes von Dorsten (d. 1481), Paltz's teacher, also cites Thomas more than any other authority. *Ibid.*, p. 213, n. 472.

[25] Ernst Wolf, *Staupitz und Luther. Ein Beitrag zur Theologie des Johannes von Staupitz und deren Bedeutung für Luthers theologische Werdegang*, (Leipzig: M. Heinsius, 1927).

[26] Wilhelm Link, *Das Ringen Luthers*, p. 192.

[27] M. van Rhijn, "Kende Luther Thomas?," pp. 153f.

in no way be considered a Thomist. Thus, "whatever else Staupitz may have been for Luther, he was not Luther's tenuous link to the world of late medieval Thomism."[28] While the important influence which Staupitz had on Luther lay elsewhere, it is nevertheless a possibility that Luther encountered at least some of Thomas' ideas in the writings of Staupitz. This, together with the example of Paltz, indicates that the role of the *schola moderna Augustiniana* in mediating Thomas to the reformer should not be ignored.

At first glance, the nominalist school may appear to be the least likely transmitter of Thomas' thought to Luther. Thus Alister McGrath has concluded that because Luther was trained in the *via moderna*, knowledge of Thomas Aquinas is "conspicuously absent" in him.[29] The supposition here is that nominalists paid little attention to the views of Thomas, and when they did, they were largely unreliable as interpreters.

One can indeed find examples to support this position. For instance, John Pupper von Goch (d. 1475) wrote a number of works in which, among other things, he attacked Thomas' theology as "Pelagian."[30] Luther, we know, read at least some of these works.[31] But, it can safely be said, he did not thereby come into contact with the "real Thomas," for as McSorley has demonstrated, Pupper's interpretation of Thomas was a seriously distorted one.[32] Moreover, Pupper can scarcely be considered a major influence on Luther.

Among more influential nominalists such as Pierre d'Ailly (d. 1420) the picture is not as clear. Luther certainly read d'Ailly,[33] and found there largely accurate accounts of Thomas' teaching. In his *Questiones* on the *Sentences*, d'Ailly cites Thomas' *Sentences Commentary*, the *Summa Theologiae* and the *opusculum* "De Potentia."[34] Though one cannot fault the accuracy of d'Ailly's interpretation, he to a large extent cites Thomas in order to disagree with him. And his citations of Thomas are relatively infrequent: one finds only fifteen of them in this "commentary" on the *Sentences*. Thus, while Luther may have learned something about Thomas from d'Ailly, it cannot have been extensive.

The same is not the case with Gabriel Biel (d. 1495). Biel was certainly the most influential of the nominalists in Luther's theological formation. Luther read Biel intensively: later in life he reports that when he did so, "my heart bled."[35] And Melanchthon reports that even in old age, Luther could still quote Biel from memory.[36] There can be no doubt that Luther had an extensive and detailed knowledge of Biel's writings. What did Luther learn of Thomas from this source?

John Farthing has recently offered a exhaustive assessment of Biel's use of Thomas in his *Collectorium* on the *Sentences* and *Canonis Missae Expositio*.[37] Surveying and evaluating all of Biel's Thomas-citations, Farthing comes to the conclusion that Biel's knowledge of Thomas was extraordinary. Thomas is cited a total of 421 times by Biel, and not merely in a superficial way.

---

[28] David Steinmetz, *Luther and Staupitz: An Essay in the Intellectual Origins of the Protestant Reformation*, (Durham, NC: Duke Univ. Press, 1980), p. 11. Cf. Steinmetz's *Misericordia Dei: The Theology of Johannes von Staupitz in Its Late Medieval Setting*, (Leiden: Brill, 1968), pp. 19-34.

[29] Alister McGrath, *Luther's Theology of the Cross*, pp. 72f.

[30] On Pupper, see David Steinmetz, "Libertas Christiana." Cf. Harry McSorley, "Thomas Aquinas, John Pupper von Goch, and Martin Luther."

[31] Cf. Luther's "Vorrede zu Gochii Fragmenta" (1522); WA 10 II, 329f.

[32] McSorley, "Thomas Aquinas, John Pupper von Goch, and Martin Luther," pp. 110-116.

[33] Cf. Heinrich Boehmer, *Luther and the Reformation*, p. 160.

[34] I rely here on John Farthing's "Preliminary Analysis" of d'Ailly's Thomas-citations in Appendix II of his "Post Thomam," pp. 341-347.

[35] WATR 3, 564, 5ff.

[36] Cited in Farthing, *Thomas Aquinas and Gabriel Biel*, pp. 199f, n. 11.

[37] For the following, see Farthing, *ibid.*, and especially his "Post Thomam," pp. 306-340. Cf. Lawrence Murphy, "Gabriel Biel as Transmitter of Aquinas to Luther," in *Renaissance and Reformation*, 19 (1983), 26-41.

Biel frequently quotes Thomas verbatim, explains Thomas' teaching at length, and seriously attempts to understand Thomas' point of view on almost all questions. Moreover, Biel refers to and quotes not only Thomas' *Sentences Commentary*, but also the *Summa Theologiae*, the commentaries on Romans and on the Gospel of Matthew, etc. Biel almost always gives an accurate reference for his citations (book, part, question, article, etc.) Nor does Biel simply cite Thomas in order to refute him: Farthing found that in 95% of these references, Biel is sympathetic to Thomas' teaching. And in assessing the accuracy of Biel's interpretation of Thomas, Farthing found that in almost 90% of these cases, no inaccuracy or distortion of Thomas' views can be discerned.

The most noteworthy exception to Biel's general accuracy in reporting Thomas's views is on the topic of the theology of nature and grace.[38] According to Farthing, "St. Thomas would not recognize as his own the doctrine of justification which Biel attributes to him. . .One whose primary access to the Thomist perspective is by way of Biel's interpretations will remain uninformed or misinformed about Thomas's doctrines of sin, grace and justification."[39] Because Biel is so accurate elsewhere, this particular glaring inaccuracy is puzzling. Perhaps it had consequences for the young Luther who did not hesitate to brand the scholastics in general as "Pelagian."

Nevertheless, this exception in Biel should not be allowed to obscure the fact that in the vast majority of cases Biel's presentation of Thomas' views is perfectly reliable. What this means is that one could indeed learn a considerable amount about Thomas by reading Gabriel Biel. The vast scope and general accuracy of Biel's Thomas-citations make it simply implausible that a reader of Luther's intelligence, reading Biel as intensively as Luther did, could remain ignorant of Thomas Aquinas. In Biel's works Luther was exposed to generally accurate presentations of Thomas' teaching. Thus it is quite incorrect to think that Luther remained ignorant of Thomas because he was trained in the *via moderna*. In fact, it was precisely in the *via moderna*, in studying the nominalist Gabriel Biel, that Luther learned more about Thomas than from any other secondary source.

Our survey of such sources for Luther's knowledge of Thomas is admittedly incomplete. It may well be that many minor secondary sources contributed to Luther's understanding in this regard. Nevertheless, what is already clear is that Luther did not come to know Thomas by way of the late medieval Thomist school. The contribution of the *schola moderna Augustiniana* to Luther's knowledge of Thomas may well have been more substantial. But it was above all in the nominalist Gabriel Biel that the young Luther was thoroughly exposed to Thomas' teaching. Even a brief survey such as this, therefore, sharply calls into question the view that Luther neither knew nor understood anything about Thomas.

When we begin to look at Luther's writings for evidence of his knowledge of Thomas Aquinas, we find in the first place that he is in possession of some miscellaneous factual information. Thus Luther was familiar with Thomas' view on the immaculate conception.[40] He knows that Thomas was a realist.[41] He seems to know of Thomas' late breakdown which decisively marked the end of his theological career.[42] He gives the correct date of Thomas' death.[43] He alludes in all probability to the condemnation of 1277.[44] And, as we have seen, he is also familiar with various legends about Thomas.[45] In short, Luther had at his fingertips a miscellany of facts

---

[38] Farthing, *Thomas Aquinas and Gabriel Biel*, pp. 150-180.
[39] *Ibid.*, p. 194.
[40] WA 1, 655, 37ff (1518).
[41] WATR 5, 653, 1ff (date unknown). Cf. WA 2, 604, 7ff (1519).
[42] WA 30 III, 562, 33ff (1533); WA 38, 148, 13ff (1533).
[43] WATR 5, 651, 7 (date unknown).
[44] WA 1, 611, 21ff (1518); WA 30 II, 383, 20 (1530).
[45] See above, Ch. I.

about Thomas. The scattered and incidental references to these facts in Luther's works probably indicates nothing more than that Luther knew what was common knowledge to most late 15th and early 16th century theologians trained in scholasticism.

One can also find other things Luther said which could be taken to imply some knowledge of Thomas. For instance, he compares Thomas to Scotus, Bonaventure and Biel, and concludes that Thomas is "more loquacious."[46] In 1518 he complains that the Thomists do not understand Thomas[47] and in later life, that no one understands Thomas anymore.[48] The obvious implication of such remarks is that in his own view, he knows and understands Thomas well.

We should also take note of the fact that Luther makes explicit claims in this regard. In 1521, Luther defends himself against Latomus' charge of ignorance. Speaking of Thomas, Luther says:

> I am convinced that my judgement in these matters is not entirely
> uninformed, for I have been well-trained in them; I have profited
> from the minds of my most learned contemporaries, and I have
> studied the best of this sort of literature.[49]

In 1530 Luther again explicitly defends his knowledge of Thomas. Speaking of the scholastics and especially of the greatest of them, Thomas, he reminds his readers that he "grew up" under these teachers and therefore knows them well.[50] And finally, in a table talk from early 1540, Luther tells his listeners that he read Thomas as a student.[51] Thus at various stages of his career Luther asserted his familiarity with Thomas. The historian rightly approaches such statements with a good measure of skepticism: clearly a "hermeneutic of suspicion" is in order. But neither should one simply dismiss Luther's claims as outright lies. Further evidence is required.

When we begin to ask what works of Thomas were actually read by Luther, it is important to recall that Luther does not explicitly cite or quote Thomas, nor does he tell us precisely which books he read. Thus, in this question, we are limited to possibilities and probabilities. The goal here is to judiciously assess both of these on the basis of the evidence available, exercising all the while extreme caution not to cross the line into the realm of pure conjecture.

First then, the possibilities must be established. What works of Thomas could Luther have read? Which writings of Thomas were readily available to Luther in either Erfurt or Wittenberg?

In the case of Erfurt, we are fortunate to have relatively complete listings of library holdings in the 15th and 16th centuries. Paul Lehmann, in 1928, published the catalogues from four Erfurt libraries: the Collegium Amplonianum, the Collegium Universitatis, the Karthause Salvatorberg and the Marienknechtskloster.[52] These listings indicate that there was available at Erfurt a collection of legends about Thomas, and this could well be the source of those that

---

[46] WATR 3, 564, 10f (1538).

[47] WA 1, 660, 5ff (1518).

[48] WA 44, 136, 6ff (1535-40).

[49] WA 8, 127, 21ff: "Arbitror igitur et mihi non esse penitus crassum in rebus istis iudicium, qui educatus in eis sim et coaetaneorum doctissimorum ingenia expertus, optima istius generis scripta contemplatus..."

[50] WA 30 II, 300, 21ff (1530): "Ich weis, das ich hie nicht liege, denn ich bin ja unter ihn auffgewachsen, hab solchs alles von ihn gesehen und gehöret. . . . Uber diese alle [Scotus und Occam] gehet Thomas Aquinas, Lerer aller lerer. . ."

[51] WATR 4, 610, 21ff (early 1540): "Ratio studiorum Lutheri . . . Scotum, Thomam, Aristotelem esse legendum. . ."

[52] Paul Lehmann, *Mittelalterliche Bibliothekskataloge.*

Luther uses.[53] As for Thomas' writings themselves, most of the minor *opuscula* were there. This includes Thomas' "De angelis,"[54] the "Officium de festo Corpus Christi,"[55] the "Contra retrahentes,"[56] etc. Many of Thomas' Aristotle commentaries were available, as were his commentaries on Boethius and Dionysius,[57] the various "Quaestiones Disputatae,"[58] and "Quaestiones de Quodlibet."[59] The whole range of Thomas' Scripture commentaries, including all the Pauline commentaries, was available.[60] There were roughly thirteen copies of the *Summa Contra Gentiles* in the Erfurt libraries.[61] They also held approximately nineteen full or partial copies of the *Sentences Commentary;*[62] and there were no less than forty full or partial copies of the *Summa Theologiae* in Erfurt![63] Finally, these libraries also had in their collections, tables and indices to the *Summa Theologiae,*[64] the so-called "Concordantia literature,"[65] and listings of topics on which there was general disagreement with Thomas' position.[66]

Unfortunately, our information on the library at the Augustinian cloister where Luther lived is only fragmentary.[67] Yet even in these partial listings, we find a representative selection of Thomas' writings.[68] Thus it is fair to conclude that quite likely Thomas' principal works were available to Luther in his own Erfurt cloister. More significantly, it is clear that when we speak of the Erfurt libraries in general, the vast majority of Thomas' works were readily accessible.

We would do well to pause here to draw another conclusion which is only indirectly related to the topic under discussion, but which is nevertheless significant for the history of Thomas-reception and interpretation. Most recent scholarship has followed Martin Grabmann in holding that it was only with the appearance of Cajetan's *Summa* commentary (completed in 1520) that the *Summa Theologiae* came to be widely regarded as Thomas' definitive and most important work.[69] Before Cajetan, Thomas' commentary on the *Sentences* was commonly accepted as his definitive writing. This view is called into question by the library holdings at Erfurt. For library holdings are surely some indication of what people read. And at Erfurt there were roughly twice as many copies of the *Summa Theologiae* as there were copies of the *Sentences Commentary*. This probably

---

[53] *Ibid.*, p. 557. The collection is entitled "Dulcis et brevis legenda de s. Thoma." On Luther's retelling of some of these stories, see above, Ch. I.

[54] *Ibid.*, p. 558; cf. p. 69.

[55] *Ibid.*, p. 557; cf. p. 137.

[56] *Ibid.*, pp. 463 and 558. Cf. pp. 557, 67, 68, and 182 for other *opuscula.*

[57] *Ibid.*, p. 558.

[58] *Ibid.*

[59] *Ibid.*, p. 68.

[60] *Ibid.*, p. 558.

[61] *Ibid.*, p. 799.

[62] *Ibid.*, p. 798.

[63] *Ibid.*, pp. 799f. In addition, many parts of the *Summa* were printed as individual and separate *opuscula.*

[64] *Ibid.*

[65] *Ibid.*, p. 558. On this literature, see my *Luther and Late Medieval Thomism,* pp. 62f.

[66] *Ibid.*, p. 463.

[67] Jan Matsuura, "Restbestände aus der Bibliothek des Erfurter Augustinerklosters zu Luthers Zeit und bisher Unbekannte Eigenhändige Notizen Luthers," in G. Hammer and K. H. Zur Mühlen, eds., *Lutheriana. Zum 500. Geburtstag Martin Luthers, von den Mitarbeitern der Weimarer Ausgabe,* (Cologne: Böhlau Verlag, 1984), pp. 315-332. Cf. Adolar Zumkeller, "Handschriften aus dem Ehemaligen Erfurter Augustinerkloster in der Staatsbibliothek Berlin -- Preussischer Kulturbesitz. Neue Aufschlüsse über Johannes von Dorsten OSA (d. 1481)," in *Analecta Augustiniana,* 40 (1977), 223-277.

[68] See Matsuura, "Restbestände," pp. 318f, 322f, and 326f. Cf also Zumkeller, "Handschriften," p. 239.

[69] Martin Grabmann, "Die Stellung des Kardinals Cajetan in der Geschichte des Thomismus und der Thomistenschule," in his *Mittelalterliches Geistesleben: Abhandlungen zur Geschichte der Scholastik und Mystik,* 3 vols., (Munich: M. Hueber, 1926-56), I, pp. 332-391.

means that in the early 16th century at Erfurt, the *Summa* had already replaced the *Sentences* as Thomas' most commonly read work.

It is also important to consider what works of Thomas were available to Luther at the University of Wittenberg. Regrettably, the evidence is not as complete in this case as it is for Erfurt. The University of Wittenberg, founded in 1502, was much younger than the University of Erfurt and therefore in all likelihood did not have as extensive a library collection in the early 16th century. Nevertheless, from its foundation until 1508, only two *viae* were represented in the theological faculty: the *via Scoti* and the *via Thomae*.[70] Thus it is very likely that the writings of Thomas were among the first library acquisitions. It is almost inconceivable that the *via Thomae* could be taught at Wittenberg for approximately fifteen years without ready access to most if not all of Thomas' writings. This is reflected in at least one of the extant catalogues covering the period 1512-1547. Here, under the heading "Theologia Latina," one finds the name of Thomas Aquinas listed more frequently than any other name, except for Albertus Magnus.[71] Though we do not know precisely which works of Thomas were there, it is safe to conclude that a wide range of Thomas' writings were accessible to Luther in the Wittenberg library. At both Erfurt and Wittenberg Luther easily *could* have read the writings of Thomas had he been inclined to do so.

One further intriguing possibility is that Luther himself possessed a copy of the *Summa Theologiae*. The key event that suggests this is the Wittenberg book-burning of 10 December 1520. It is clear that Luther himself wanted to burn the papal bull, the books of canon law, and perhaps also the *Summa Angelica* of Angelus de Clavassio. Johann Agricola was in charge of organizing the event, and we know that on the morning of December 10, "he was still trying to collect Thomas Aquinas' *Summa* and Duns Scotus' commentary on the *Sentences* from the Wittenberg theologians."[72] But not one of the Wittenberg theologians was willing to part with his copy! The implications are clear: first, some Wittenberg theologians in 1520 possessed a copy of the *Summa Theologiae*. And if this is true, is it not plausible that Wittenberg's star theologian himself possessed a copy? The second telling detail is that none who owned a copy were willing to part with it. And this may very well apply to Luther himself. In any case, it is significant that while the circle of Wittenberg theologians in 1520 were willing to dispose of a good number of books, they were reluctant to consign the works of Thomas to the flames.

It has now been established that Luther could have read the writings of Thomas both at Erfurt and at Wittenberg. But what is the likelihood of his having done so? This is certainly the most decisive question. At the same time it is the most difficult, for in general the evidence is less than conclusive. Nevertheless, the available indications must be pointed out here, and an attempt made to draw conclusions with regard to these probabilities.

The various editions of Luther's works occasionally represent statements as quotations from Thomas. Upon closer examination these all turn out to be incorrect: they are all summaries, or at most paraphrases of Thomas. All, that is, except one: Luther in 1521 gives a direct quotation of Thomas' hymn "Verbum Supernum," albeit in German translation, without citing Thomas as the

---

[70] For further details and documentation, see my *Luther and Late Medieval Thomism*, pp. 112f.

[71] Ernst Hildebrandt, "Die kurfürstliche Schloss-und Universitätsbibliothek zu Wittenberg, 1512-1547," in *Zeitschrift für Buchkunde*, 2 (1925), 34-42, 109-129, 157-188. See pp. 159, 163 and 173.

[72] Martin Brecht, *Martin Luther*, p. 423. For further details and documentation, see *ibid.*, pp. 423ff, and p. 533. Note that in 1538, speaking about Thomas, Scotus, Bonaventure, Biel and Occam, Luther asserted: "I still have the books that used to torment me so." WATR 3, 564, 7f; tr. from LW 54, 264.

author, and in the context of refuting Thomas' view![73] This is the single quotation from Thomas that is to be found in Luther's works, and it sheds little if any light on our present question. For this hymn was thoroughly integrated into the body of "common knowledge" by the 16th century.

Thomas' Aristotle commentaries were also widely known and used in the early 16th century. They were the foundation of courses taught at Wittenberg during Luther's early years there, and thus it comes as no surprise that Luther was familiar with them. He was to some extent aware of what went on in the courses of his colleagues. But what Luther knew of Thomas' Aristotle commentaries he quickly came to dislike, so much so that he mounted a campaign in 1518 and 1519 to have them dropped from the curriculum.[74] Elsewhere, Luther implies that he is familiar with Thomas' commentaries on Aristotle: in 1520, he bluntly asserts that he knows Aristotle better than Thomas did. Such a claim clearly carries with it the implication that he has studied Thomas' Aristotle commentaries.[75] Yet we have no direct evidence that Luther was well-read in these works. And indeed, there are some indications to the contrary. For instance, Luther more than once accuses Thomas of following Averroes,[76] and yet he shows no awareness of Thomas' critique of Averroes. A thorough reading of Thomas' Aristotle commentaries would make one aware of this. Furthermore, we have already shown that Luther's understanding of the way in which Thomas used Aristotle was inadequate.[77] But we have also seen that Luther's lack of comprehension in this regard was equalled or even exceeded by some leading Thomists, such as Prierias.[78] The picture is therefore clouded. Luther probably lacked an extensive first-hand knowledge of Thomas' Aristotle commentaries. Comparatively speaking, his acquaintance with these writings fell far below the level of a contemporary such as Cajetan. And yet it may have been equal or better than that of some Thomists such as Prierias.

Luther's knowledge of Thomas' Scripture commentaries is equally dubious. He read and used the *Glossa Ordinaria* of course, and mistakenly attributed it to Thomas. This is in itself revealing since Thomas cites the *Glossa Ordinaria* in his own commentaries. Thus wide reading in Thomas' commentaries should suggest to the reader that the *Glossa Ordinaria* is not from Thomas' hand. Still, this mistaken attribution was a common one in the 16th century: in ascribing it to Thomas, Luther was following a widely held opinion.

Luther was doubtlessly aware of Thomas' commentaries on Scripture, but there is no evidence to indicate that he read them. He refers several times to the Pauline commentaries which seemed in the 1520's to be gaining in popularity. They were reprinted at least three times between 1522-32,[79] and Luther reports in 1522 that according to the Thomists, no one wrote better on St. Paul than Thomas.[80] Luther disagrees, adding that Thomas' Pauline commentaries

---

[73] WA 7, 391, 16ff (1521). For full details and documentation see the section on the Lord's Supper above, Ch. II. In addition one also finds in Luther's works two possible allusions to Thomas' hymn "Adoro te devote" (Vivès 32, 823). The first occurs in a sermon of 1523 (WA 12, 291, 11ff), and the second in a sermon from 1537 (WA 47, 172, 15f). Again, this hymn was well known in the early 16th century; modern scholars question its authenticity (Chenu, *Toward Understanding Saint Thomas*, p. 344). Furthermore, the allusion is so vague as to tell us nothing about Luther's knowledge of Thomas.

[74] WABR 1, 262, 3ff (1518); 1, 349, 13ff (1519); 1, 350, 23ff (1519); and possibly also WA 1, 651, 1 (1518).

[75] WA 6, 458, 18ff (1520).

[76] WA 25, 219, 13ff (1532-34); and WA 43, 94, 3ff (1535-45).

[77] See the section on Aristotle above, Ch. II.

[78] *Ibid.*

[79] H. Jedin, *A History of the Council of Trent*, I, p. 366.

[80] WA 10 II, 309, 12ff (1522).

"betray Christ."[81] How this could be flatly asserted without perusing these works is an open question. But there is no direct evidence to indicate that Luther ever did.

On the face of it, it is more likely that Luther possessed a more extensive acquaintance with Thomas' commentary on the *Sentences* of Peter Lombard. For this work was believed at least by some to be Thomas' principal work. Luther was of course well aware of its existence; according to him, Thomas was one of the first to write a commentary on Lombard's *Sentences*.[82] While Luther could well have consulted this work as a student, there is no direct evidence of thorough reading. This is only implied in some of Luther's statements. For instance, when Luther says that Scotus' *Sentences* commentary is better than that of Thomas,[83] the clear implication is that he has read both. The evidence, however, only permits us to conclude that Luther probably had a basic familiarity with the work.

The various *opuscula* of Thomas, though available, were not widely read or cited in early 16th century theological circles. Even in the writings of self-avowed Thomists, one rarely comes across references of these works. Thus it is all the more surprising that Luther displays a first-hand knowledge of one of them, namely the small work bearing the title "De Substantiis Separatis," or alternatively "De Angelis."[84] In 1529 Luther first referred to this work as "De Substantia Angelorum," a conflation of its two titles.[85] But when he once again spoke of this work in 1532-33, he correctly gave the title as "De Angelis."[86] The earliest editors of Luther's writings did not render these as titles, probably because they were not aware that Thomas had written such a work. But Luther's references are almost certainly to this *opusculum*: he names it, and he refers to teachings of Thomas which are found in this work.[87] Moreover, it is unlikely that Luther's knowledge in this case comes from a secondary source. This *opusculum* is rarely cited even by 16th century Thomists, nor do others such as Biel use it. Luther must have had occasion at some point to read it. His recollection of this work is an incidental one, and thus it is quite possible that Luther had read more of the *opuscula* than just this one. In any case, it must be acknowledged that it was not common for non-Thomist theologians in the early 16th century to have read Thomas' *opusculum* "De Angelis."

There is also strong evidence to suggest that Luther read at least parts of the *Summa Contra Gentiles*. First, in a sermon on Genesis 29 in 1523-24, Luther reports Thomas' view on Jacob's perfect virtue despite his incontinence.[88] Although Luther's recollection here is not perfectly accurate, it is nevertheless significant for it is a small detail in a large body of writings. It is referred to by Thomas only once, in the *Summa Contra Gentiles*.[89] It is not mentioned in the *Sentences* commentary, the *Summa Theologiae*, or the *Glossa Ordinaria*. Nor is this teaching of Thomas passed on by Biel, who does not use the *Summa Contra Gentiles*. It seems likely, therefore, that Luther read the work for himself, or at least parts of it. And his recollection of this minor point suggests that his knowledge of the work was not superficial.

Second, in a table talk of 1532 Luther compares the *Summa Contra Gentiles* with the *Summa Theologiae*. In his view, the *Summa Contra Gentiles* was more widely read "in the schools."

---

[81] WA 10 II, 310, 12ff (1522). For another possible reference to Thomas' Pauline commentaries, see WA 5, 644, 19ff (1519-21).

[82] WA 36, 511, 6ff (1532).

[83] WATR 1, 117, 31f (1532).

[84] For full details and documentation on what follows, see the section on Angels above, Ch. II.

[85] WA 29, 673, 17ff (1529).

[86] WA 40 III, 50, 19ff (1532-33).

[87] Again, details and documentation are to be found in the section on Angels above, Ch. II.

[88] WA 14, 405, 1ff (1523-24). For full details and documentation, see the section on Scripture above, Ch. II.

[89] *SCG* III, 137 (Vivès 12, 439).

But, while he finds the *Summa Theologiae* "tolerable," the *Summa Contra Gentiles* is "ridiculous."[90] A comparison such as this strongly suggests some knowledge of the two works. Luther's remark is not simply a derisive statement about Thomas' writings in general. He knows that they vary in quality, and he is familiar enough with them to clearly prefer some over others. This is hardly the kind of remark one would expect from one who knew nothing specific about these books.

Third, Luther shows some knowledge of the nature and purpose of the work. In a table talk from 1533, he refers to the *Summa Contra Gentiles* as Thomas' "catechism."[91] While historians today continue to debate its precise character, it is quite correct to see this book in general as a "catechism," intended to teach the structures of faith to non-Christians.

Fourth, in this same table talk from 1533 Luther mentions a minor point which Thomas makes in the *Summa Contra Gentiles*. According to Luther, Thomas teaches here that infused faith and mortal sin can co-exist in the same person.[92] Thomas does indeed say this in the work.[93] But what is more, it is a minor detail: only one sentence in the entire book deals with the issue! Luther's recollection here is difficult to reconcile with the view that he had only a general familiarity with the work.

Indeed we have already suggested the hypothesis that sometime between the years of 1522 and 1528, Luther read the treatise on grace in the *Summa Contra Gentiles*.[94] While this hypothesis is an attempt to account for the evidence, it cannot be conclusively proven. Nevertheless, it remains highly probable that Luther at some point in his career read widely in the *Summa Contra Gentiles*.

A strong case can also be made for Luther's having a first-hand knowledge of the *Summa Theologiae*. Before summarizing the evidence for such a claim, it will be necessary to dispel certain confusions and misconceptions which have played a large role in the scholarly discussion to date. The first of these has to do with Angelus de Clavassio (d. 1495) and his *Summa de casibus conscientiae*. In the early 16th century this work was widely known and referred to as the *Summa Angelica*, and thus it became a source of confusion for later interpreters.

Some modern scholars for instance mistook it for Thomas' *Summa Theologiae*. Thus when Luther mentioned it, they assumed he was referring to Thomas. So, for instance, when Luther speaks of the *Summa Angelica* in his lectures on Isaiah of 1527-30,[95] Wilhelm Link in 1940 regarded this as the one indication which clearly attested to a reading of Thomas![96] Translations of the passage, in the meantime, did nothing to correct the error:

> I spent a great deal of work on the angelic summary for the scholastic theology. [Multum enim opere in angelicam impendi summam ad scolasticam illam theologiam.][97]

---

[90] WATR 1, 117, 31ff (8 June 1532): ". . . Secunda secundae und prima primae war leydlich, aber man lase es selten in scholis. Interim legebantur ridiculi libri contra gentiles etc." More will be said about the "prima primae" below, in connection with the *Summa Theologiae*.

[91] WATR 1, 191, 11ff (1533): "Summa Thomae contra Gentiles, dies ist sein catechismus. . ."

[92] *Ibid*. The quote continues: ". . . ibi dicit fidem infusam posse stare cum peccato mortali. Quo quid potest magis dici impium?"

[93] *SCG* III, 154 (Vivès 12, 461). For full details and documentation see the section on Justification above, Ch. II.

[94] Book III, caps. 147-163 (Vivès 12, 449-468). See the section on Justification above, Ch. II.

[95] WA 31 II, 454, 16ff: "Multo enim opere in angelicam impendi summam ad scolasticam illam theologiam. Expertus tamen sum, quod nihil effecerim." This statement occurs in the context of a discussion of pacifying the troubled conscience.

[96] Wilhelm Link, *Das Ringen Luthers*, p. 192, n.3.

[97] LW 17, 250.

More recently scholars such as M. van Rhijn cited the same passage as an indication that Luther had read Thomas.[98] But clearly the statement has nothing whatsoever to do with Thomas' *Summa*.

To complicate matters, other scholars have attributed the error to Luther himself. Thus some have held that Luther confused the *Summa Angelica* of Angelus de Clavassio with the *Summa Theologiae* of Thomas. And this is then taken to be a clear indication of Luther's ignorance of Thomas! Such a blunder would of course indicate that Luther was familiar with neither the *Summa Theologiae* nor the *Summa Angelica*. But there is no evidence of such a mix up in Luther, and in fact many indications to the contrary.

Luther frequently mentioned the *Summa Angelica* of Angelus de Clavassio. In fact, this is one of the books which he had consigned to the flames along with the books of canon law in 1520. It was a popular manual for confessors, "which Luther believed shared the responsibility for the great Anfechtungen which contemporary confessional practice induced."[99] Precisely because this work was so intimately related to his own experience, it was one of the few books that he truly despised. He was only too familiar with it. Nor can we say that he confused the work with Thomas' *Summa*. For instance, in a 1518 sermon, Angelus is mentioned as one of the *followers* of Thomas.[100] And in his "Explanations of the 95 Theses" of the same year, Luther clearly distinguishes between the two, citing first Angelus' opinion and then naming Thomas as the source of this opinion.[101] Again in the same work Luther says that Angelus follows the opinion of Francisco de Mayronis, who was born after Thomas' death.[102] There is no need to multiply evidence such as this. Clearly, Luther knew Angelus de Clavassio, and could not have confused the *Summa Angelica* with Thomas' *Summa Theologiae*.

Another piece of evidence which has played a large role in the scholarly discussion of Luther's knowledge of Thomas is the fact that he used the term "prima primae" in referring to the *Summa Theologiae*: "The secunda secundae and prima primae were tolerable, but one seldom read them in school."[103] One who used the term "prima primae," so the argument goes, can have only the most minimal familiarity with the *Summa* because there is no such part in the book. At first sight this seems to be a telling indicator: no one who knows Thomas would make such a mistake.

Yet the argument is called into question, first, by the mere fact that Luther's words occur in the table talk. They are thus a *report* of what Luther said. This particular remark is one recorded by Viet Dietrich, who lived in Luther's home and served for a time as his amanuensis. Though Dietrich is now given credit for generally capturing the substance of Luther's remarks, he took only skeletal notes in these conversations and filled in the details later. Though his accounts are "reasonably trustworthy in reporting the subject matter and the directions which the conversation took," they do not "reproduce word for word what was actually said at Luther's table."[104] Thus it is extremely hazardous to build an argument on one word in the table talk (in this case, the word "primae"). Moreover, it is highly unlikely that Dietrich himself knew much about Thomas or his works. (He was educated at Wittenberg between 1522-29, when Thomas was not part of the curriculum.) He was quite capable of making the error which has traditionally been attributed to Luther.

---

[98] M. van Rhijn, "Kende Luther Thomas?", p. 153.

[99] M. Brecht, *Martin Luther*, p. 424.

[100] WA 1, 384, 14ff.

[101] WA 1, 568, 4ff.

[102] WA 1, 568, 1ff. Mayronis' dates are ca. 1280-1327.

[103] WATR 1, 117, 31ff (8 June 1532), quoted above n. 90. LW 54, 39 translates this as "The second question of Part II and the first question of Part I . . ." This is clearly mistaken.

[104] Theodore Tappert, "Introduction to Volume 54," in LW 54, p. xxiii.

Then too, the argument fails to take into account the widespread use of these terms in the scholastic tradition in which Luther was trained. We have already described Biel's extensive and largely accurate use of Thomas Aquinas. In referring to Thomas, Biel constantly uses the terms "prima pars," "prima secundae," "secunda secundae," and "tertia pars."[105] It is difficult to see how one could read Biel, let alone "memorize" him without becoming familiar with these terms. The same usage is common in Pierre d'Ailly and others whom Luther doubtlessly read. And one also finds this usage among Luther's early Thomist opponents, and even in letters written to Luther.[106] In short, the terms are so much part of the early 16th century scholastic milieu that Luther would have to have been extraordinarily obtuse had he not been familiar with them. It is highly unlikely that the "prima primae" error is his.

In addition, the context in which this remark occurs makes it improbable. Luther is comparing parts of the *Summa Theologiae* with another work by Thomas. He clearly prefers the *Summa* or at least some sections of it. And he complains that it is seldom read in the schools.[107] Such a comparison between two of Thomas' works makes no sense unless Luther knows something about both of them. Otherwise, why would he not simply dismiss *both* works as "ridiculous," instead of singling out one of them? And furthermore, his complaint that the *Summa Theologiae* is seldom read in the schools is utter nonsense if we suppose that he does not even know the most basic things about that work. In fact, no sense can be made out of this particular table talk if we assume the view that Luther knew nothing of the *Summa Theologiae* and that he utterly despised it.

As we shall see, there is some evidence that Luther read at least parts of the *Summa Theologiae*. This evidence too speaks against the view that Luther made the inexcusable blunder of using the term "prima primae," and thereby demonstrated his ignorance of the *Summa Theologiae*. But if he did not say "prima primae," as I have argued, and if the error is to be attributed to Viet Dietrich, then what did Luther really say? There are really only two possibilities: either "prima pars" or "prima secundae." My own surmise is that Luther said "prima secundae." The remark would then have been: "the secunda secundae and the prima secundae were tolerable..." This interpretation I think is preferable to "prima pars" because it seems clear that Luther would have sooner designated the *prima secundae* as "tolerable" than the *prima pars*. To say this, of course, is to imply that Thomas' teaching on topics like human psychology, law, and grace was more tolerable to Luther than his teaching on topics like natural theology, theology of creation, and angelology. Luther's actual critique of Thomas on some of these issues seems to bear this out.[108]

The direct evidence for Luther having read at least parts of the *Summa Theologiae* can be briefly summarized. In the same table talk of 8 June 1532, Luther recounts how as a young student theologian, he was required to take one question, and from it prepare nine corollaries. Taking the two words "God created," he turned to Thomas and found there one hundred questions on the topic.[109] This incidental recollection of Luther means, first of all, that Luther may well have also turned to Thomas in other cases. Second, it is almost certainly a reference to the *Summa Theologiae*: there are nowhere near this many questions on creation in the *Summa Contra*

---

[105] For examples see John Farthing, *Thomas Aquinas and Gabriel Biel*, p. 224, n. 27; p. 201, n. 24; p. 202, n. 26; p. 207, n. 12.

[106] E.g. WABR 2, 22, 671 (1520). Hieronymus Dungersheim to Luther.

[107] See quotation above, n. 90.

[108] See the relevant sections above, Ch. II.

[109] WABR 1, 177, 31ff (8 June 1532): ". . . Cum essem iuvenis theologus et deberem facere ex una quaestione novem corrolaria, accipiebam haec duo vocabula: Deus creavit, da gab mir Thomas wol 100 quaestiones drauff. . ."

Gentiles, and the *Sentences Commentary* treats at most some seventy questions on creation. In the *Summa Theologiae*, on the other hand, there are more than one hundred questions on creation in the *prima pars*. Thus, it must have been to this work that Luther turned. Luther certainly knew the content of the *prima pars*, and it is highly probable that at some point he read widely in it.

This is corroborated by evidence from a sermon preached by Luther on December 26, 1537. Here he refers to Thomas' speculation on how angels communicate.[110] This is almost certainly a reference to Thomas' treatment of the issue in the *prima pars*, question 107. For there is no other likely place where Thomas treats this question, nor does Biel refer to Thomas on this question.[111] Thus we have here in Luther a clear and impressive recollection of a relatively obscure question in the *prima pars* of the *Summa*. This is not what one would expect from a person who possessed merely a cursory overview of the work.

In regard to the *prima secundae* and *secunda secundae*, we have already argued that Luther saw these as "tolerable," and preferable to the *Summa Contra Gentiles*. It is important to underscore the fact that Luther did not utterly despise the *Summa Theologiae* or regard it as worthless. One senses here a grudging recognition of greatness even in a book which contained, from his point of view, great error. And we recall too that Luther did *not* want to burn it along with other books of scholastic theology and canon law in 1520.

There is also reason to believe that Luther was familiar with the contents of the *secunda secundae*. In another table talk from 1532, Luther indicates his awareness that it deals with moral matters.[112] This kind of evidence should no longer be surprising. Indeed, in the light of Biel's extensive and wide-ranging summaries alone, it would be astonishing if Luther did *not* know what the *secunda secundae* contained.

Finally, we also find in Luther some indication of a knowledge of the *tertia pars*. In connection with a critique of Thomas' view on baptism in a sermon in 1538, Luther actually summarizes Thomas' teaching in question 62, article 4.[113] Again, this is a minor section in the *tertia pars* and Luther's knowledge of it is impressive. It may be a surprisingly accurate recollection of something read many years earlier. More likely, as I have argued, Luther consulted the *Summa* as he prepared for this sermon.

The foregoing considerations make it utterly implausible to suggest that Luther knew nothing of the *Summa Theologiae*. Luther almost certainly read at least parts of this work, and thus it must be included in the inventory of those works of Thomas with which Luther had a firsthand acquaintance. Likewise, as I have suggested, the *Summa Contra Gentiles* and the *opusculum* "De Angelis" should be included in this inventory. There is considerably less reason to believe that Luther had firsthand knowledge of Thomas' commentary on the *Sentences*, his Scripture commentaries, and his commentaries on Aristotle. While Luther was familiar with these works, one could not make the claim that he read widely in them. In the final analysis, therefore, it can be said that Luther acquired a considerable knowledge of Thomas by reading at least some of his principal works. This knowledge, along with that gleaned from secondary sources, may not add up to what one might call expertise in Thomas Aquinas. Nevertheless, these sources gave Luther substantial exposure to the theology of Thomas. Denifle's characterizations of Luther as an "Ignorant" or a "Halbwisser" are, in this case, clearly inappropriate.

---

[110] WA 45, 351, 20ff.

[111] For details and documentation see the section on Angels above, Ch. II.

[112] WATR 1, 135, 11f (Summer/Fall 1532): "In moralibus Scotus et Occam idem sunt. Scotus in quatuor sententiarum, Thomas in secunda secundae maxime laudantur."

[113] WA 46, 168, 8ff. For full details and documentation see the section on Baptism above, Ch. II.

Admittedly, it is one thing to read Thomas or to read about Thomas, and quite another to fully understand his theology. In the present context I have not dealt with the depth of Luther's understanding of Thomas. This was one of the subjects of inquiry in Chapter II, and here only the briefest recapitulation of the results is necessary. On the subject of experience, Luther accurately perceived a fundamental difference between Thomas and himself, and this perception entails a good understanding of Thomas's theological method. Luther's appreciation of the way in which Thomas used Aristotle was inadequate, but nevertheless better than that of some Thomists such as Prierias. Luther showed only slight interest in Thomas' exegetical method. On indulgences, Luther again grasped Thomas' teaching better than some of his Thomist opponents; and on penance, while Luther was at some points misled by these Thomists, he at the same time rightly questioned their comprehension of Thomas. On the Lord's Supper, Luther's understanding in all probability was derived largely from Gabriel Biel, and it was substantially accurate. There are minor errors in Luther's understanding of Thomas on monastic vows, but over all, it is substantially correct; he probably read Thomas on this subject shortly before 1523. On justification the understanding of the young Luther was oversimplified and far from accurate, probably due to his dependence on Biel; after being exposed to Thomas' teaching, probably in the *Summa Contra Gentiles* in the mid-1520's, his misconceptions seem to have been corrected to some extent. On the subject of law, Luther seriously misapprehended Thomas, probably due again to his reliance on Biel and Usingen. On baptism, Luther's understanding of Thomas was technically correct but nevertheless distorted. Luther's grasp of Thomas' teaching on the subject of angels was accurate. On the subject of papal authority we find in Luther a minor distortion, probably attributable to the extreme papalism which was almost unanimous among contemporary Thomists. Luther's understanding of Thomas on purgatory was correct. And finally, Luther's assimilation of Thomas' doctrine of images was likewise accurate. Thus on many of the topics examined in this study, Luther's understanding of Thomas cannot be faulted. Not only did Luther read a considerable amount by and about Thomas, but his understanding of Thomas in general was not superficial.

One final dimension of the entire issue should not escape our attention. When we speak of Luther's knowledge of Thomas Aquinas, we are always speaking in comparative terms, whether consciously or unconsciously. Thus when it is said that Luther's knowledge is "considerable" or "substantial," the question is "in comparison to what?" Surely it would be inappropriate to measure Luther's knowledge against the standard of 20th century Thomas-scholarship, though ultimately it is from this vantage point that all final judgments of accuracy must be made.[114] The appropriate comparisons are obviously Luther's 16th century contemporaries. Thus, in saying that Luther possessed a relatively substantial knowledge of Thomas, we mean this to be understood with reference to other early 16th century theologians. Due to the present state of scholarship, we know little about other 16th century theologians' knowledge of Thomas. While full comparisons must await this future research, a few suggestions along these lines may help to indicate direction and orientation.

It can be said categorically that Luther's knowledge of Thomas is superior to all 16th century theologians with a non-scholastic, humanistic background. Philip Melanchthon may serve as an appropriate test case. Melanchthon quotes Thomas in his *Apology for the Augsburg Confession*,[115] and we know that he consulted Thomas' works in preparing his lectures on the Gospel of John.[116] Yet is would be folly to suppose that he had deep familiarity with Thomas' thought. The same could be said of John Calvin. There are a total of five references to Thomas

---

[114] For further elucidation of the hermeneutical problem involved here, see above, Introduction.
[115] Tappert, *Book of Concord*, p. 260.
[116] David Steinmetz, *Luther in Context*, (Bloomington: Indiana Univ. Press, 1986), p. 58.

in his *Institutes* and various commentaries.[117] His "scholastic opponent" is, in fact, a straw man -
- an artificial construct that corresponds to no actual scholastic.[118] It is safe to say that his grasp
of Thomas' thought was minimal. Neither one of these humanist-trained theologians can rival
Luther when it comes to knowing Thomas Aquinas.

Turning to scholastic-trained theologians in the early 16th century, the Thomists are the
ones which would logically be expected to surpass Luther in their knowledge of Thomas. Many
of the more prominent among their number -- Cajetan for instance -- certainly do.[119] Here there
is no comparison. But the same is not necessarily true for some of the lesser Thomists of that
age. Karlstadt, in his years as a Thomist, seems to have seriously misunderstood Thomas.[120] And
we have seen in the present study how Thomists such as Prierias and Tetzel were in some cases
less reliable interpreters of Thomas than Luther.[121]

The fairest comparison would certainly be to non-Thomist, scholastic-trained theologians in
the 16th century such as John Eck. While our conclusions about Eck's knowledge of Thomas must
remain provisional until a complete analysis is done, a cursory look at some of his principal works
is already revealing. In his Vienna disputation of 1517, the only references to Thomas are found
in six theses directed against him.[122] Eck's 1518 response to Karlstadt contains no mention of
Thomas.[123] *De Sacraficio Missae* (1526) has five references to Thomas' well-known treatment of
the issue in the *Tertia Pars*.[124] Eck's *Enchiridion* (1525-43) refers to Thomas a total of eight times
either in the text or in the marginalia.[125] A selection of Eck's German writings mentions Thomas
not at all.[126] The same is true of a sample of his exegetical work.[127] In his 1538 *Epistola de
Ratione Studiorum Suorum* Eck reports that in 1502 he heard the Thomist Dietrich von Süstern's
lectures on the *Summa Theologiae*.[128] And finally, in his annotations on the first book of
Lombard's *Sentences*, we find a total of eight references to Thomas.[129] Though this survey is
incomplete, a general picture already begins to emerge from it. To begin with, it is clear that Eck
read some of Thomas' writings firsthand. Not only did Eck receive his training in the scholastic
tradition, but he remained committed to it until the end of his life. Obviously he valued Thomas'
views and in all probability continued to consult Thomas' works throughout his career. At the
same time, it must be acknowledged that we do not find a wealth of Thomas-citations in Eck.
Moreover, Eck was thoroughly familiar with Biel, and at least some of his Thomas-citations come

---

[117] Armand LaVallee, "Calvin's Criticism of Scholastic Theology," (Harvard Univ Dissertation, 1967), p. 263.

[118] *Ibid.*, p. 237.

[119] See my *Luther and Late Medieval Thomism*, pp. 123-153.

[120] *Ibid.*, pp. 111-122.

[121] See e.g. the section on Penance and Indulgences above, Ch. II.

[122] Johannes Eck, *Disputatio Viennae Pannoniae Habita (1517)*, ed. Therese Virnich, CC 6, (Münster: Aschendorff, 1923).

[123] Johannes Eck, *Defensio Contra Amarulentas D.Andreae Bodenstein Carolstatini Invectiones (1518)*, ed. Joseph Greving, CC 1, (Münster: Aschendorff, 1919).

[124] Johannes Eck, *De Sacrificio Missae Libri Tres* (1526), eds. Erwin Iserloh, Vinzenz Pfnür and Peter Fabisch, CC 36, (Münster: Aschendorff, 1982).

[125] Johannes Eck, *Enchiridion Locorum Communium Adversus Lutherum et Alios Hostes Ecclesiae (1523-1543)*, ed. Pierre Fraenkel, CC 34, (Münster: Aschendorff, 1979).

[126] Johannes Eck, *Vier Deutsche Schriften Gegen Martin Luther, den Bürgermeister und Rat von Konstanz, Ambrosius Blarer und Konrad Sam*, eds. Karl Meisen and Friedrich Zoepfl, CC 14, (Münster: Aschendorff, 1929).

[127] Johannes Eck, *Explanatio Psalmi Vigesimi (1538)*, ed. Bernhard Walde, CC 13, (Münster: Aschendorff, 1928).

[128] Johannes Eck, *Epistola de Ratione Studiorum Suorum (1538)*, ed. Johannes Metzier, CC 2, (Münster: Aschendorff, 1921).

[129] Johannes Eck, *In Primum Librum Sententiarum Annotatiunculae D. Iohanne Eckio Praelectore*, ed. Walter Moore, (Leiden: Brill, 1976).

directly from this source. Thus, while one can say that Eck knows Thomas Aquinas, there is no evidence that would tempt us to call this knowledge comprehensive or profound.

If Eck is representative, i.e. if he can be taken as the "average" non-Thomist, scholastic-trained theologian in the early 16th century, then we have a standard over against which Luther can be measured. The evidence presented in this Chapter makes it quite conceivable that Luther's knowledge of Thomas would indeed measure up well in such company. Modern Luther-scholarship has for too long a time seriously underestimated Luther in this regard.

RETROSPECTUS

"Thomas Aquinas -- the source and foundation of all heresy, all error and the obliteration of the Gospel": this verdict, though issued by Luther early in his career (1524), stands as his summation and final judgement on Thomas. This entire study should be seen as an effort to rightly understand what Luther meant by these words. For everything else that Luther said about Thomas must be regarded as a clarification and elaboration of this statement.

A long line of modern scholars has taken the view that Luther was simply unqualified to say this. The assertion obviously implies a considerable knowledge of the one to whom it refers. And Luther to a large extent lacked such a knowledge. This position, however, is untenable. A close examination of all Luther's references to Thomas reveals that his knowledge of Thomas was respectable. Modern scholarship can no longer dismiss Luther as an "Ignorant" in this regard. Luther's knowledge of Thomas was sufficient to compel us to take seriously his condemnation of Aquinas as "foundation of all heresy."

Nevertheless the statement should not be understood to imply an utter contempt and destain for Thomas. Luther's view of Thomas was in fact in some ways fairly ambivalent. On a personal level, Luther had both positive and negative things to say about Thomas. One finds in Luther many abusive characterizations of Thomas, but they are at least partially balanced by laudatory comments. Taken together, Luther's statements on the person of Thomas indicate that he harbored a kind of grudging respect for Thomas. He recognized, in short, Thomas' stature as a theologian.

Yet great theologians can be mistaken. And we have examined in detail the various issues on which Luther thought Thomas was. On a whole range of themes, from basic methodological ones like the role of experience in theology, to relatively insignificant topics like the veneration of images, Luther found Thomas wanting. On the various issues his understanding of Thomas was sometimes perfectly accurate and in other instances seriously distorted. Moreover, Luther's critiques on these issues varied from the trenchant to the trivial. Though Luther, in his sweeping indictment, calls Thomas the "foundation of all heresy," this is belied by the fact that in many instances Luther's concrete objections are curiously unemphatic. Though some of Thomas' errors are grave in Luther's view, one senses that for him, none in themselves spell disaster for the church or for theology. The most fundamental problem for Luther lies not with the theological mistakes Thomas made, serious though they may be.

Great theologians are sometimes wrong, and this is to be expected. The problem arises, however, from the fact that they are often influential. It was this which was of the highest concern for Luther: the authority accorded to Thomas by his followers was misplaced. This more than anything else was, from Luther's point of view, fatal for the church and for theology. Thomas made errors, but *the* error was that of his followers.

We have traced in detail Luther's view of what authority Thomas ought to have in the church and in theology. His teachings should be treated as nothing more than theological opinions; as such they are quite allowable even though mistaken. Thus, for example, Thomas' view of transubstantiation, though it is erroneous, is one of several permissible opinions; Thomas need not be condemned as a heretic for it. In principle, Thomas should have the same authority as any other great theologian in the church. His teaching falls into the realm of theological opinion -- a realm in which St. Paul's dictum to "Test all things" applies.

However, the actual authority which Thomas in fact possessed, according to Luther, was another matter. In this connection, we find in Luther a comprehensive view of the evolution of scholastic theology from the 13th to the 16th centuries. And the key to this development was the role played by the teaching of Thomas Aquinas. To begin with, the scholastics themselves, though they revered Thomas, held that Thomas had erred in some matters. Despite his greatness, his views were treated as theological opinions alongside those of others. Thus the "Wegestreit" (the conflict between the *viae*) developed and persisted up to Luther's own time. But in his own time a decisive turning point had been reached -- one which in fact represented the resolution of the "Wegestreit." The pluralism of the "Wegestreit" had now given way to the decisive triumph of Thomism. Thomas was now regarded as an infallible teacher, and all that he said was treated by his followers as dogma. What Thomas had humbly offered as opinion was now regarded as infallible teaching. Not only was there now a Thomist hegemony in theology, but the church itself had become the "Thomist Church." And this, in Luther's view, was the real disaster. Thomas had indeed been wrong about a good many things, but the crucial error was that of his followers in transforming his opinions into articles of faith. Luther never acknowledged himself to be heretic, unless "heresy" be taken to mean disagreement with Thomas Aquinas. In that case he accepted the label willingly. Eventually he also accepted the consequence of this designation as heretic, namely, his own final farewell to that part of Catholicism which in his view had become the "Thomist Church."

Still, the historical Thomas could scarcely be held accountable for all these developments. Thomas suffered a cruel fate at the hands of his followers, just as Luther feared he himself would. What this suggests is that for Luther, the real problem with Thomas was not Thomas but Thomism. Had his followers not elevated Thomas to the status of infallible teacher, he would not have become "the source and foundation of all heresy, all error and the obliteration of the Gospel."

BIBLIOGRAPHY

1. Primary Sources

Book of Concord. T. Tappert, ed. Philadelphia: Fortress, 1959.

Eck, Johannes. *Defensio Contra Amarulentas D.Andreae Bodenstein Carolstatini Invectiones (1518).* Joseph Greving, ed. CC 1. Münster: Aschendorff, 1919.

-. *Epistola de Ratione Studiorum Suorum (1538).* Johannes Metzler, ed. CC 2. Münster: Aschendorff, 1921.

-. *Disputatio Viennae Pannoniae Habita (1517).* Therese Virnich, ed. CC 6. Münster: Aschendorff, 1923.

-. *Explanatio Psalmi Vigesimi (1538).* Bernhard Walde, ed. CC 13. Münster: Aschendorff, 1928.

-. *Vier Deutsche Schriften Gegen Martin Luther, den Bürgermeister und Rat von Konstanz, Ambrosius Blarer und Konrad Sam.* Karl Meisen und Friedrich Zoepfl, eds. CC 14. Münster: Aschendorff, 1929.

-. *In Primum Librum Sententiarum Annotatiunculae D. Iohanne Eckio Praelectore.* Walter Moore, ed. Leiden: Brill, 1976.

-. *Enchiridion Locorum Communium Adversus Lutherum et Alios Hostes Ecclesiae (1525-1543).* Pierre Fraenkel, ed. CC 34. Münster: Aschendorff, 1979.

-. *De Sacrificio Missae Libri Tres (1526).* Erwin Iserloh, Vinzenz Pfnür und Peter Fabisch, eds. CC 36. Münster: Aschendorff, 1982.

Erasmus, Desiderius. *Opus Epistolarum Des. Erasmii Roterdami.* P.S. Allen, ed. Oxford: Oxford Univ. Press, 1922.

Gerson, Jean. *Joannis Gersonii Opera Omnia.* Vol. 1. E. du Pin, ed. Antwerp: Sumptibus Societatis, 1706.

Luther, Martin. *D. Martin Luthers Werke: Kritische Gesamtausgabe.* 114 vols. Weimar: Böhlau, 1883ff.

-. *Dr. Martin Luthers sämmtliche Schriften.* 23 vols. Johann Georg Walch, ed. St. Louis: J. J. Gebauer, 1880-1910.

-. *D. Martini Lutheri opera latina varii argumenti ad reformationis historiam imprimis pertinentia.* 7 vols. Frankfurt and Erlangen: Heyder and Zimmer, 1865-1873.

-. *Luther's Works: American Edition.* 55 vols. J. Pelikan and H. Lehman, eds. St. Louis: Concordia, 1955-1987.

Mantuanus, Baptista. *Opus Aureum in Thomistas,* in P. Kristeller, ed., *Le Thomisme et la Pensee Italienne de la Renaissance.* Montreal: Inst. d'Études Médiévales, 1967, pp. 129-185.

Thomas Aquinas, *Thomae Aquinatis Opera Omnia.* 34 vols. Paris: Vivès, 1871-82.

-. *Summa Theologiae.* 5 vols. Rome: Mariètti, 1948.

-. *Summa Theologica.* 3 vols. New York: Benzinger, 1947-48.

2. Secondary Literature

Althaus, Paul. *The Theology of Martin Luther.* Philadelphia: Fortress, 1966.

Aubert, Roger. *Le Problème de l'Acte de Foi: Données Traditionelles et Résultats des Controverses Récentes.* Louvain: Publications Universitaries de Louvain, 1950.

Bacht, Heinrich. "Luthers 'Urteil über die Mönchsgelübde' in Ökumenischer Betrachtung." *Catholica,* 21 (1967), 222-251.

Boehmer, Heinrich. *Luther and the Reformation in the Light of Modern Research.* London: G. Bell, 1930.

Bornkamm, Heinrich. *Luther in Mid-Career, 1521-1530.* Philadelphia: Fortress, 1983.

Brecht, Martin. *Martin Luther: His Road to Reformation, 1483-1521.* Philadelphia: Fortress, 1985.

Chenu, M.D. "'Maître' Thomas est-il une'autorité'?" *Revue Thomiste,* 30 (1925), 187-194.

-. *Toward Understanding Saint Thomas.* Chicago: Regnery, 1964.

Clark, Francis. *Eucharistic Sacrifice and the Reformation.* London: Darton, Longman and Todd, 1960.

Collins, James. *The Thomistic Philosophy of the Angels.* Washington: Catholic Univ. Press, 1947.

Congar, Yves. "St. Thomas and the Infallibility of the Papal Magisterium." *The Thomist,* 38 (1974), 81-105.

Davis, Kenneth. *Anabaptism and Asceticism: A Study in Intellectual Origins.* Scottsdale PA: Herald Press, 1974.

Delius, Hans-Ulrich. *Augustin als Quelle Luthers: Eine Materialsammlung.* Berlin: Evangelische Verlagsanstalt, 1984.

Denifle, Heinrich. *Luther und Luthertum in der ersten Entwicklung.* 2 vols. Mainz: F. Kirchheim, 1904-09.

Ebeling, Gerhard. *Evangelische Evangelienauslegung: Eine Untersuchung zur Luthers Hermeneutik.* Munich: C. Kaiser, 1942.

-. *Lutherstudien II: Disputatio de Homine.* Tübingen: Mohr, 1977.

Eckermann, Willigis. "Die Aristoteleskritik Luthers: Ihre Bedeutüng für seine Theologie." *Catholica,* 32 (1978), 114-130.

Edwards, Mark. *Luther's Last Battles.* Ithaca NY: Cornell Univ. Press, 1983.

Farthing, John. "Post Thomam: Images of Thomas Aquinas in the Academic Theology of Gabriel Biel." Duke Univ. Dissertation, 1978.

-. *Thomas Aquinas and Gabriel Biel: Interpretations of St. Thomas Aquinas in German Nominalism on the Eve of the Reformation.* Durham NC: Duke Univ. Press, 1988.

Gerrish, Brian. *Grace and Reason: A Study in the Theology of Luther.* Oxford: Clarendon, 1962.

Gilson, Etienne. *The Spirit of Medieval Philosophy.* N.Y.: Scribners, 1936.

Grabmann, Martin. "Aristoteles im Werturteil des Mittelalters." *Mittelalterliches Geistesleben: Abhandlungen zur Geschichte der Scholastik und Mystik.* 3 vols. Munich: M. Hueber, 1926-56. II: 63-102.

-. "Die Stellung des Kardinals Cajetan in der Geschichte des Thomismus und der Thomistenschule." *Mittelalterliches Geistesleben.* I: 332-391.

Grane, Leif. *Contra Gabrielem: Luthers Auseinandersetzung mit Gabriel Biel in der Disputatio Contra Scholasticam Theologiam, 1517.* Copenhagen: Gyldendal, 1962.

-. "Luthers Kritik an Thomas von Aquin in De Captivitate Babylonica." *Zeitschrift für Kirchengeschichte,* 80 (1969), 1-13.

-. "Die Anfänge von Luthers Auseinandersetzung mit dem Thomismus." *Theologische Literaturzeitung,* 95 (1979), 241-250.

-. *Modus Loquendi Theologicus: Luthers Kampf um die Erneuerung der Theologie (1515-1518).* Leiden: Brill, 1975.

Grisar, Hartmann, *Luther.* 3 vols. Freiburg: Herder, 1911.

Grislis, Egil. "The Manner of Christ's Eucharistic Presence According to Martin Luther." *Consensus: A Canadian Lutheran Journal of Theology,* 7 (1981), 3-15.

Grossmann, Maria. *Humanism in Wittenberg, 1485-1517.* Nieukoop: B. De Graaf, 1975.

Hamm, Berndt. *Frömmigkeitstheologie am Anfang des 16. Jahrhunderts: Studien zu Johannes von Paltz und seinem Umkreis.* Tübingen: Mohr, 1982.

Headley, John. *Luther's View of Church History.* New Haven: Yale Univ. Press, 1963.

Hendrix, Scott. *Luther and the Papacy: Stages in a Reformation Conflict.* Philadelphia: Fortress, 1981.

Hermes, Astrid. "Zur Verständigung zwischen Martin Luther und Thomas von Aquin." *Una Sancta*, 33 (1978), 229-236.

Hildebrandt, Ernst. "Die kurfürstliche Schloss- und Universitätsbibliothek zu Wittenberg, 1512-1547." *Zeitschrift für Buchkunde*, 2 (1925), 34-42, 109-129, 157-188.

Hilgenfeld, Hartmut. *Mittelalterlich-traditionelle Elemente in Luthers Abendmahlsschriften.* Zurich: Theologischer Verlag, 1971.

Hovland, Warren. "Anfechtung in Luther's Biblical Exegesis." In F. H. Littel, ed., *Reformation Studies and Essays in Honor of Roland H. Bainton.* Richmond VA: John Knox, 1962. pp. 46-60.

Janz, Denis. "A Reinterpretation of Gabriel Biel on Nature and Grace." *The Sixteenth Century Journal*, 8 (1977), 104-108.

-. *Luther and Late Medieval Thomism: A Study in Theological Anthropology.* Waterloo: Wilfrid Laurier Univ. Press, 1983.

Jedin, Hubert. *A History of the Council of Trent.* vol. 1. St. Louis: Herder, 1957.

Kasten, Horst. *Taufe und Rechtfertigung bei Thomas von Aquin und Martin Luther.* Munich: C. Kaiser, 1970.

Kleinhaus, A. "Paulus von Burgos." *Lexikon für Theologie und Kirche.* Vol. 8, p. 230.

Kohls, Ernst-Wilhelm. "Luthers Verhältnis zu Aristoteles, Thomas und Erasmus." *Theologische Zeitschrift*, 31 (1975), 289-301.

Kristeller, Paul. *Le Thomisme et la pensée italienne de la Renaissance.* Montreal: Inst. d'Études Médiévales, 1967.

-. *Medieval Aspects of Renaissance Learning.* Durham NC: Duke Univ. Press, 1974.

Kühn, Ulrich. *Via Caritatis: Theologie des Gesetzes bei Thomas von Aquin.* Göttingen: Vandenhoeck und Ruprecht, 1965.

La Vallee, Armand. "Calvin's Criticism of Scholastic Theology." Harvard Univ. Dissertation, 1967.

Le Goff, Jacques. *The Birth of Purgatory.* Chicago: Univ. of Chicago Press, 1984.

Lehmann, Paul. *Mittelalterliche Bibliothekskataloge Deutschlands und der Schweiz, Vol. 2: Erfurt.* Munich: C. H. Beck'sche Verlagsbuchhandlung, 1928.

Leijssen, Lambert, "Martin Bucer und Thomas von Aquin." *Ephemerides Theologicae Lovaniensis*, 55 (1979), 266-296.

Lescoe, F. ed. *Saint Thomas Aquinas: Treatise on Separate Substances.* West Hartford: St. Joseph College Press, 1963.

Link, Wilhelm. *Das Ringen Luthers um die Freiheit der Theologie von der Philosophie.* Munich: C. Kaiser, 1955.

Löhr, Gabriel. *Die Kölner Dominikanerschule vom 14. bis zum 16. Jahrhundert, mit eine Übersicht über die Gesamtentwicklung.* Cologne: Kölner Universitätsverlag, 1948.

Lohse, Bernhard. *Mönchtum und Reformation: Luthers Auseinandersetzung mit dem Mönchsideal des Mittelalters.* Göttingen: Vandenhoeck und Ruprecht, 1963.

-. "Cajetan und Luther: Zur Begegnung von Thomismus und Reformation." *Kerygma und Dogma*, 32 (1986), 150-169.

Lortz, Joseph. *Die Reformation in Deutschland.* 2 vols. Freiburg: Herder, 1962.

-. "Basic Elements in Luther's Intellectual Style." in J. Wicks, ed., *Catholic Scholars Dialogue with Luther.* Chicago: Loyola Univ. Press, 1970. pp. 3-33.

Mandonnet, P. "Les titres doctoraux de saint Thomas d'Aquin." *Revue Thomiste*, 17 (1909), 597-608.

Matsuura, Jan. "Restbestände aus der Bibliothek des Erfurter Augustinerklosters zu Luthers Zeit und bisher Unbekannte Eigenhändige Notizen Luthers." In G. Hammer and K. H. Zur Mühlen, eds., *Lutheriana. Zum 500. Geburtstag Martin Luthers, von den Mitarbeitern der Weimarer Ausgabe*. Cologne: Böhlau, 1984. pp. 315-332.

McCue, James. "Luther and Roman Catholicism on the Mass as Sacrifice." *Journal of Ecumenical Studies*, 2 (1965), 205-233.

-. "The Doctrine of Transubstantiation from Berengar through the Council of Trent." in P. Empie and T. Murphy, eds., *The Eucharist as Sacrifice*. Minneapolis: Augsburg, 1967. pp. 89-124.

McGrath, Alister. *Luther's Theology of the Cross: Martin Luther's Theological Breakthrough*. Oxford: Blackwell, 1985.

-. "John Calvin and Late Medieval Thought: A Study in Late Medieval Influences upon Calvin's theological Development." *Archiv für Reformationsgeschichte*, 77 (1986), 58-78.

McSorley, Harry. *Luther: Right or Wrong? An Ecumenical-Theological Study of Luther's Major Work 'The Bondage of the Will'*. N.Y. - Minneapolis: Newman-Augsburg, 1969.

McSorley, Harry. "Some Forgotten Truths about the Petrine Ministry." *Journal of Ecumenical Studies*, 11 (1974), 208-237.

-. "Thomas Aquinas, John Pupper von Goch and Martin Luther: An Essay in Ecumenical Theology." in J. Deschner, L. Howe and K. Penzel, eds., *Our Common History as Christians: Essays in Honor of Albert C. Outler*. Oxford: Oxford Univ. Press, 1975. pp. 97-129.

-. "Luther: Exemplar of Reform -- Or Doctor of the Church?" in E. Grislis, ed., *The Theology of Martin Luther*. Winnfield, B.C.: Woodlake Books, 1985. pp. 27-52.

Meissinger, K. *Der katholische Luther*. Munich: Lehnen, 1952.

Meyer, Harding. "Fundamental Difference--Fundamental Consensus." *Ecumenical Trends*, 15 (1986), 38-41.

Mostert, Walter. "Luthers Verhältnis zur theologischen und philosophischen Überlieferung." in H. Junghans, ed., *Martin Luther von 1526 bis 1546*. 2 vols. Göttingen: Vandenhoeck und Ruprecht, 1983. I: pp. 347-368.

Murphy, Lawrence. "Gabriel Biel as Transmitter of Aquinas to Luther." *Renaissance and Reformation*, 19 (1983), 26-41.

Oberman, Heiko. *The Harvest of Medieval Theology*. Grand Rapids: Eerdmans, 1967.

-. *Werden und Wertung der Reformation: Vom Wegestreit zum Glaubenskampf*. Tübingen: Mohr, 1977.

-. "Wittenbergs Zweifrontenkrieg gegen Prierias und Eck: Hintergrund und Entscheidung des Jahres 1518." *Zeitschrift für Kirchengeschichte*, 80 (1969), 331-358.

O'Donovan, Louis, ed., *Henry VIII's Assertio Septem Sacramentorum, 1521*. N.Y.: Benzinger, 1908.

Overfield, James. *Humanism and Scholasticism in Late Medieval Germany*. Princeton: Princeton Univ. Press, 1984.

Paulus, Nikolas. *Geschichte des Ablasses im Mittelalter: Vom Ursprunge bis zur Mitte des 14. Jahrhunderts*. Paderborn: Schöningh, 1922-23.

Pelikan, Jaroslav. *Luther the Expositor: Introduction to the Reformer's Exegetical Writings*. St. Louis: Concordia, 1959.

-. *The Growth of Medieval Theology*. Chicago: Univ. of Chicago Press, 1978.

-. *Reformation of Church and Dogma*. Chicago: Univ of Chicago Press, 1983.

Pesch, Otto. *Theologie der Rechtfertigung bei Martin Luther und Thomas von Aquin: Versuch ein systematisch-theologischen Dialogs*. Mainz: Grünewald, 1967.

Pesch, Otto. "Luthers Kritik am Mönchtum in Katholischer Sicht." in H. Schlier, E. Severus, J. Sudbrack, and A. Pereira, eds., *Strukturen Christlicher Existenz: Beiträge zur Erneuerung des Geistlichen Lebens*. Würzburg: Echter Verlag, 1968. pp. 81-96, 371-374.

-. "Existential and Sapiential Theology -- the theological Confrontation between Luther and Thomas Aquinas." in J. Wicks, ed., *Catholic Scholars Dialogue with Luther*. Chicago: Loyola Univ. Press, 1970. pp. 61-81, 182-193.

-. "Paul as Professor of Theology: The Image of the Apostle in St. Thomas' Theology." *The Thomist*, 38 (1974), 584-605.

Pfürtner, Stephan. *Luther and Aquinas -- A Conversation: Our Salvation, Its Certainty and Peril*. London: Darton, Longman and Todd, 1964.

-. "Das reformatorische 'Sola Scriptura' -- theologischer Auslegungsgrund des Thomas von Aquin?" in C. H. Ratsschow, ed., *Sola Scriptura -- Ringvorlesung der Theologischen Fakultät der Phillipps-Universität*. Marburg: Elwert, 1977. pp. 48-80.

Polman, Pontien. *L'Élément Historique dans la Controverse religieuses du XVIe Siècle*. Gembloux: Duculot, 1932.

Poschmann, Bernhard. *Penance and the Anointing of the Sick*. N.Y.: Herder, 1964.

Preuss, James. *From Shadow to Promise: Old Testament Interpretation from Augustine to the Young Luther*. Cambridge MA: Harvard Univ. Press, 1969.

Ritter, Gerhard. *Via Antiqua und Via Moderna auf den deutschen Universitäten des XV. Jahrhunderts*. Heidelberg: C. Winter, 1922.

Scarisbrick, J. J. *Henry VIII*. Los Angeles: Univ. of California Press, 1968.

Schenk, Max. *Die Unfehlbarkeit des Papstes in der Heiligsprechung: Ein Beitrag zur Erhellung der theologiegeschichtlichen Seite der Frage*. Freiburg: Paulusverlag, 1965.

Schüssler, Hermann. *Der Primat der Heiligen Schrift als theologisches und kanonistisches Problem in Spätmittelalter*. Wiesbaden: Steiner, 1977.

Schwiebert, Ernest. *Luther and His Times*. St. Louis: Concordia, 1950.

Seckler, Max. *Das Heil in der Geschichte: Geschichtstheologisches Denken bei Thomas von Aquin*. Munich: Kösel, 1964.

Seeburg, Reinhold. *Text-Book of the History of Doctrines*. Grand Rapids: Baker, 1977.

Smalley, Beryl. *The Study of the Bible in the Middle Ages*. Notre Dame: Univ. of Notre Dame Press, 1964.

Stamm, Heinz-Meinolf. *Luthers Stellung zum Ordensleben*. Wiesbaden: Steiner, 1980.

Steinmetz, David. *Misericordia Dei: The Theology of Johannes von Staupitz in Its Late Medieval Setting*. Leiden: Brill, 1968.

-. "'Libertas Christiana': Studies in the Theology of John Pupper of Goch (d. 1474)." *Harvard Theological Review*, 65 (1972), 191-230.

-. *Luther and Staupitz: An Essay in the Intellectual Origins of the Protestant Reformation*. Durham NC: Duke Univ. Press, 1980.

-. *Luther in Context*. Bloomington: Indiana Univ. Press, 1986.

Stock, Ursala. *Die Bedeutung der Sakramente in Luthers Sermonen von 1519*. Leiden: Brill, 1982.

Tavard, George. *Holy Writ and Holy Church*. N.Y.: Harper and Row, 1959.

Van Rhijn, M. "Kende Luther Thomas?" *Nederlands Archief voor Kerkgeschiedenis*, 44 (1961), 153-156.

Von Rohr, John. "Medieval Consolation and the Young Luther's Despair." In F. H. Littel, ed., *Reformation Studies and Essays in Honor of Roland H. Bainton*. Richmond VA: John Knox, 1962. pp. 61-74.

Vorster, Hans. *Das Freiheitsverständnis bei Thomas von Aquin und Martin Luther*. Göttingen: Vandenhoeck und Ruprecht, 1965.

Weier, Reinhold. *Das Theologieverständnis Martin Luthers*. Paderborn: Bonifacius-Verlag, 1976.

Weisheipl, James. *Friar Thomas D'Aquino: His Life, Thought and Work*. N.Y.: Doubleday, 1974.

-. "Thomism." *New Catholic Encyclopedia*, vol. 14, pp. 126-135.

Wicks, Jared. *Cajetan Responds: A Reader in Reformation Controversy*. Washington: Catholic Univ. Press, 1978.

-. "Roman Reactions to Luther: The First Year (1518)." *Catholic Historical Review*, 69 (1983), 521-562.

Wiedermann, Gotthelf. "Cochlaeus as Polemicist." in P.Brooks, ed., *Seven-Headed Luther: Essays in Commemoration of a Quincentenary, 1483-1983*. Oxford: Clarendon, 1983. pp. 195-205.

Wolf, Ernst. *Staupitz und Luther. Ein Beitrag zur Theologie des Johannes von Staupitz und deren Bedeutung für Luthers theologische Werdegang*. Leipzig: M. Heinsius, 1927.

Zumkeller, Adolar. "Die Augustinertheologen Simon Fidati von Cascia und Hugolin von Orvieto und Martin Luthers Kritik an Aristoteles." *Archiv für Reformationsgeschichte*, 54 (1963), 15-37.

Zumkeller, Adolar. "Handschriften aus dem Ehemaligen Erfurter Augustinerkloster in der Staatsbibliothek Berlin --Preussischer Kulturbesitz. Neue Aufschlüsse über Johannes von Dorsten OSA (d. 1481)." *Analecta Augustiniana*, 40 (1977), 223-277.

Zur Mühlen, Karl-Heinz. "Luther und Aristoteles." *Lutherjahrbuch*, 52 (1985), 263-266.

INDEX